D0616671

Acknowledgments

I want to thank my wife Joyce, who once again was patient as another book demanded so much time and energy. I also thank Judy Littlebury, to whom this volume is dedicated. Not only has she inspired much of my professional work, but she also assisted in editing these pages. My brother John helped in editing as well, even with this time consuming task hitting his life at the worst possible time.

I appreciate the work of Karen Gray and her staff at Acacia Publishing for their help in completing this project.

As with so much of my career, I have been influenced in this project by my Mother and Father, Rosemary and Guy Ziegler (yes, I am Rosemary's Baby). In addition to eating everything on my plate, my parents taught me to make the most of my talents and opportunities and then share what I have with others. With this goal of sharing I offer these pages to you, and I hope you find some useful ideas and reflections on working with children.

Contents

Foreword

I want to first welcome you to the latest fruits of my life long learning process of working with challenging children. I learn the most when I am working directly with a difficult child, and I am open to the lessons available. I will repeatedly encourage the reader to do the same with the teacher in your life, who is disguised as an emotionally disturbed child. If you find in these pages helpful ideas and recommendations, you may want to take a look at my previous books, if you have not already done so. In this volume I will continue my belief of speaking plainly and not being politically correct. In fact, you will find in these pages that I take several positions that are not currently popular. I do not have being provocative as a goal, but I will speak out when I believe the latest fad in working with difficult children is dead wrong.

Two concepts in the title of this book bear immediate scrutiny. The first is what is meant by the term "impossible children." Do I subscribe to the belief of many professionals, administrators and parents that some children are simply "impossible," and will demonstrate failure regardless of what resources are provided?

I have to begin my answer to this question by saying that there are impossible situations that parents, teachers and even therapists find themselves in, but the term "impossible" better describes situations than it describes children. I work every day with children who were impossible in some settings but not in ours. The term impossible is often used to describe both the frustration of adults who have worked valiantly to provide a child the ingredients of success, and the prospects of further efforts to succeed that have repeatedly failed in the past. Many of us find ourselves in impossible situations with children whose needs demonstrate the insufficiency of our ability to meet them. We may not be able to accomplish the task of helping a very challenging child due to inadequate resources, full understanding of what is required, or willingness on the part of all adults in the child's life to commit to and stick to a plan to help the child. However, such situations actually say more about adults than about children.

I don't want to sidestep the initial question, is there such a thing as an impossible child? I would have to say my experience points to an optimistic answer that there are not impossible children, just impossible situations. I have made a career built around coming up with the answer to how to help children nearly always described by one or more adults as "impossible." I have worked as a psychologist/therapist with thousands of families and caseworkers who hoped I could help with their impossible child. The programs for children that I have helped start in my career have primarily focused on children no one seemed to be able to help. The outcomes the children have had over time have been exceptionally positive. Specifically, the program we have for the most damaged and difficult children has been called by numerous experts the most successful program of its kind they have ever come across.

There is a price for success (although it is preferable to the price of failure), that I am reminded of with each new referral for a child who on paper appears to have needs that no one could possibly meet. The price of success is yet another opportunity to take up that challenge and see if our team can once again do the impossible. Do we always accomplish our goals? No. I can look back on my career and remember five children for whom I felt like I had no answers. But I also can't say for sure that our work failed. My list had six names on it before last fall, when one of these children contacted me as an adult and gave our program credit for changing her life. At the same time, I can't say that because it appeared to me that I was not able to reach these children, that they were unreachable. Sometimes we are like farmers who plant fruit trees that only many years later will bear the first fruit from all our labor. But after more than thirty years of having a very high rate of success with difficult children, I approach each new case with humility but also with confidence.

Since there have been so few children that I have found to be unreachable with the right combination of ideas, resources and hard work, then other than in the title, I will not describe children as impossible throughout the book. Instead you will find the terms difficult, troubled, and traumatized used instead. Periodically I may even use such fond descriptions as little Typhoid Mary, domestic terrorist, and Dennis Rodman Jr. (nothing personal, Dennis). I use such terms at times not to be negative, but I find laughing, although it may not always be funny, preferable to crying. As in my previous books, I will use humor frequently, even when describing very serious situations that are anything but funny for those involved.

The second concept in the title of this book that deserves comment is what I mean by "success." I want to make it clear that having success with difficult children is a complex subject. I continually find that different people have very different ideas of what success with difficult children is. A parent might want an adopted child to be much more like the image the parents hoped the child would be when they first adopted. Caseworkers want a child to stop being a problem so other children on the caseload can get some attention. My idea of success is quite different than either of these definitions of success.

To define success, I will begin by saying what success is not. Having success with a difficult child is not synonymous with finding a cure to the child's problems. Cures are rare enough that I don't expect or even hope for an absence of problems with a difficult child. Success is not to hand back to the parents the quiet life they had before the child darkened their door. However the child came into the family, be it through birth or adoption or a decision to be a foster parent for the child, the parents cannot turn back time and have the life they used to have. It will not happen, so get over the idea and move on.

To me, success is finding the internal and external resources to face the challenges presented by the child, and seeing a gradual but unmistakable movement in a positive direction for everyone. This meaning of success includes a significant and continual investment of energy by the parents. Success also means that the parents are open to and involved in their own personal growth as individuals, as parents, and as couples or families. When we invest a significant amount of personal resources into something and we accomplish our goals, there is no better way than this to describe success. This type of success requires that the goal is difficult and the journey demanding, with an uncertain future. When accomplishments are easy or quick, we find little reward in such success. But since there is no such thing as quick or easy success with difficult children, hard earned accomplishment is pretty much all that is available (other than hard earned failure).

I use one primary internal measure of success. Despite the amount of effort, worry or tears along the way, success is when the end result gives back to me a deep psychic or spiritual energy. This is similar to the inner spring of living water talked about in the Bible. This is tapping into the universal energy discussed in Taoism and other spiritual belief systems. Any adult who defines success as finding peace and quiet is looking in the wrong direction. Difficult children demand our best efforts, and when we give this, we are rewarded with a sense that we have provided the missing tools for the child to build a life on a more firm foundation. This foundation has a chance to offer the child and others both quality of life and personal fulfillment. However, even when we are successful, we are not necessarily rewarded with a calm household. What I have learned so far about living is that it is apparently not designed to be easy, and it is not for wimps. Parenting a difficult child is an even more demanding journey than what life itself requires of us.

When I started the task of writing this book, I originally had three different books in mind. With the amount of time a book takes from beginning the task until it is available in print, my struggle was to decide which of my three topics was most important. What I decided to do was to follow the theme of the book *Raising Children Who Refuse To Be Raised*, and combine multiple perspectives related to difficult children. This allowed me to incorporate each of the three areas into one document. Although each section would need to be somewhat abbreviated, doing the book this way would force me to condense and integrate the topics into one volume. The reader will have to decide if I was successful.

This volume integrates two elements of my last two books. From the first book I have taken a wide angle view, and discussed multiple issues related to very difficult children. Most parents of troubled children will tell you of their frustration in having to read a dozen books to cover all the problems their child presents. At the same time, these difficult children are not simply a challenge in one environment. They create problems for parents, teachers, therapists, coaches, pastors and most any other adult involved in the child's life. It began to make sense to me to include in one volume a discussion of not only management techniques for parents, but also a section on educating the difficult child, looking at complex issues of treating trauma related issues, and many other topics.

The second element comes from my second book, *Traumatic Experience and the Brain*. I will include here both case examples and summary comments at the end of each chapter.

Readers have commented on the helpfulness of both of these aspects of the last book.

Another element found in this book in Chapter 8 is an expansion of the detailed steps of the important components of trauma therapy. The ten steps of trauma therapy are outlined in Chapter 10 of *Traumatic Experience and the Brain*. In this volume I go into more detail.

In Section I will be found the first four chapters. Chapter 1 provides the big picture perspective on why in the battle between parent and child, the parent must win for everyone to come out ahead. In this chapter can be found a discussion of power struggles and control issues as well as tantruming behavior. This chapter sets the tone of the rest of the book with an overview of each issue and specific interventions designed to help the parent prevail on the domestic battlefield.

Chapter 2 is about teaching responsibility. Unless you plan to be around the child the rest of your days, the responsibility for the child's actions must eventually be turned over to the child. It is never too early to begin working on teaching responsibility, because it does not come naturally to children.

Chapter 3 addresses the concept of positive discipline. This topic includes the challenge of making sure that parenting is not built upon punishing children, but teaching them how to succeed in a family, at school and in the community. Eight principles of positive discipline are covered, including the use of logical consequences. This chapter is a good overview of successful parenting methods.

Chapter 4 completes the first section with a review of violence and what to do about it when it comes from the child you are working with or parenting. A brief look at violence in our culture provides the setting and the challenge of raising children prone to violence with a message that is often different than the message the child receives from the news, entertainment, and sports. I also respond in this chapter to the recent movement in our country to "protect the rights of children to do what they want to do." I have still not found this in the Bill of Rights, but to some this includes the right that a child should not be physically prevented from damaging property, harming self or harming others. Effective tools to work with violence are covered.

Section II takes a close look at the psychological needs of troubled children. A principle that runs throughout the book is that unless we understand the child, we will be unable to either manage or successfully meet the child's needs.

Chapter 5 covers an often overlooked issue that as bad as child abuse and neglect was, what can be worse for the child is being deprived of the growth and learning that was missed due to the abuse. Ten critical needs of traumatized children are reviewed.

Chapter 6 looks at the effects of trauma on the individual. A discussion of attachment and trauma is provided. An overview of trauma and brain development is presented. The chapter concludes with a list of the effects of trauma, followed by how perception is altered by traumatic experiences.

Chapter 7 takes a close look at the many issues that come up in the process of trauma treatment. The discussion includes symptoms of trauma, the conclusions of research concerning trauma therapy, and the chapter ends with an overview of the basic components of effective trauma therapy.

Chapter 8 goes into a step-by-step process of the ten steps of trauma treatment. This chapter is a further development of chapter ten of *Traumatic Experience and the Brain*. Each step in the process is followed by specific suggestions. The chapter stresses that these ten steps must be addressed, but how they are addressed will depend on the style and approach of the therapist.

Chapter 9 looks into the most intensive form of mental health treatment in a residential setting. The chapter discusses why this level of care has been the target of criticism. The most common arguments against the use of residential care are addressed along with a response. The discussion leaves no doubt that effective residential care remains an important component of an overall system of care for difficult children.

Section III moves into a look at adopting and educating troubled children. It is difficult to discuss either without also spending some time on attachment problems that are produced by childhood trauma.

Chapter 10 begins the third section with a new way to view adoptions with a difficult child, and the resulting impacts on parents and on the family as a whole. There appears to be a parallel between the impact of trauma on an individual and the impact of some very difficult adoptions on the family. Suggestions are provided to prevent long term negative effects of traumatic adoptions. A unique model of adoption is also discussed.

Chapter 11 provides a detailed look at disorders of attachment. This chapter is designed to be somewhat less technical than the discussion of attachment in *Raising Children Who Refuse To Be Raised*. Biological and neurological aspects of attachment are reviewed. The chapter then goes into what to do to correct attachment problems. The chapter points out that attachment therapy is not just for professionals; in fact, most of the effective interventions for attachment problems are done by families. The final discussion is an attachment model used in the author's residential program for the most serious cases of attachment disorders.

Chapter 12 goes into the challenges of providing an effective education for children who resist the process. Components of successful schools with difficult children are presented. One model of an approach that has been found to be successful is discussed.

The book concludes with a review of what makes the difference between the parent, teacher or therapist who succeeds with a difficult child and one that does not. Hint —

success does not equate to the amount of effort you put into the endeavor.

Chapter 13 attempts to pull the many points made in the book together into one discussion of the common elements of people and programs that are successful with difficult children. The chapter covers attributes of successful individuals and strategies that work with children. A discussion is also included of working with traumatized individuals as adults. The chapter and the book conclude with a look at the possibility of "no lose parenting."

Before we begin, there is one more comment I need to make. There are few things in life less humorous than a child who has been badly abused. It is also not much fun nor is it funny to parent or teach one of these difficult children. However, I believe one aspect of resilience and a person's ability to continue an arduous task is the ability to bring some humor to the most difficult challenges. Taken out of context, humor can look odd or even inappropriate. However, our ability to laugh at ourselves and the difficulties we face can help recharge our batteries. The reader will find humor appearing frequently in these pages.

If you are offended by the humor and you find absolutely nothing funny about the situations being covered, I have two suggestions. First, you can ignore my attempts to lighten up the seriousness of the task at hand; or you could take a moment to ask yourself if you have lost your ability to look at the world in a humorous way. I attempt to set a light hearted tone at the beginning of each chapter with an actual quote from the difficult children I have worked with over the years. It may not have seemed funny to the adult working with the child at the time, but I think you will agree that difficult children do "say the darnedest things."

Part I

Mission Impossible — Or Is It?

Parenting and Behavior Management That Works

The children were filling out a school form and came across an empty box that said "Gender" without male and female to check. When the children turned in the form, here were some of the listed genders: "Mermaid," "Human Boy," "Tired and Sad," "Don't have one," "No clue," "Never mind," and "Princess." [Makes being a male or female seem pretty boring.]

Chapter

1

The Battlefield with Challenging Children

Ten years ago, Judy Littlebury and I put together a booklet for parents who were doing their best to raise difficult children. In some ways all children are difficult to raise, but the focus of our booklet was on children who had a traumatic past and, often, multiple family placements. This would include children in foster care, adoptive homes and many children with one or both biological parents. We called the booklet *Mission Impossible – Or Is It?* (Ziegler & Littlebury, 1994). After Tom Cruise read the booklet, he was able to persuade a film studio to recreate the Mission Impossible series from the 1970s, resulting in the two wildly popular movies over the last four years. This isn't exactly true; OK, it isn't true at all; but if Tom had read it, he would find that fighting international criminals isn't nearly as difficult as raising a troubled child. With the passage of ten years, parents continue to indicate that the booklet's ideas and suggestions are as useful today as when it was written. For this reason, I have decided to expand on some of the suggestions from *Mission Impossible* in this first section.

I start this chapter with the understanding that many people object to some of the analogies that I use. In this case, the offensive analogy to some people is my use of the term "battlefield." It is not to be controversial that I use a term like this, and, at times, equate parenting difficult children to a war zone. My reason for using this term is that I have, at times, experienced parenting, like a battle, and the majority of parents I communicate with resonate with the concept and feel better understood with what they are living through. My goal is certainly not to perpetuate warfare or a battle of wills between children and their parents; however, even if I didn't call it a battlefield, it still feels like one to very large numbers of parents. I use this term with a primary goal to outline a win-win scenario for the child and the parents. I believe that such an outcome is possible with the ongoing battles of parenting. I understand and agree with individuals who prefer to see parenting in a paradigm of caring and support — with the child learning to respond to the parent with respect because they experience respect from the parents.

Parenting based on a supportive and nurturing relationship with the child is the ultimate win-win between a parent and a child. However, traumatized children, who present continual hurdles to being parented, usually have a history that precludes starting from the position of caring and respect going both ways. The children I will talk about most often in this book are the children who go out of their way to disrespect adults, and take caring and support and throw them back into the face of the parent.

Some people may believe the difficult children described in this book are rare. If so, they need to speak to most foster parents, many adoptive parents and nearly every parent who has put in the love and hard work to parent a child who has been the victim of child abuse or neglect at the hands of a drug addicted mother, male sperm donor (to me, fathering a child is more than a biological event), or boyfriend du jour. I have no interest in vilifying the parents who have neglected or in some way traumatized a child. In most cases they were facing economic or personal situations that made being a parent a steep climb at best. In many cases, the parents of today are the traumatized children of the past. This fact alone should be sufficient reason to invest in our domestic wars much more than in our foreign wars.

Todd Tried To Control Everything But The Weather

After years of practice, Todd had controlling adults down to a science. He surveyed the situations he was in, identified the weak areas of adult structure, and found out the power buttons to push with the adults. In his early years, Todd found himself in control of his family by default with a parent who was involved in drugs. Control equaled survival to Todd and his sister. Todd even had his psychiatrist believing he would likely never change. In our treatment program we invited Todd to have fun and be a child, but we told him we understood that he would have to test us for control first. He tried repeatedly to control every situation. Sometimes he won a round, but overall he lost most of the skirmishes. We continued to suggest he try harder to control everything until he was ready to just be a kid and have fun. There was no observable change for months, but after ten months of struggle Todd gradually left control to the adults, other than occasionally testing, as he turned his attention to having as much fun as possible. At the end of treatment he was greatly improved and now is like any normal child; he only controls adults who let him.

In parenting, the term "battlefield" refers to the situations when the child resists the positive efforts of the parent to help the child. Parenting a difficult child requires more than doubling your positive efforts to help the child. In many cases, the harder the parent tries, the harder the child resists. This is why I have written in the past that a great deal of TLC is needed to parent a difficult child. As you may suspect, TLC does not stand for tender loving care, which generally works with normal children. Tender loving care with difficult children often sets up the parent to be a huge target for the child, whose daily agenda is to resist your best efforts to be a good parent. The TLC I suggest stands for: **T**ranslating the meaning of the child's behavior, **L**earning from each situation to be a better and more effective parent, and **C**ontrol as in being in control of ourselves and the family environment. More on this subject can be found in chapter 10 of *Raising Children Who Refuse To Be Raised* (Ziegler, 2000).

Nearly all foster or adoptive parents start out believing that they have the time and the love to give a child to make a huge difference in the child's life. Fortunately, most of the time this turns out to be the case. However, the percentage of children for whom this does not turn out to be the case are most often the children battling their parents. When parenting these children, being in a battle may be unavoidable at times, but what must be avoided are power struggles.

Power Struggles and the Control Issue

The most distinctive dynamic of raising a difficult child is a struggle for control. For many children with a history of child abuse, it is understandable why they have control issues. They have learned the hard way that adults cannot be trusted with either large or small issues. The motto of these children is "get it for yourself, or forget it." Although it is easy to see why some children struggle for control, the problem is that this struggle continues even when it is not in the best interest of the child. This initial adaptive response to the environment becomes counter-productive; and these children seldom see when they make a wrong turn and begin working contrary to their own personal interests. The primary reason children lose sight of want they want and settle for control is that control becomes paramount, not what they wanted in the first place.

It is not unusual for a controlling child to be completely inconsistent in her stated position, but very consistent with control. For example, the ten-year-old female who loves to go to the mall, today decides she wants to stay home when the family is going to the mall and says, "I hate the mall." Immediately her mother reminds her that she loves to go to the mall (in an attempt to use logic). The child is being completely consistent with wanting to control the situation, although she is inconsistent within her stated reason. Rather than let the child's logical inconsistency drive you to drink, it is important to see how the child is viewing the situation — the content is secondary to who is in control.

Juan Liked To Keep Adults Off Balance

Juan was in the early stages of residential treatment. He loved to see if he could confuse adults in large and small ways. Each situation was another chance to throw adults off balance. During a class I was teaching, he raised his hand when I asked a question. When I called upon him he smiled and said, "I didn't have my hand up, I was stretching," while holding back a small grin. Later in the class I asked many other questions and now Juan wanted to speak. Each time he raised his hand I said with a smile, "Juan is still stretching so I'll call on Tim." After this happened three times, Juan said in a frustrated tone, "You are just doing this to me on purpose." A couple of minutes later I came back to Juan and said, "Are you ready to make a deal with me that when your hand is up you are wanting to be called on?" He said, "OK," and eagerly participated the rest of the class. This was a very small matter, but the message was clear to Juan. The next day he told his roommate, "Don't lie to Dave, it never works."

The above example points out the first step of working successfully with the controlling child — understand why the child is doing what she is doing. The reasoning (or lack of reasoning) on the child's part may not seem logical to you, but it makes perfect sense to the child. When translating the reason behind the problem behavior of a difficult-to-raise child, I suggest the parent always consider the possibility the child either wants attention (positive or negative), or the child wants to be in control. There are many times that the motivation behind the behavior is neither of these two, but there are many more times that one or both hits the target right in the bull's-eye. If we do not understand the thinking and inner motivation of the child, the child will be one step ahead of the parent as we will see with Juan.

I have a sports analogy for this important step. Before there were professional basketball players right out of high school who were enticed by signing bonuses similar to the gross national product of some small countries, there were some very smart men who played the game. One of these was Bill Russell, who once described how he provided himself with an advantage over an athlete who may have been larger or more athletic. He studied his adversary and what the opponent liked and did not like to do on the court. If he did a good job, this knowledge of how the other player competed could provide him the winning advantage before the game even began on the court. Bill would find this method very useful if he was a foster or adoptive parent of a controlling child. On the court, the goal is to beat the opponent and win the game. However, the parent must first beat the opponent in order for both parent and child to win the game. This is a critical point for the people who object to thinking of parenting as a battle to be won. The goal of good parenting is always to help the child grow and learn, while encouraging the child to enjoy the process by modeling enjoying the process yourself. Until you win the control battle, you will find the child putting hurdles between you and being that good parent.

If you have had control battles in the past with your child, it is reasonable to expect more in the future. The surprise attack is a favorite control maneuver of the controlling child. Let's use the example of ten-year-old Sara, a young lady whose favorite activity is to go to the mall, except when you want her to do so. If the family is ready to go and Sara digs in her heels, the whole family is affected. However, anticipating this was a possibility could have given the parents a chance to arrange child care on a standby basis. When Sara protests that she would rather die than go to the mall, you can smile and say, "We thought you might not want to have too much fun all in one day with a movie and dinner at the food court in the mall, so we asked Aunt Mildred to stay with you." Her response will likely be "That is just fine with me," but do you believe her? The truth may not be in her words, but in her energy and body language.

This brings up another controversy with difficult children. I advocate being playful with interventions like the one in the previous paragraph. I have several reasons for this. The most effective intervention is one where the child has some insight over her behavior. I find it helpful to have the child know that you know what she is doing. In this way she may, in fact, get what she was demanding to get, but you both know that she paid a high price — being exposed. I like to consider the long-term with parenting interventions. For example, the next time the family goes to the mall, I might first have the parent mention to Sara, "We are all going to that new movie at the mall and you are invited, but we are guessing you won't want to go so we can call Aunt Mildred again." I would expect something back like, "No way, Mildred smells bad and won't let me do anything. I'm going to the mall." She wants you to believe your last intervention did not work; do you believe her?

Being playful with interventions not only helps the child consider what she is doing, but it provides a very important message about control. The best way to tell the child she is in control is to get upset, which is an ineffective intervention used by most parents on the planet. I will guarantee the child made a mental note of what upset you, and she will try this again several times before the next full moon or next sunset, whichever comes first. The opposite is to be in control of your own response and not get upset when Sara wants to take you for a control ride. When a control maneuver does not work, the child often looks elsewhere. Being playful indicates a message to the child that you are not being negatively affected, and your feelings are not available for her to control. Some parents ask, "But what if she does make you angry?" My response is, "Of course you will be angry at her sometimes; that is what she is trying to do, but do you want to let her win this round of the match?" If the child has you upset, do what you can to get back on your feet, and you can later tell someone else how upset you were. When parenting normal children it is helpful to express honest feelings because this helps the child learn how to act in ways to gain your approval. However, to a child who has a very different agenda, sharing your honest feelings about their actions will likely reinforce the behavior and give her ammunition against you.

The primary objection I have heard about using humor with interventions is that sarcasm is disrespectful. My response is that I agree, sarcasm is not respectful and has no place in good parenting. Being playful is not sarcasm. The term sarcasm is often incorrectly linked with being facetious or ironic, but they are not the same. Mr. Webster indicates that sarcasm means "making a mocking comment intended to wound someone." Wounding a child is never good parenting. A playful or facetious remark is not intended to hurt the child, but by changing the literal meaning of what is being said, you are making a point with the child. The situation with Sara provides an example. After staying with Aunt Mildred the first time rather than going to the mall with the family, the next time the parent says with a smile, "You would probably have more fun with Aunt Mildred than going to the mall, should I call her?" The smile indicates that you both know what is going on and your actual message is something like, "Is being controlling this time more important than seeing the new movie at the mall?" So why not just say your message straight? From my experience, controlling children frequently get stuck, and being playful can help them get unstuck. Sometimes you have to throw a curve ball to the child to slow her down just enough to make the point.

The intervention with Sara can also help illustrate the best intervention with controlling children. Instead of you confronting the child, have the child confront herself. Children with major control issues often seek control over their parent as the highest priority. If you attempt to say the equivalent of, "do as I say, or else," the child will generally choose "or else." If the child is able to act in a way to counter your parental decisions, a controlling child will often do so. However, if you are skillful enough to lay out the choices and consequences, the child is given the chance to decide. At times, having a choice is enough for the child to avoid a controlling stance. At other times, you have to be skillful enough to lay out alternatives so that the child must internally ask, "Do I want quality time with smelly Aunt Mildred, or do I want to see the new movie and get pizza at the mall?" It is important that you communicate that either way is fine with you. You may internally hope the child chooses a fun family event at the mall, but if you signal that in any way, you could inadvertently be encouraging the child to choose the opposite of what you want in order to win the control contest.

Each of the points being made with controlling children is designed to have the parent avoid being a target for the controlling child. If the controlling child is not sure which decision you prefer her to make, she is unclear how to oppose you. If you provide consequences for behavior without communicating that the situation upsets you, the controlling child is not sure how to attempt to control your emotions. This is a prime example of the statement that the adult must win the control battle for both the adult and the child to win in the end. By not being a big target, the parent encourages the child to develop other reasons for her decision rather than to "drive you to an early grave," as my 80-year-old grandmother used to say.

Another method of disrupting the automatic control mode of the child is the fine art of distraction. Many parents unsuccessfully use the same methods with difficult and controlling children as they do with other children. The adult calmly speaks directly to the child and tells the child exactly what is expected (generally a good idea in parenting), and the controlling child thinks to himself, "Thanks for letting me know how to try to get control over you," and declines to cooperate. Even if the parent uses humor, choices, or not giving the child a target to shoot at, the seriously controlling child may still decide to do what he thinks is the most disruptive. To anyone who at this point is thinking, "Is this guy kidding, do children really go to such extremes to be controlling and disruptive?", my answer is, yes, absolutely. But don't take my word for it; call any parent of a difficult child. The reason I know what these parents will say is that I have spoken to thousands of parents as well as personally parented these children for over twenty years.

Controlling others begins as a way to ensure the child's own survival. Afterward it becomes automatic or a habit that the child has little reason to change. You must give the child a reason to change this stance toward others and help him get unstuck when he finds himself in the control rut. Distracting the child can help him get out of the rut. Most parents are familiar with distracting toddlers — when the toddler becomes stuck wanting only one specific toy that is unavailable, the toy disappears and a more interesting alternative appears. The toddler may still protest, but if this is unsuccessful at getting what he wants, he usually will consider his other option. Older children are very similar, but the parents must be more sophisticated in their methods to distract the child. An example might be to bring up the issue of the movie at the mall with Sara well before it is time to go. If she begins to respond in a controlling manner, you can indicate that you don't have time to talk about it and she can think it over. She may be in a different frame of mind later in the day, particularly if you provided more interesting choices than fun with Aunt Mildred.

I ask parents to consider that controlling children will often try to prevail and attempts to control are inevitable. However, power struggles are different and always a losing proposition for the adult and for the child. The difference between an attempt by the child to control and a power struggle is the engagement of the adult. The minute the child says, "No, I won't do it," and the adult says, "Oh, yes, you will," the power struggle is well on its way to taking hold and everyone losing. So what else can a parent say when the child says, "No?" There are many responses I would suggest the parent use before, "Go ahead, make my day!" A power struggle is a recognition by the adult that the child is now a worthy adversary. The moment an adult communicates that the contest is on, the child is elevated from being a kid to being an opponent with the adult; and this always reinforces controlling maneuvers because the child gains more status. When the child says, "No" I often smile, and suggest the child think it over. I will return shortly, give the child a couple of choices with a time limit to decide, use distraction, use humor or set up some playful way to help the child see what is going on. All of these responses ignore the attempt at power and control by the child, and the adult clearly establishes that the child's invitation to a power struggle did not work with the adult.

Tantrums

Perhaps the quickest way to signal the challenging child that you are not available for power struggles is to learn to manage tantrums. Tantrums are not restricted to children, adults have them all the time. People throw tantrums for a variety of reasons, but the most common is to express to people around them that things are not going the way the person throwing the tantrum prefers. Children are no different; they communicate their displeasure not by filling out a form for the family suggestion box — they scream, cry, throw things and make a maximum clamor to ensure that everyone in your zip code is aware that the child is unhappy. Tantrums are a wonderful place to start to get the upper hand in the power and control battle with children. In the mind of a child, a well-played-out tantrum is a serious display of power. The response of adults determines how successful the tantrum was and provides information to the child regarding how frequently this method should be used in the future. Ergo, if I received everyone's attention and, even better, if I upset an adult, tantrums are the way to go.

The best tantrums (from the child's perspective) are those that bring the environment to a halt and disrupt everyone and everything. For this reason, tantrums in public places are personal favorites of some children. Tantrums are difficult for adults to deal with, which is why they provide the child with a sense of power and control. It is difficult to be around a child throwing a tantrum, much less to be in a public place where other adults assume this little fallen angel has your last name. Tantrums are so blatant in motivation and in implementation, they are actually some of the easier power plays by a child for parents to extinguish.

Public tantrums are somewhat more difficult to address, so we will start with tantrums at home and school. Tantrums come in many forms and can occur for a variety of reasons. It is always a good starting place to translate the behavior, and ask yourself, "what is behind the tantrum and what does the child hope to gain?" Remember to always consider if control and attention are potential motivations. Depending on the age of the child, tantrums usually do not have a strong cognitive foundation. Tantrums are usually amplified emotional displays, although there are some children, much like Oscar-winning actors, who can turn an emotional display on and off as they choose. One of the goals of handling a tantrum is to bring a level of thinking into the situation for the child.

Doug's Tantrum Time

Doug was in a rut and this was most obvious at bedtime. He would find a reason to get upset just about bedtime each evening. Each of his tantrums was handled with little energy, but it became so predictable we changed the environment with an intervention. I told everyone in the family that we had something special this evening, so we would stop evening play a little early. Before Doug had a chance to find a reason to tantrum that night, I got everyone together and said we would begin to structure Doug's tantrum into the schedule and we would all rate him on how good the tantrum was. Doug was speechless for a minute and everyone waited for his evening tantrum. Finally, Doug told everyone he would not do it. The children expressed disappointment because they wanted to rate his effort. Over the next three nights we met for Doug's tantrum time, but he never obliged. He continued to have tantrums at other times in the day but this disrupted the rut of his evening tantrums.

Many tantrums are not conscious maneuvers by the child. Abused and particularly neglected children can have an instantaneous negative response to a variety of events, such as unanticipated changes, disappointments, surprises and not getting exactly what they want when they want it. These children move directly to emotional displays without the situation coming to the attention of the brain's reasoning centers. As with other interventions with difficult children, it becomes the job of the adult to provide from the outside what the child lacks on the inside — thinking through the situation. However, before we will be successful in interjecting some rational thought into the awareness of a tantruming child, we must be able to absorb the initial blast.

Since a tantrum is predicated on maximum commotion and disruption, it is important that the behavior does not achieve its intended results or it will be coded into the child's experience as a success. Children are like adults — what worked for us in the past generates our preference in the future. If tantrums get the child what he is initially seeking, the tantrum has been reinforced and will be repeated. However, if the child does not get the desired result after repeated tantrums, there is a greater possibility that the child will try something else to get what he or she wants.

The first response to a tantrum is to respond to the child in a way the child does not expect. The child plans on upsetting or frustrating you and is most successful when the tantrum makes you angry. Being able to frustrate an adult, which is pretty easy with many of us, is a clear indicator to the child he is winning the battle. Within a short period of time, a difficult child will be able to sense exactly what will push the buttons of the adult he is targeting. Adults often make it easy for the child to find our emotional weaknesses; we simply react to what the child says or does and the child makes a mental note.

If the purpose of a tantrum is to disrupt the situation or to frustrate or anger the adult, the best interventions will ensure that the situation is minimally disrupted and the adult does not emotionally react as the child expects. Working with tantrums brings us back to the "C" in my TLC model, which stands for control. It is critical that the adult maintains control of emotional reactions to the child's misbehavior. As parents, we must maintain control over our emotions and reactions or the child gains the emotional upper hand. It is also important that we maintain control of the environment, so that the child is not successful in disrupting what is going on.

I have encountered schools and treatment programs that remove everyone from the situation when a child begins to be disruptive. For example, when the child starts a tantrum in the special education classroom, the teachers have the other students leave the room until the situation is resolved. If others find this helpful, fine, but I would advise against taking this course of action. It is a very powerful message to give the child that he can disrupt everyone in the classroom, and make everyone stop what they are doing and go elsewhere whenever he decides to be a problem. I remove the child from the situation so he cannot disrupt others.

The primary ingredient of a tantrum is an audience. Many children go to their rooms and cry and even throw things, but a tantrum requires that someone either knows or witnesses your emotional and behavioral explosion. Most tantrums end within minutes or even seconds when the audience is no longer available. This is a key step to extinguishing tantruming behavior in the long run — respond to tantrums by eliminating the audience. This can be done by removing the child from the situation, or by not giving the child's actions your undivided attention.

At the point the audience has been removed, and you have translated the behavior and determined what the child is wanting, you can now offer the child your thoughts on how he can modify his approach to have a better chance of getting what he ultimately wants. For example, Bert begins to yell and cry because another child is playing with the toy he wants. If Bert notices that no one is being disrupted by his outburst, he will probably change his response to something like grabbing the toy, attacking the other child, or turning up the volume on the tantrum. These are all methods to exert more power over the situation. I would tell Bert he needs to go to his room, and when he is finished being upset we will talk about better ways to have a turn with the toy. If this sounds much too easy, it really isn't. It may take a number of times to successfully reach this child who has learned in the past that adults can be controlled and pushed to react to his power plays. But if you maintain your cool, most children will change. I have worked with children extremely skilled at controlling adults, who within a short time actually say to me, "Tantrums don't work with you."

I said this discussion would come back to tantrums in public places. I admire the skills of children who are able to pick a time and place that makes responding to tantrums extremely difficult. I make this point to show that I work with children, in part, to learn from them, which is the "L" in the TLC model. I hope to learn to be a more effective parent every day, and this will only happen if children stretch my skills at counteracting their skills. Some of you may be thinking, "I would be fine with taking the day off from learning to be a better parent if the child decided to cooperate." I agree, but I am always prepared to learn, and in my world I don't have to wait long for the next lesson.

Public places do not change the primary response to tantrums: 1) Translate the behavior; 2) Stay in control of your emotions, reactions and the environment; 3) Remove the audience; and 4) Help the child think about better ways to get what she wants. A public environment primarily changes two factors — it makes it more challenging to remove the audience and it requires a new level of internal control on the part of the adult. Regardless of the setting, it remains important to remove the audience. If you are in a movie theater, it is time to head for the exit with the child. If you are on the city bus, it is time to get off at the next stop. If you are at the playground, it is time to move away from the other children.

The increased inner control required of an adult dealing with a tantrum in a public place is needed to handle the response of other adults, not the child. Everyone has a better idea about how to raise your child, just as you have a better idea about how they could raise theirs. You must be able to withstand the silent looks or vocal judgments from other adults in the public setting. If they are not wearing a police badge, I suggest you ignore the looks, comments, or advice of adults more than willing to demonstrate their ignorance about handling your difficult child. Allowing such people to judge you or verbally reacting to them is more than they deserve. Some of the most harsh judgments may come from your extended family. If the tantruming child can get adults to have some conflict, all the better. It is not easy to walk out of the church with a screaming child in tow. Although this is not your favorite experience, it is just another opportunity that comes with parenting a difficult child.

As I mentioned earlier, there are many types of tantrums and each intervention to address tantrums needs to be specific to the situation at hand. There are many ways that children have tantrums that are designed to upset the adult in the situation. Many times the child chooses an issue that he knows will get the adult fired up, such as lying, stealing, violence or sexual behavior. When the adult takes the bait, the child uses that opportunity to let the feathers fly. Many adults do not see the connection between the events and the subsequent tantrum. It is important to realize that children are capable of baiting adults in order to set up a tantrum. If you are a step ahead of a child doing this, you have many alternatives you can use, including deciding the time and place to deal with the situation. Anticipation and having a battle plan ready can be invaluable.

WAYS TO WIN THE BATTLE

✓ Use "TLC" — **T**ranslating, **L**earning and being in **C**ontrol of yourself and the environment.

✓ Children need the assurance that the adult is in charge, even if they struggle for power and control.

✓ Work to understand what is behind behavior.

✓ Plan ahead, be one or two steps ahead of the child.

✓ Instead of getting upset, be playful with interventions that catch the child off balance.

✓ Don't be an easy target, have the child confront himself or herself.

✓ Learn to distract the child.

✓ Eliminate the audience with tantrums.

✓ With tantrums, use four steps: 1. Translate the behavior, 2. Stay in control of yourself, 3. Remove the audience, 4. After it is over help the child see there are better ways of getting what she wants.

When asked to make a wish list for her birthday, the confident four-year-old said, "Don't need to, I already told God!"

Chapter

2

Helping Children Master Responsibility

The primary job of a parent is to help a child to grow and mature. Maturity is synonymous with responsibility. As parents we must prepare children to understand the situation they are in, to determine how to respond to the situation, and then work with the consequences of their actions. These are all very complex steps. It is common for adults to observe that troubled children do not distinguish themselves in the area of responsibility. Children who have behavioral and emotional problems are not the only ones who struggle with responsibility. All too frequently another corporate executive is in the news being charged with a white collar crime who says, "I am innocent and I look forward to my day in court to prove it." Apparently the hope is we will forget such a statement by the time the trial occurs and the verdict comes back guilty as charged. Too often confident claims of innocence are euphemisms for, "Just wait and see how long it takes for my highly paid attorneys to get me out of this mess." There are certainly exceptions, but corporate America has not set the best example of responsibility.

It is not just corporate America that struggles with responsibility. After all, we live in a country where the motto could have been Life, Liberty and the Pursuit of Responsibility. Instead we collectively hold our freedom and our desires to be paramount over altruism and self-denial. Even in the halls of power, more than a few inhabitants of the White House have struggled with being responsible. Given the complexity of learning to be responsible, it may seem beyond the grasp of a troubled child. That is just what such a child would like you to believe, but don't buy it. We must insist that our presidents, our corporate executives and our children act responsibly. It is precisely the individual who attempts to avoid being held accountable who needs an external structure, and with children this external structure consists of the parent, the teacher, and other important adults in the child's life.

After a few general comments, I will lay out some ideas intended to help parents with the difficult job of teaching responsibility to a child who is less than excited about the concept. My first comment I alluded to above. I believe that with all that is right about our American culture, there are some issues that are not right, and responsibility is on the latter list much too often. Perhaps we struggle with responsibility in America, in part, because our nation's early inhabitants were not very good at obeying rules, although most would say they had good reason for this. When our forefathers set up communities and a governing structure, they took great pains to put an emphasis on individual rights, not the rights of the community over the individual. With a slightly different orientation by our founding fathers, the Bill of Rights could just as well have been a Bill of Responsibilities. Our nation started with an emphasis on the individual to a degree not seen previously in either the western or eastern worlds.

We continue to see the results of a mindset where the rights and freedoms of individuals are often protected over the well-being of the community. We ensure that insulting people are able to speak. We allow pornography in the name of free speech. Whether you are for or against the American Civil Liberties Union, it has clearly made a cause of protecting the most distasteful and offensive opinions and acts by individuals, regardless of the effect on the larger community. The ACLU is actually a direct extension of what our founding fathers had in mind for our government, although this statement would ruffle any good conservative, a term that used to include conserving the constitution.

In our American culture, we detest and at the same time are fascinated by irresponsible figures. We have radio personalities who try to be more shocking than the next guy. We entertain ourselves with movies and books that depict the latest loner, criminal, or rebel without a cause. Some actors and famous athletes forget who they really are and become the public stereotype of the bad boy or girl. Hit movies are rarely rated "G" because they do poorly at the box office if they present nothing objectionable, and popular music is not designed to be liked by grandmas. It is an unfortunate fact that the quickest way to become famous in America is to do something extremely irresponsible, a reality not lost on President Reagan's gunman, John Hinkley, Jr., or the latest teen who takes an automatic weapon to school with the intent to use it.

There is much more that could be said about the tenuous state of responsible behavior in our culture. I touched on this subject above because with all the hard work of a parent to teach a child responsibility, there are many other voices giving the child a very different message. We may not be able to silence all the confusing noise coming at a child, but as parents we need to know what the child is hearing and from what sources.

I believe children gravitate to heroes. Unfortunately, our culture seems to have lost the true meaning of what a hero is. In America, too many of our heroes are athletes who make obscene amounts of money. Heroes are also movie actors and actresses who pretend to be someone else for a living — what is heroic about that? Other heroes have power and influence, but don't always use it for the good of others. We seem to have lost an important ingredient of any true hero and that is responsibility. Children seem to pick heroes such as the rap singer who can put the most offensive words in one sentence, the young female singer who shows more skin in a concert than you would see in most locker rooms, or the professional wrestler who is threatening and violent for a living. As parents, we need to offer other alternatives of true heroes who were responsible for themselves and others, and made a difference in our world. Such extraordinary people can be found, like Mother Teresa, the Dalai Lama, Rosa Parks, the young man in Tiananmen Square who stood in front of and stopped several tanks, or the friend of the disabled coworker who stayed by his side in the World Trade Center to the end. I believe it is the job of the parent to bring to the attention of the child individuals truly worthy of admiration. If you don't help children learn what a true hero is, our culture will fill the void with someone modeling values we do not want our children to admire.

My last general comment about this topic, before we discuss ideas for teaching responsibility, is to take a closer look at the many children with histories of abuse who spend much of their day denying responsibility. I often mention a dynamic that I observe with challenging children that they speak and act in opposites. What I mean by this is that the content of their statements may be the opposite of what they are thinking and feeling. For example, the child who says, "I hate this family," may actually be saying, "Why are you all being so nice to me when my birth family never was? It bothers me that I am beginning to like it here." I have found that sometimes children have a similar dynamic when it comes to responsibility. When a child constantly says, "It was not my fault," or "I didn't make the mistake," they may actually be thinking and feeling, "I'm the one who never does anything right." Some children learn from their past (either by the words of abusive adults or by experience) that bad things happen around them. These children internalize responsibility for negative outcomes. These are the children who believe they are the "bad seed." I have worked with numerous children who begin treatment with the theme, "it is everyone else who is messed up, not me," but later in treatment they confess that they believe they are the true problem in most situations. I suggest you consider this dynamic of speaking in opposites if you have a child who fanatically denies all levels of responsibility.

Tina Doesn't Make Mistakes

Overall, Tina was a good employee, hard working and dedicated to her job. Things were fine as long as things were fine. If a problem came up, Tina was the first to spot it and the first to identify the cause of the problem — someone else. It became clear that she was an equal opportunity blamer, as long as the fault lay as far from her as possible. She wasn't always careful in her blaming and was frequently wrong, which did not seem to distress her. I wondered how to alter this dynamic. One day when Tina was bringing a relatively minor problem to my attention along with the perpetrator from her perspective, I asked, "Is this your mistake?" There was an immediate, "No!" then silence, and finally tears. Tina was a little abused child in a grown-up body. Over time she was able to tell me that she was told by her family that she was the problem in the home, something she unconsciously did not want to have happen in her work. People grow up, but trauma often remains.

Like many other protests, it may be helpful to consider if a child denying any responsibility is actually thinking the opposite, that he or she is responsible for everything that has gone wrong. If this is true with the child you are working with, you can see that it may be counterproductive to continue to confront the child with more and more responsibility he may rightfully have. The result could be more denial since he may be thinking that if he accepts even the slightest responsibility, it will become obvious to others what he already knows — that all the problems are his fault.

Mastering Responsibility

We start our task with the acknowledgment that teaching responsibility is a very difficult and complex job, especially in an environment that often works against us. However, we can and must succeed in this job or the child and society will ultimately be the losers. Teaching responsibility is equally as difficult as teaching empathy, self-denial or moral decision making. In other words, it is one of the most difficult tasks of a parent. From the primitive reasoning of a child's mind, why would anyone ever say they broke the window if they could blame someone else? It just doesn't make sense to get yourself in trouble. Why would someone think of others when there is a real opportunity to score big for yourself? Just ask the convicted corporate executive — the temptation is formidable. As difficult as the task of teaching responsibility is, parents do a pretty good job with most children. For the most part, the way to teach responsibility to troubled children is very similar to other children, it just may take some adjustments as well as more concerted effort.

There is no trick or easy-to-follow formula for teaching responsibility; however, I like to break down this challenge with the help of the letters in the word *master*. A master of anything means you have put in the time and effort to understand and achieve the desired outcomes by continual practice until it becomes second nature. This may be the distinguishing feature between either the CEO who does right and the one who does wrong, or the child who does right or wrong: what is second nature to the person? As in any pursuit, it does not work to wait until a critical time to demonstrate important values and decisions; one must operate responsibly in many small ways to enable responsibility to become second nature with large issues. If someone stretches the truth or cheats just a little as a daily style, there is little question what the person will gravitate to when the chips are down and the stress is high. The following are some thoughts on teaching a child to MASTER responsibility.

Modeling Responsibility Yourself

You knew it was coming: step number one is to teach by modeling. Of all the sophisticated approaches in learning theory, none has outperformed the power of children learning from what they observe from others, in particular, what they observe from parents. To the dismay of many adults, they cannot have it just one way and have the child only following their good example. In fact, it is more frequent that children learn the negative behavior from parents first, even though the positive behaviors are also absorbed. Our greatest influence on children is our silent teaching by our actions. The smokers of tomorrow are much more likely to come from a parent who smokes; the children of convicted criminals are much more likely than their peers to be involved in crime. However, the converse is also true that children are more likely to live by spiritual and ethical principles when they have parents who live in this way. In a behavioral way, the Biblical admonition is true that the sins of the parents come to rest on their children, but the same can be said of the virtues of the parents as well.

A point often missed by parents may be one of the most important aspects of teaching responsibility — admit and correct your own mistakes in the presence of children. Some parents believe that when they make a mistake, it is a good idea to keep it quiet so the child does not know, and the parent can save personal embarrassment. However, this reasoning takes away a wonderful opportunity to teach several essential aspects of responsibility. To admit to a child that you have made a mistake, first of all, models taking responsibility for your actions. How often do we expect children to do this, and how are they to get better at admitting mistakes if they do not see this modeled by parents? It also gives the child the message that mistakes are made by everyone and can be forgiven and overcome. Admitting a mistake is a statement of personal strength that we want our children to learn how to do. So, go out of your way to admit your errors, apologize to those negatively affected and commit to making positive changes — that is, if you want your child to learn to take these steps.

Being a parent for a child is one of the best reasons there is to be the best person you can possibly be. Many people make life improving changes at the point they become parents. However, too many other parents believe they can continue negative habits and somehow shield their child from learning the wrong way to live. This is not intended to be a self-help book, but you would be wise to stop reading at this point and ask yourself what you should change about yourself to be a healthier person in mind, body and spirit, and then make a commitment to yourself to work on this, if not for yourself, then for your child's sake.

An Environment Where Responsible Behavior Is the Norm

Human beings are instinctively predisposed to be social creatures. We are incapable of survival in our early years and generally throughout life without the presence, support and assistance of a social network. Social creatures rely heavily on learning from the example of others. For this reason, as parents we need to look around and see what example is being set by relatives, friends, and all family members. One of the critical reasons parents need to be aware of the social group children interact with as they grow older is the power of modeling on the child. There is a significant difference in the values modeled in a street gang and in a church group.

The environment around a child demonstrates how conflict is handled; it lays out expectations for children regarding the balance of meeting our own needs and the needs of others. Gandhi, an excellent example of personal responsibility, once defined community as the act of voluntary renunciation. In other words, we get along with others to the degree we are able to defer our personal wants and desires and consider others. Our families are the first community that children experience. How well do the members of your family demonstrate the ability to think of the needs of others in the family as well as thinking of their own personal needs? The odds are the child will grow up with a similar disposition. In Adlerian psychology, and in conventional wisdom, there is usually a dynamic created with families with only one child. There is no need to share with others, to do things the way another child wants to do it, or to negotiate throughout the day to balance your needs with those of siblings. The result may be an individual who struggles more with deferring personal needs for the needs of others. This certainly does not always happen, but it points out the impact of environmental modeling and practice.

There are several qualities of a family environment that teach responsibility. Families that have members who think of each other model to children to do the same. Parents who listen to their children model being listened to in return. Homes that demonstrate family members taking pride in personal space promote in the child the respect for the property of others and of self. Parents who discuss disagreements and strong feelings demonstrate responsible ways to handle conflict. Parents who discuss moral questions with children present demonstrate the process of careful consideration of decisions. Each of the components of responsible decision-making and responsible behavior needs to be present in the environment of a child if responsibility is to be effectively learned.

Stop Irresponsible Behavior Before It Becomes a Habit

There is no way around the fact that what you allow, you condone; and what you condone, you support. This is true in world events and it is true in families. I agree with the advice to parents to pick your issues, but this cannot turn into giving ground to children on a wide variety of issues related to responsibility. Children modify the way they test the rules as they mature. Watch a toddler do what she knows is off limits as she checks to see if the adult is going to hold firm. As children grow older they continue to test the limits, and adults maintaining a high standard of responsibility remains important.

The goal of teaching responsibility is to have the child demonstrate, through repetition, behaviors and choices that reflect thoughtful consideration of the situation. Practice makes perfect, well, at least pretty good. Repetition combined with reinforcement helps the child's brain to develop positive, habitual responsibility. Just as positive habits can develop, negative ones seem to develop even more easily. Irresponsible patterns are reinforced when they are not challenged, not corrected and the environment is one of a false good/bad dichotomy. No one is responsible all the time and certainly not children. Punitive responses, rather than discipline that teaches, create an environment where it is not safe to make mistakes. A child who fears making a mistake adapts with a wide range of negative responses, from being passive, to secretive, to denying responsibility for actions — all prompted by the fear of punishment. An environment that teaches responsibility accepts the fact that everyone in the family makes mistakes, and that these are excellent opportunities to learn more responsible choices and behaviors.

Close Was A Good Start For Richard

Sometimes as parents we forget that this race is a marathon and not a sprint. A marathon run requires endurance, determination and a lot of work before it is time to rest. Richard helped me remember this lesson. There were so many problems with his behavior, his attitude, his hygiene, and his loud, often unpleasant personality. Where to begin? To top it off, Richard would oppose you or disagree with you just because you were an adult. I broke his many issues down to small units. I began to work on one or two at a time. I changed the issues frequently so he could not figure out my goal, and therefore it would be harder to oppose it. He was visibly confused that I ignored some obnoxious behavior (not on my list that day) while I complimented him on some other issue. "What is the fun of fighting with adults when they don't fight back," was the look I saw on his face. Over time he began to cooperate with me, but I watched as he successfully engaged other adults in the type of battle that was his specialty. Richard had found another sprinting adult, and the game had begun!

It is more accurate to consider responsibility on a continuum rather than all or nothing. Parenting can help the child by shaping approximations of responsibility. Just as the parent needs to correct irresponsibility, a parent can also point out how a child who does well can do even better. Shaping behavior must be done to prevent the child from feeling criticized and believing he can never do anything right. A good way to teach responsibility is to find the best aspect of any behavior and reinforce and build upon this foundation. It also works to think out loud with the child about how your own decisions in situations could have demonstrated even more responsibility than they initially did. The parent who opens his or her own performance to discussion teaches a child to do the same.

The best time to shape behaviors is as early as possible. We know from information on brain development that habitual behavior has a physiological component within the brain. Negative and positive behaviors and attitudes tend to develop into patterns, in part, because of the way the brain processes information. The more developed a pattern is, the more resistant it is to change. When a parent first sees an issue that needs correction, there is literally no time like the present to teach a better way to handle the situation.

Teach Responsibility at the Youngest Possible Age

In the same way that early correction improves the chances that a parent will be successful in preventing bad habits and promoting good habits, teaching children early in childhood always has more lasting results than the same effort in later years. There is no question that a person can learn new behaviors at any age of life, but the amount of effort it takes increases as the child's age increases. I believe there is a very good reason that the popular book *All I Really Need To Know I Learned in Kindergarten* (Fulghum, 1990) was not titled *All I Really Need To Know I Learned in Graduate School.*

Teaching children about responsibility is not only a good idea when the child is young, but there is a strong scientific reason to do so. We now know from research about how people learn that there are critical periods in life where learning takes place at a highly accelerated pace. For example, the critical period of learning language (expressive and receptive) is between 18 and 36 months of age. Like language, many of the critical periods of learning are in very early childhood. Part of the downside of this discovery is that many troubled children were being neglected or abused during critical learning periods and missed very important opportunities to grow and develop in a variety of areas.

Responsibility is like other important lessons children need to learn in that it must be taught in increments based on the developmental level of the child. Moral reasoning will be taught differently to a 3-year-old and a 13-year-old. The important areas of responsibility such as correctly understanding the situation, consideration of others, formulating a response, and learning from actions, can and should be taught to children very young in a way the child can understand. To the question "when is it time to teach responsibility?" the answer is "as early as possible."

It is a good idea with all children, but particularly with young children, to have them practice various aspects of responsible decision-making and behavior. Repetition is the key to many types of effective learning. At times it is good to have children practice or even mimic behavior that they resist. Even in these situations, the repetition has a positive influence on the way the brain processes the new approach. This lends some credibility to the phrase "fake it until you make it."

Expect Responsible Behavior Every Time

Although everything covered in this chapter can be used with all children, the particular focus we have is with troubled children. Although the principles are the same, specific interventions can be quite different. The odds are good that the troubled child you are thinking about as you read this is a child who has taken on many adults before you came into the picture and has prevailed against many, possibly all of them. One of the differences between teaching responsibility to your biological child and doing so with your foster or adopted child is that the latter often has a history that you must overcome to move forward in a positive direction. Responsibility is an attribute for which troubled children seldom come up and ask for instruction. Why should they? They would prefer to think only about personal needs and ensure that they maximize what they want and minimize what they don't want.

This orientation is often the opposite of your agenda for them as their parent.

I have noticed that a favorite tactic of troubled children is to present such an overwhelming display of misbehavior that the child trains the adult to systematically lower the expectations they have for the child. Beware of this trap — it will end in failure for both you and the child.

Children use a variety of methods to extinguish your behavior of correcting them by linking an aversive behavior to your correction. Let's try that again: children like to punish adults who correct them. If you think that smart adults would never fall for this, think again. It is startling how many adults who work with troubled children have been trained by the child to modify the precise instruction the child needs.

There are a number of ways that children train adults to lower their expectations. Children often have tantrums when corrected. This behavior is nearly always a signal to me that the child needs more, not less, practice related to the issue at hand. Children will intensify the negative behavior when you focus on it. I tell parents to expect this and to be prepared to handle the initial reaction. The child is telling the adult, "Go ahead and make my day." I suggest you go right ahead with working on the issue at hand, regardless of the ways the child punishes you for doing so. In fact, I often tell the child I am raising my expectations based upon their negative reaction, which proves there is more work needed on the issue.

One technique that may help with children who punish you when you work with them on responsibility is to predict that they might do so. It is common for many children not to do something that you predict they will do. This is unlikely to be because of added personal insight; it is more likely that they refuse to have you believe you are correct. You can predict a child's behavior by saying something like, "You will probably want to throw a tantrum, but we are going to talk about your behavior today on the school playground." This often takes the child by surprise, and disrupts the child just enough to change the outcome. Don't try to use this approach every time or you will be giving the child the cue to begin a tantrum.

Expecting responsible behavior every time can take the form of having a focus on the small issues in a situation. I have found with many troubled children that when I work on the small issues, the large issues tend to come up less often. For example, when I transport one or more troubled children in a vehicle, I make it clear each and every time that safety will not be compromised. We do a checklist before I start the vehicle: seat belts, space, voice level, rules for the trip, and anything I might anticipate would come up. At the first sign of even a small issue, I may pull the vehicle over to the side of the road and make any needed correction. I tend to avoid problems with loud, acting out children at a time that safety could easily be compromised. Another example is at dinner time. There are a number of very clear issues that are relatively minor that I enforce at meal times. I expect children to make polite requests, eat correctly with utensils, and chew with their mouths closed. When I focus on these relatively minor details, the more blatant misbehavior at meals is rare, even with twenty emotionally disturbed children at the same dinner table!

Reinforce Responsible Behavior Each Time You See It

Although it is a very difficult job to teach responsibility, particularly to a troubled child, the best methods are relatively straightforward and good common sense. This is especially true for this last discussion point related to reinforcement. Over 100 years ago, the new field of social science called psychology was making great strides in understanding human behavior. Some of the new principles being developed were coming from scientific experiments with animals and became known as behaviorism. While some of these experiments took place before the Wright Brothers' first flight, the principles are as valid today as they were initially. One of these behavioral principles is reinforcement.

Briefly stated, the principle of behavioral reinforcement is that any behavior that results in consequences either desirable or undesirable to the child will influence the child's behavior.

Positive reinforcement occurs when a child has a desirable outcome from the behavior which promotes or "reinforces" the child to repeat the behavior. Negative reinforcement also affects behavior, but is often misunderstood. Negative reinforcement has nothing to do with negative energy from the parent or the child, it simply means that something desired is withheld, prompting the child to change his or her behavior to regain the desired result.

Both positive and negative reinforcement are important components of teaching responsibility. It is essential that children of all ages notice that demonstrating responsible behavior results in desirable outcomes. Many parents take the position that they expect responsibility, and the child does not deserve something special just for doing what he or she is supposed to do. This parenting style does not take advantage of reinforcement, which has been found to be one of the most effective means to shape behavior. Withdrawing desired consequences is also an effective way to reinforce the types of behavior the parent wants to promote from the child. It is always a good idea to frame withdrawing desired outcomes not as punishment, but as a means for the child to refocus before returning to obtain the desired result from responsible behavior.

Another aspect of understanding behavior is that, generally, what is not reinforced tends to decrease in frequency. This is one way to extinguish or decrease an undesirable behavior, which is to not reinforce it. With this principle in mind, it is useful to consider what happens when a child shows some level of responsibility but receives no external reinforcement (either a comment, a privilege, or a reward). In such a case, the demonstration of responsibility may actually decrease in frequency. This principle is the foundation for the emphasis on providing young children with more praise than criticism. Being able to have this balance leaning in the direction of praise can be very challenging, indeed, when parenting a troubled child.

Jack's Training Program

It is not just adults who use reinforcement to achieve their goals; so do difficult children. Jack was the most difficult type of troubled child. His abuse was so severe and he was so young that he would win by losing. By this, I mean he would do anything to anyone who opposed him, regardless of the consequences to himself or the adult. When Jack came to our program, I was told in no uncertain terms not to directly say, "No" to him, or he would hurt himself and you and ruin the rest of the day. Don't ever say "No" to a difficult child? That was a new one. My immediate guess was that Jack was training the adults through negative reinforcement to act the way he wished them to act. He would link peaceful behavior with getting what he wanted. I listened to the advice not to tell him "No," but I went a different direction. I told him "No" frequently. He responded as I was warned he would, which was his training program. I let him know his response told me that he needed more practice hearing "No," so I would say "No" even when I normally would say "Yes," until he could handle it. He did his best, but it was not good enough to train me.

This very quick look at principles of behavioral conditioning leads to the conclusion that it is a very good idea to reinforce responsible behaviors each time you notice such behaviors. It is also a good idea to get beyond the internal resistance some adults have to giving children frequent praise. At times a parent will say, "She just did that so I would notice and praise her for it." Rather than such behavior being an undesirable manipulation on the child's part, if she actually is doing something positive in order to get the adult's praise, this is very good news. The best dynamic that can be developed between a parent and a child is for the child to consider his or her behavior based upon the values being put forth by the parent and wanting to please the parent. This is an approval motivation on the part of the child. Whenever you experience that the child is wanting your approval, do your best to give such approval if it is linked to approximations of responsibility.

CHECKLIST FOR TEACHING RESPONSIBILITY

✓ Responsibility does not come naturally to children; it must be taught and mastered.

✓ Don't get frustrated if it takes considerable time and effort to begin to see results.

✓ There is no substitute to your modeling or being a good example.

✓ Your home must be a place where responsible behavior is the norm.

✓ Work to eliminate irresponsible behavior before it becomes a habit.

✓ The younger you teach responsibility, the more return you will get on your investment.

✓ Don't let the child train you to lower your expectations, expect responsible behavior every time.

✓ Use principles of behavior reinforcement to encourage the child to learn responsibility.

When his therapist was speaking to him about not chewing his fingernails, the seven-year-old had an idea, "Maybe you could put tobacco sauce on my fingernails." [Please pass the sauce!]

Chapter

3

Positive Discipline

Successful parenting is all about finding the balance between doing enough and not doing too much. Parenting requires a balance between being firm and holding out high expectations, but not demanding too much of a child. No less an authority on child rearing than the Bible admonishes parents not to nag children lest they lose heart. At the same time, we have talked in previous chapters about communicating high expectations in order to give children the confidence to become what they are capable of becoming. The motivation of the parent, along with the way parenting is received by the child, will determine whether the parent finds a successful balance.

When a parent has high expectations of a child, this can be either helpful or unhelpful to the child. The first factor that determines which it will be depends on what the parent wants to accomplish. It is essential that corrections from a parent are designed to build up the child, not tear down the child. Children do a very good job of fulfilling the expectations adults have of them. If an adult communicates expectations of poor behavior, generally the adult will get just that. However, if a correction is stated in a way to help the child see his or her potential, the result has a much better chance of producing a positive outcome.

The motivation of the parent in correcting the child is not the only important dynamic of whether it is likely to be a successful intervention. The other important element is how the energy and the words of the adult are received by the child. The parent may be sending one message, yet a very different message is received by the child. This is particularly true for children who have a background of abuse. A frequent disposition created by abuse of a child is a negative sense of self-worth. "If I were a good person, why would my dad have treated me like he did?" This is not always verbalized, but it is nearly universally a thought abused children have. Since the parent of an abused child is fighting a negative sense of self in the child, it is essential to consider how parental corrections are received. We can anticipate the child hearing a much more negative message than we intend, and we can counteract this by choosing our corrective words carefully. The parent can also translate the child's affect and response to understand the message the child received, regardless of the message that was intended.

Parenting is fundamentally about teaching the child life skills by example, by instruction, and by making corrections each and every day. If the child witnesses poor modeling from adults, or if the child experiences each instruction and every correction as a statement the adult does not have faith in the child's ability to do a good job, parenting can quickly become a losing proposition for both parent and child. The point has already been made that ineffective parents communicate to the child, "Do as I say, not as I do." Parents have complete control over the type of example they set for the child. A parent also has some control over how the child receives instruction and correction based on the way the parent approaches the child.

To help find a balance for parents on the continuum of doing enough but not too much, and correcting the child but not being overly critical, I suggest the concept of **positive discipline**. The English language is rich in the history of how words derive their meanings. It can help to understand a word by considering its etymology or the origin of the word's initial meaning. Discipline is a word that has unfortunately lost some of its initial meaning, and when it comes to parenting, it is important to get back to what discipline should be about. Discipline comes from the Latin word *discere,* meaning to teach. Discipline in modern usage is often equated with penalizing someone. However, when it comes to successful parenting, discipline cannot be punishment; it is not harsh correction, or being confrontational in a punitive way. The word punishment also provides us with a helpful understanding of its meaning based on its roots. Punishment also comes from a Latin word *poenire,* meaning to cause someone to undergo pain or suffering or to subject someone to a harsh penalty for a wrongdoing. Punishment has stayed closer to its original meaning, as we can see from terms like capital punishment.

Positive discipline means to teach a child how to better handle a situation by employing a positive intervention. Before discussing positive discipline further, it may be helpful to ask the question, "So what is so wrong with punishing a child to teach him not to misbehave? Are you suggesting I coddle the kid?" To answer this question, I will first acknowledge that punishing children does change them. Many times it decreases the misbehavior (not always), but it makes several unintended changes as well. When punished, children often lower their internal expectations of their own behavior — they often get down on themselves and view themselves in a negative way. Some children fight back and protest any type of punishment. Punishment can easily become the battleground of a power struggle.

Crafty children see punishment as an excuse to punish either the parent and family or to punish someone more vulnerable than themselves. Although punishment, such as spanking a child for using coarse language, can have an immediate effect of reducing the problem behavior, it does not tend to generalize to other situations. The child may come out of the situation thinking, "I need to stop saying 'goddamnit' around him, but he can't control me when he isn't around." Other children respond to punishment based on modeling and learn to punish right back. Difficult children can often dream up more creative ways to punish adults than most adults can come up with ways to punish children (this does not include abusive parents). The answer to the question, "Why not use punishment?" is that there are much more effective ways to parent a child, and the most important aspect of parenting is what works the best in the long run.

As important as teaching is in discipline, just as essential is a positive approach to teaching. There are many subjects that we have all been exposed to as children and adults. The areas of learning that we tend to gravitate to are those where we show a level of skill and aptitude. Since we are new to the topic area, we look to others to provide us with information as to how well we are grasping the material. I hope to stay far away from advanced mathematics in any form the rest of my life. You might guess from this attitude how proficient I was throughout my schooling. Yes, you are correct, my blood pressure goes up when I see an "x" or Greek letter in a sentence. I know this is not true for many other people who love mathematics and see it as a challenging adventure. Although I cannot cite specific research as support, I believe that learning is facilitated by having fun. There are not many examples I can give from my life of learning situations that left a lasting mark on me that were negative experiences. In fact, I changed my career focus away from a field more than once due to intensely negative experiences with professors. On my way to an advanced academic career in philosophy, I ran into very closed minded, judgmental professors, and I didn't want to turn out like them. I now see that the reverse was true for me as well. One of my earliest positive experiences as a freshman in college was with a professor who taught a field I eventually went into, psychology. This makes little logical sense to have others decide for me, but the impact was nonetheless dramatic. There has been repeated research that when a teacher encourages a child, the child tries harder and learns more. As a parent, a positive orientation is definitely the way to go.

I will cover a number of suggestions that are related to positive discipline. This is not an exhaustive list, and they are listed in no particular order. The orientation for each of the following suggestions is to go into positive parenting with the goal of using every situation possible as an opportunity to teach and not to give the child painful (physical or emotional) consequences for wrongdoing. In other words, teach, don't punish.

Your Parenting Will Be More Positive if You Are More Positive about Parenting

Children are not the only ones who do better in a positive environment and in a positive frame of mind. Parenting a difficult child likely means that you cannot rely on the child to keep you or the household in a positive state. A favorite tactic of children who focus on power struggles is to get you upset, and when you oblige, the child believes he or she has won that round. You will have little chance of staying positive if you take your lead from your child, as many of us have found out the hard way. We must maintain a positive disposition, either from our own internal resources, or from others who support us. I am not asking the impossible here. When you start and end your day with World War III, I am not asking you to hum to yourself "Don't Worry, Be Happy." However, I am saying that as an adult and as a parent, you are responsible for your feelings and your mood; don't blame your boss, the national debt or your child for your negative disposition. All the child did was to invite you into the negative world he lives in most of the time — it was your choice to accept the invitation and stay around for awhile.

I said these suggestions were in no particular order, but the overriding point is that it is not possible to be positive when you are thinking and feeling negatively. It is not only possible to stay positive in the face of parenting a challenging child, it is imperative that you do so. The best way to stay positive is to see positive results from your parenting, but before you become an expert at this, there will be some dark days when you will need the help of a partner, a friend, your rabbi, or dial-a-prayer.

Troubled children do not often give you praise and support (and when they do, watch out) — praising you is not in their job description. These children are supposed to externalize their internal struggles if they are ever to learn a better way to live. As a therapist, if my client comes into each session with a smile, I know we are not getting to where we need to go. Strong negative reactions from children are actually intimate communication, and a parent must learn to see the importance of this energy coming out so you can work with it. If you are not sure you believe this, simply make a list of your greatest fears and then go share the list with someone who has power over you and whom you do not trust — does that raise your blood pressure somewhat? It is a similar type of risk for the child to share real feelings with you.

The best indicator of whether you will stop parenting challenging children as soon as possible, or will choose to continue to do so for years to come, is if you have learned how to recharge your batteries regardless of the child's response to your efforts. Most any parent can feel positive when things are going well; it is the expert parent who has found an inner spring of positive energy during the days, weeks or years of drought working with Genghis Khan Junior, or little Miss Typhoid Mary. We all have our own ways to bounce back when times are tough. If you are not sure you know how to do this, put this book down immediately and give this issue your undivided attention. *Negative adults are not good at positive discipline.* But even if you know that your inner spring is helped by aerobic stamp collecting, anaconda wrestling or playing with bobble head dolls of actors who became governor of California, this is only a start and there is much more to positive discipline.

Was Paul Getting Worse?

I received a message with the note "please get back to me ASAP," which is normal for the calls I get. When I contacted the adoptive parents of eight- year-old Paul, I spoke to his adoptive mother. We had spoken some months previously and after implementing some suggestions I offered, there was a two-month period where things had gone smoothly. Now it was anything but smooth, and the parents were in a controlled panic. Was Paul getting worse? This is not always an easy question to answer on the phone, but this time I was pretty sure about what I told her. The problem was that after several months of little in the way of problem behavior, Paul was showing more anger, frustration, and irritation with family members. His negative expressions were difficult to take, but the fear was he was becoming more distant. I offered a different interpretation. Paul was initially quiet in the family, watching to see if there were any threats. Then he allowed himself to join in, but with little emotion or contribution. Now Paul was safe enough to express strong feelings. I told his mom that the crucial question was "are his new feelings real or fake?" The answer was immediate, "very real." Then Paul was not getting worse, although he may be more challenging to manage, but he was showing intimacy (real emotions), which usually begin with negative emotions. To gauge improvement, look first to whether expressions are genuine, rather than if they feel positive to you. Real comes first, positive comes later.

Use Logical Consequences

The very best teacher is life itself. The best way to facilitate learning is to allow the child to learn directly from experience. Naturally this is not always an option — the hot stove, the deep end of the pool and a street with a speeding automobile are not places a parent can let a child learn by direct experience. For most other situations, the consequences of one's choices and actions can be powerful learning tools.

At times, the parent can assist the child in learning from her actions, but to be effective, the situation must flow naturally or logically. The parent is often able to amplify the natural consequences of choices. This is called logical consequences, and is one of the very best techniques for parents. Too often parents come up with a response to the misbehavior of a child that is excessive or unrelated to the behavior itself. What this can tell the child is that the parent is being unfair, is picking on the child, or is wanting the child to fail. Why else would he be sent to bed before his favorite TV show just because he got in trouble at school? If the child doesn't see any connection between the behavior and the consequence, little is learned other than you don't want them to have things they like. However, if the child is not careful with the Easter egg and it falls and breaks, the child experiences a direct connection between the behavior and the result. At the time the child may feel badly, but the opportunity to learn from experience is available. An effective parent will look for opportunities to help a child learn from experience.

A logical consequence, meaning a result is directly linked to the cause, helps a child to directly learn from mistakes. A parent can use these opportunities to help the child see that mistakes are made by everyone, and they are not a sign that something is wrong with the person. Rather, mistakes are opportunities to learn how to handle a situation to achieve a more desirable result. Children who are taught to consider a positive benefit coming from mistakes will be way ahead of their peers, who are used to being criticized whenever they make mistakes, because a parent has made the point that mistakes are wrong.

A related learning that comes from logical consequences is the all important understanding of cause and effect. The child may need to learn that the reason she failed the test was not because the teacher hated her, it was because she put off studying until the last minute. Children often have magical thinking. They can grow up believing they can wish something to happen and it will. The harsh reality of living is that there is usually a very direct link between what we do and what result we get in life. It is to a person's credit if they learn this lesson early in life, because all too many adults overlook the connection between what they are putting out to the world and what they are getting back in return. Someone who does not operationally understand cause and effect will be unable, in most situations in life, to learn from experience.

Marcus Learns An Expensive But Poignant Lesson

One of the most obstinate boys I have lived and worked with was Marcus, who never heard a rule he didn't want to break. Like many other badly abused children, he fought for control by often doing the opposite of what was expected of him. As he entered his late teen years, he went out on his own and got an apartment and part-time job. Our primary concern for Marcus was whether he would seriously break the rules of society, as he had in our program, and wind up in jail. One day the call came, "This is Marcus and I am using my one phone call to have you come get me out of jail." After speaking to the police about the incident, we chose to have Marcus learn from life what he did not learn from our words and our therapy. It turned out that Marcus was leaving the grocery store and picked up a Kit Kat bar and put it in his pocket at the check stand. A store employee saw this and called security who confronted Marcus getting on his bike outside the store. He grumbled and tried to hand the security guard the money, but instead he was arrested. The company had started a new policy of prosecuting all shoplifters, large items or small. Marcus spent three nights in the county jail. Although obstinate, he was not a large or rough kid, and he was very scared of his fellow jail mates over the three days. Marcus told me, "Never again." The incident was six years ago, and there has been no more jail time or law violations we are aware of. Life, and in this case jail, can teach some profoundly strong lessons.

The best way to teach a child is to help the child see the naturally occurring results of his or her actions. Even the smartest children will do their best, at times, to ignore the obvious. Amplifying cause and effect will make it more clear to the child, although he may not give you the satisfaction of acknowledging the obvious. If you want a child to learn from his actions, help the child see what comes back based on what he does. You can do this by explaining to the child with no requirement that he agree with you. As a parent, you can also do this by linking misbehavior with a consequence that logically flows from the child's behavior. In the previous example of misbehavior at school, going to bed early had no direct connection. However, instituting a signed card from the teacher on attitude and behavior at school each day linked with work done at home that was not completed at school, is a more direct consequence. You do not have to be an expert at parenting interventions instantaneously when the child does poorly. I suggest that parents give themselves some time to cool down, use their heads, consult another adult and consider alternatives. Isn't this exactly what we teach our children to do? Logical consequences are not always easy to figure out, so tell the child you will let him know after dinner what you plan to do about the fact he is home late without a good reason. The extra time to think about the situation and your response often helps your creativity. Feel free to think of a few negative things you could imagine doing in response to the child, then clear your head and get busy teaching the child by helping them experience the natural course of events based on poorly-thought-out behavior.

Stay in Control of Your Emotions and Reactions

Control is a pivotal concept with troubled children. They want it and you cannot let them have it, or at least not as much as they want. There are very few things the child will not do to obtain the upper hand. We can understand why this pattern happens so frequently and see the direct link with being vulnerable to adults in the past and paying the price. But regardless of how much sense this behavior makes to us, we still need to ensure that the child does not take over the environment, primarily because the result will be damaging to the child and everyone else as well. We discussed control in Chapter 1 — it is the "C" in the TLC model of parenting. There are several important distinctions that must be made about the meaning of control when it comes to effective parenting.

Control for the effective parent is different than the control the child fights to have. It may seem the same on a specific issue, but it is not the same overall. The child wants to outwit and outlast the adult out of a defensive or protective motivation. A parent wants to outwit the child to help the child learn effective life skills, so the motivation is different. The child wants to control everyone and everything, while the parent wants to create a setting that is safe and stimulating to the child. Control to the child is all about breaking rules and being actively or passively non-compliant. The parent uses control to provide limits that are intended to help the child better understand what is expected. Since the control of the parent and the control of the child are very different issues, if the parent starts sounding like the child, it is time to reassess. Parents do not want to find themselves saying, "Because I said so, that's why," "I still make the rules in this house," or "You will get to do that when I am good and ready to say you can." Such statements have accepted the child's meaning of control and are throwing back at the child what the child is communicating to the parent. There is a basic problem with the "I am in charge because I am bigger" style of parenting, as any parent who has relied heavily on physical punishment finds out during teen years, when the parent may no longer have the physical advantage. Our power cannot rest in our size advantage over the child. If you find yourself mimicking the same type of control you experience from the child, it is time to take a close look at who is really in charge of the household. It may not be you who is setting the tone.

Since the parent has to demonstrate a different type of control than the child, the question comes up: "What is control and what or who is being controlled?" Let's start with what control isn't. In addition to control not being the power mongering of the troubled child, control is not about making other people do what we want. This is called being controlling, not being in control. As parents, we do not control what the child says, how the child feels, what the child thinks or how the child chooses to respond to situations. A parent who controls the words, the feelings, the thoughts, and the responses of the child is simply delaying the time when the child does these things for him or herself, and the result will usually be vastly different when this inevitable change occurs. One way to say this is that a parent cannot control what goes into or comes out of a child, at least not legally. You can put the food on the table, but you can't force him to eat. You can punish all you want, but the bedwetting will likely continue in a shaming atmosphere. You may not want to hear George Carlin's seven words that can't be said on television coming out of the mouth of your little darling, but putting duct tape over his mouth is only legal in Saudi Arabia.

There are some things we can and must control. We can control ourselves, our emotions, our behaviors, experience and the atmosphere of our environment. To allow a troubled child to control any of these things is to quite literally give up our personal power. A child who can do any of these things will not respect you, and without respect you will lose the war. Don't let a child get you angry or you become a target for the child. We all get angry working with difficult children. When this happens, switch with your partner or take some time for yourself to calm down. Don't let the child force you to act in a certain way or the child will see this as winning the power struggle and will do the same thing in the future. Any family that has sent up the white flag and admitted that the difficult child has everyone walking on egg shells, has parents not looking forward to when school gets out, or dreading bath time, will usually admit that the child is setting the tone of the household. I can guarantee you that if a controlling child is able to set the tone of the house, the child will not change, because she has achieved her goal.

For the parent, control is not about who is stronger, bigger, smarter or more experienced. For the parent, control enables the adults to create the setting that can best help the child learn and grow. If the child has a better idea (it does happen on occasion) the parents who are in control for the right reasons will gladly make a change because they are not focused on whose idea it was. Generally, children have little or no idea what they need to grow and develop. Children are too preoccupied with what they want, to have time for what they need. Children who grow up to be childish adults have the same problem. There is no way around the fact that with parenting comes the all important job of denying wants in order to provide needs. None of us liked hearing "No" while we were growing up, but we would never have grown up emotionally if we didn't. If you can't bear to not give a child all the things she wants, you will not be the parent she needs.

The New Day

What discriminates humans from the rest of the animal kingdom is the ability to self-reflect and make personal changes in thinking, feelings and behaviors. However, when humans live a life that is reactive to all that is around them, this aspect that sets them apart from other animals is not much in evidence. Abused children develop highly reactive patterns. They go through their day wanting many things, but remembering all their disappointments and failures rather than all the good things they have received. These children often expect the negative patterns they have experienced to continue. Before you can even respond to them they have often reflected or even said something like, "You won't keep your promises like everyone else." What abused and troubled children need is to learn how to start fresh in life, how to self-reflect and make changes within themselves, and allow events around them to potentially turn out well for a change. This need fits nicely with one of the principles of positive discipline called the "new day."

The new day concept is both for the child and the adults to start over each morning with the possibility that today will be better. The child can learn to believe that things may have been bad in the past, but today can improve. Yesterday the child may have had repeated problems with everyone and everything, but today is a new opportunity to do it all better and to have things turn out differently. For the parent, the new day is a hope and a belief that we have a new canvas, and today's painting will be better than yesterday's. If parents cannot truly believe this, they trap the child in a continuous loop of problem behavior met with frustration in a negative cycle. The new day must begin with the parent, and all the signals to the child must be the message that the child can make small and large changes. The child will initially be confused by this and then not know how to go about this differently. It is helpful for the parent to point out very specific steps the child can take and then show the child that these changes will get a much different response from everyone around them than problem behavior.

The new day is also a very practical concept. It is important to generally start every morning with a new slate. Particularly with young children, it is often not helpful to have multi-day interventions. Although you might like to tell the child, "You don't get desert for a month," you will probably find that after missing the first desert they will not remember their own problem behavior, and they will see you as the problem. In general the new day starts each day fresh, even logical consequences from the day before may inadvertently connect today with yesterday's problems, so a new day is just that — a fresh start.

The new day is not necessarily connected with 24 hours or each morning. It can be a principle that can be used with time periods throughout the day. The younger the child, the shorter time frames the adults need to work in. Toddlers can start a new day after their nap, elementary children may have had a rough day at school, but they can be greeted after school with a fresh start at home. For the most part, it is a good idea to give children multiple times each day to start fresh as a teaching tool to learn that they can self-reflect and have a positive influence on their behavior and experience.

Obviously, the new day is not always called for. At times, you will want to have consequences at home directly related to misbehavior at school. At other times, you may want to connect tonight's bedtime with the behavior from last night. Older children, and particularly with children who misuse the concept of the new day (as in "I will throw a tantrum then ask to start fresh right afterwards"), you will need to have consequences that take place over time. When 12-year-old Allen breaks his brother's radio, Allen will need to earn money to replace the radio, which might take some time. Although the new day is not necessarily linked with a 24-hour day, it can still be used to help children learn that they are the masters of their own experience, and what they put out will influence what they get back.

You Don't Teach Well When Angry

There may be some things that people do well when they are angry, but teaching a difficult child is not one of them. As we have discussed, the job of the parent is to protect and to teach the child, and people don't send out a protective energy when angry. Parents also tend not to make creative or even sound decisions when experiencing anger.

It is important to make this point about anger because one of a child's most powerful tools is to successfully influence the emotions of the parent. If the child can get the parent to feel something based on the child's actions, it is experienced as being in control of the adult. In a way, it is being in control of the adult's affect. If the parent knew that the child was going to try to get the upper hand by acting in a way to elicit anger from the parent, a successful parent would make sure that this manipulation of the parent's emotions would not produce the results the child was seeking. There are few tactics that are as common as this among troubled children and the parents who attempt to work with them.

Discipline is complex. As soon as we have a small or large success with an intervention, we want to try it again. This is not unlike the child who believes she is successful at getting the parent angry by stealing and wearing mom's makeup. If this approach, in fact, angers either mom or dad, the child thinks, "That worked pretty well, I'll have to remember that maneuver." However, the odds are that any particular intervention that works one time may fail miserably the next time. Just as the parent would hopefully learn from the last time the child produced anger, the child may also learn how to counter your best laid plans. The complexity of effective discipline takes significant brain power. Parents who have raised a challenging but normal child, and then attempt to raise a troubled child, know that the goals may be the same but the route to get there is altogether different. Anger and other strong emotions shut down critical brain power that is needed to counter negativity with positive discipline. The adrenaline that is produced by anger, frustration, and disgust will often prevent the parent from being as creative as needed to win the battle and win the war for both sides.

As an adult you may have never had someone in your life be as upsetting as the bundle of joy you refer to as your foster, adoptive or difficult biological child. These children have often spent years fine-tuning their ability to identify and then press the panic button adults hide from others. These children know that everyone has their weakness, and they study adults to find these weaknesses. Some adults oblige the child by laying out on the table what makes them angry. Many of these children will quietly think to themselves, "Thanks for saving me the time and effort to find out what upsets you." At the same time, most of this book is about understanding why children are difficult in the first place. The goal is to understand their needs, so you and the child can move forward with positively meeting these needs.

I am not saying that it is not part of being a positive parent to get angry at times. Anger is one way to underscore your point to a child that something is important. My question to the parent is, "did you or did the child decide in this situation that you would be angry?" If you do decide to express anger, then plan on doing your creative parenting at a time when you do not have adrenaline coursing through your veins. Anger can be a part of parenting if the parent is deciding how to feel. To become angry around the child can be helpful for the child to see that you may be very upset but you do not harm others, as some adults likely have in the child's past. But to make this work, do not let the child decide the place, the time and the reason for you to become angry. The only lesson the child is likely to learn is how to push your anger button.

Parenting Is a Team Sport

A reality that I do not believe can be denied is that parenting a challenging child is not something one person can do well. This does not mean that I condemn all single parents to be failures. Many single parents do very well, but the ones who do well do not try to go it alone. Parenting takes a village, or, said differently, parenting is a team sport.

The world that children grow up in requires that multiple adults play a role in their learning and development. One adult cannot raise a child alone; the child also needs a grandparent, teacher, minister, coach, big sister, swim instructor, scoutmaster, caseworker and other safe adults who each provide an important ingredient to their learning. It is natural for children to learn from multiple adults. Throughout history children have had the advantage of watching and learning from the personalities and the skills of many adults. We now have more insulated families than at most times throughout history. Close extended families are the exception rather than the rule. There are school districts in America that have more single parents raising children than traditional nuclear families with two parents. Although the modern world has changed the complexion of families, the needs of children have not changed.

Children learn more by modeling than any other teaching. The pressures on single parents usually require that one person does the job of mom and dad as well as teacher, counselor and best friend. These are roles that one person alone cannot do well. Even in a two parent family, there is still a need for other adults who can assist in the long-term job of helping a child learn the required skills he will need to be a success in life.

Challenging children have a habit of coming to the attention of everyone around them. They do not make it easy for anyone to help them. Facing the reality of twenty-eight children in her classroom, Ms. Smart may not initially be thrilled with the opportunity to learn from your challenging child. But school is second only to the family home in importance for young children. Ms. Smart needs to join the team, and with the support of other members of the team she can view your child as an opportunity to make a real difference — which she will remember is why she went into teaching in the first place.

The initial position of the school, church, girls club, or scout troop is often to ask the parent to take care of the problem behaviors in the home before sending the child back. However, the parent must meet with everyone involved and ask for the critically needed assistance of all the adults in the child's life. This is often a considerable challenge. As a parent, you need to be prepared to hear how many other children are vying for attention and time. You must be able to sell all the adults on the child's need to have each of them on the same team.

Some members of the team will not necessarily work with the child or even know them well. As the parent, you will need one or more friends to help you recharge your batteries and maintain your sanity. As the parent of a difficult child, you will need to be around other people who are not like your child who is constantly trying to control you or do the opposite of what you ask. If your friend has lots of advice for you, all bad, then make it clear that you can enjoy time with her, but the topic of parenting a difficult child is off-limits.

If your child is very good at being really bad, then he knows the fine art of setting adults against each other. This must be one of the first discussions for members of the team. You must put out on the table that when your poor misunderstood child reports torture, mayhem, and criminal activity in your home, the adult needs to give you a call to check it out before dialing 911. You must do the same in return when the child tells you the teacher is vicious and cruel and takes children into a hidden room if they misbehave and some are never seen again. Make a commitment to call the teacher before calling the FBI or school board. You cannot have a team if everyone is off balance because the child has all the adults suspicious and investigating each other.

There is nothing particularly easy about multiple adults helping to raise a child. It is similar to several cooks in the kitchen, everyone has a style, a preference and an opinion on every aspect of the child's needs. However, there is one basic choice with a troubled child: you can either have the adults fighting each other, or you can have them working as a coordinated unit in helping meet the child's needs — even though opinions will be different at times. As with any team sport, you will succeed or you will fail as a team.

What Are You Doing To Terry?

I attended a school meeting concerning a seven-year-old in our program. The teacher and assistant principal started the meeting stating strong concern for what we were doing in our treatment program, because Terry was rapidly changing from a model student into a discipline problem. I was quite surprised at this energy since Terry was progressing well in treatment. I asked how he demonstrated being a "model student" in the past. The answer was that he did not talk out in class, he never left his seat without permission, and was not as demanding as he was starting to be. I asked if he turned in his school work in the past and they said, "Well, no." Didn't he sit in back of the class and daydream in the past? "Well, yes, but he wasn't a behavior problem," was the reply. Is a child who sits passively and isn't learning a model student because he doesn't cause problems for the teacher? I had a lot of work to do to help the school staff see that this depressed young man needed to come out of his shell, get more active and express himself more, even if he was now more demanding and challenging. The school staff understood and worked with me the rest of the year without complaining that he was getting worse. Sometimes we need to reconsider how we measure progress.

Distinguish Between the Child and the Behavior

A deceptively simple aspect of positive discipline is often overlooked by parents — seeing the difference between the child and the child's behavior. If a parent does not make this distinction, then the predictable response to the child will be consistently negative, because a troubled child's behavior is typically negative.

It is critical for the parent to be able to distinguish the difference between the child and the child's behavior because the child does not have this discriminative ability. The child has learned from repeated interactions with adults that because he does bad things, he is bad. The main problem with this logic is that the child knows that bad people, which he knows he is, do bad things, and the cycle is repeated. This negative feedback loop is strengthened with every passing day until the child does not trust anyone who would trust him. As Woody Allen once said, "I would never join a club that would have someone like me as a member." This ironic joke for adults is a death trap for the child, a death of the child's spirit and the child's potential.

Humans are profoundly affected by their perceptions of self and events around them. An athlete who is cheered on by a favorable crowd literally reaches new heights, while the world class athlete who begins to doubt herself loses before the starting gun goes off. Children have a habit of being more straightforward and brutally honest than adults. Children do not have the sophistication to hide the fact that they view themselves as bad and not worthy of doing well and being praised for it. If the child will not directly tell them, it is important for the parent or therapist to figure out what the child is thinking. If the child does not have a positive sense of self, the child's behavior will consistently demonstrate negativity.

In such situations, the parent must interrupt the negative cycle from the outside. The child has neither the insight to change this pattern nor the confidence to do so if he knew how. This cycle of negative perceptions, producing negative behaviors, resulting in negative outcomes, reinforcing negative perceptions, is a cycle that is the ultimate blind spot for the child. The child is both blind and deaf to this pattern. For the child, she does not see a pattern, she sees an ugly reality. The result can develop into a lifelong pattern of failure, disappointment and ultimately depression. This is a cycle that can only be disrupted from the outside, and the parent, and at times the parent and therapist, are in the best position to provide this lifeboat to the child.

Distinguishing between the child and the child's behavior is not a complex concept; it is a very practical aspect of disciplining the child. The parent is in the strongest position with young children to help the child form a self-image. The parents must verbalize the internal image they want the child to have. If the parents only point out mistakes, the child will believe he makes too many mistakes and ends up believing he *is* a mistake. Parents must integrate the internal image they want the child to have with each correction they give the child. For example, most parents would not hesitate to say to a child, "It was wrong for you to hit your sister." However, if the child has a negative sense of personal worth, this statement will say to the child, "You showed again that you are bad by doing such a horrible thing." However, it is relatively easy to distinguish between the child and the behavior in this situation, "I am disappointed that you chose to hit your sister because I know you can show Dad a better way to act." You are disappointed in the behavior, but you maintain confidence in the child. Even if you do not have confidence in the child, you need to find some, or you will hand the child more reason to have a negative internal self-perception. With each correction to a child, practice separating the person from the behavior, it is not such a bad idea to practice this with your spouse as well.

The question every adult of a troubled child must ask is, "Is my goal to reinforce the child's negative self-perception, or is my goal to help the child develop a positive sense of self?" That is not a very difficult question when it is so plainly stated. Being able to consistently distinguish the person from the behavior will go a long way toward achieving a positive outcome in the child.

More Praise than Criticism

For many of the same reasons as distinguishing the child from the behavior, the balance of praise and criticism must lean in the positive direction. Like many other aspects of parenting a challenging child, this simple principle is not so simple to implement. Just how does a parent find enough reasons to praise a child, when the child demands hundreds of corrections a day? You will have need to find the answer with your child, or you will perpetuate the cycle of providing the child with an external negative view to solidify the internal negative view the child already holds tightly.

There is no easy formula for the balance of praise and criticism, but I often suggest that a 5-to-1 ratio is a good place to start. If you were hoping for a simple majority of praise, perhaps 51% of the time, think again. Among troubled children there is a concept I refer to as amplification. Put simply, the child amplifies the negative messages she hears because this message fits her internal self-perception. When positive messages are provided, she either seems confused, "He must have made a mistake, did he forget who he is talking to?" or the positive message simply does not penetrate the child's internal defenses. So think about it. If at work your boss yelled at you every few minutes in disappointment of your work performance, how long would you maintain a positive view of what you were doing? For most of us, if a boss yelled even once, we would be devastated. The principle of amplification means that every negative statement you make to the child goes over the loudspeaker and is received much stronger than you intended. For this reason, successful parents will need to make sure they word corrections carefully and amplify positives until the child learns to hear the positive messages.

To complicate matters, it will not work to throw false compliments at the child throughout the day. At times, a troubled children can be more perceptive than adults of false praise. You must be real and you must be positive. If you were thinking, "Easier said than done," I would agree. However, praise does not need to be for major issues. Don't wait for the child to bring home a report card loaded with A's and B's before you praise the child's school work. If you are not the type of parent to give a lot of praise to others, go to the nearest mirror and ask yourself why. Could it be because you were given very little praise among all the criticism when you were a child? If so, give this child more of what she needs than you received. It is also helpful to tell your partner or therapist that you want to do a better job in this area and ask for support to do so. The only way to eventually get more positive behaviors than negative ones is to start early and often to give the child much more praise than criticism.

You Don't Teach a Child to Tell the Truth by Asking for a Lie

Let's face it, it is in our nature to react to people who don't tell the truth. We say things like, "That person cannot be trusted," or "The only thing you really have is the integrity of your word — lose that and what do you have left?" Perhaps the only thing that adults are even more reactive to than someone who tells lies is someone within the family who lies. Families handle lying with various degrees of proficiency. Some parents understand that young children concoct stories for various reasons; but when a child is older, stories become lies and the level of concern raises exponentially. The truth is that it is very difficult to trust someone who will directly lie to you. However, when it comes to children telling the truth, this is like every aspect of growing up: children must learn how and when to be truthful.

Just like some adults, children lie to help their chances of getting something they want or to avoid getting something they don't want. Young children also lie as a form of magical thinking, thinking that saying something is true over and over will make it true. There is also crazy lying that appears to have no rhyme or reason involved. There are many other types of lies, but the most frequent for children are the first two — getting something or avoiding something.

It surprises me how many parents think that telling the truth should come naturally to children; however, it does not. What comes naturally to children is to maneuver within the environment to get as much as possible of what they want and to avoid as much as possible of what they don't want. The first tool children use to accomplish this is physical activity. The toddler picks up the shiny vase to play with it or she picks up the lima beans to get the slimy things off her plate. As the child develops, the second tool a child uses is language. Children use language before they learn words. They look at what they want, point at it and make sounds to communicate they want it. When faced with something they don't want, such as an immunization at the doctor's office, they first try to get away and they make loud noises to scare away the doctor. As language progresses, the child learns words that substantially help in the process of both obtaining and also avoiding. The initial use of language to the child is therefore to aid in this process. The child does not start with the concept that language is to accurately reflect external reality or objective truth. Language is a subjective tool and can be altered to suit the need of the moment. Lies are a common result of this mode of thinking.

Children need to learn to report accurately. The huge step of reporting accurately, even when it may hinder getting what they want or avoiding what they don't want, may take quite a while and is measured in years, not days. The tendency to use language to obtain what we want never completely goes away. We can see this dynamic with white collar crime among corporate executives, political leaders testing to see what the public will believe, and even pastors who secretly fondle their young parishioners after a sermon on hypocrisy. Some of these adults who struggle with using language to avoid the truth are learned men and women. Our knowledgeable lawyers of today struggle with truth just as the scribes and lawyers of the Old Testament temple. After all it was Pontius Pilate, the educated Governor of Judea 2,000 years ago, who first said, "And what exactly is the truth?" Or a more recent example of a Rhodes scholar inhabiting the oval office who said, "that depends on what *is* means." If very smart adults struggle with telling the truth rather than telling lies to manipulate the truth, why would anyone be surprised that children do the same?

When we teach a young person to tell the truth, we must acknowledge that it is actually counterintuitive. For the child, the truth often does not get him what he wants or help him avoid what he does not want. I always suggest parents begin teaching the truth from a practical perspective and not a moral one. I suggest you not lead with the argument that truth is right and lies are wrong. We know this is accurate and must be grasped at some point in childhood, but it is step 47 and not step number 1. First teach the child to accurately report information so she will be believed by you and others. The fairy tale "the boy who cried wolf" points out the initial importance of telling the truth. This story is less about the moral importance of accurate reporting than the practical importance of being believed to avoid being the wolf's lunch.

I will not give a step-by-step method of teaching a child to tell the truth because it would be a book in itself, although, come to think of it, I have not come across such a book. However, in the process of teaching a child to tell the truth, it is important to avoid teaching a child to lie. There are actually many ways adults inadvertently teach deception and lies rather than the truth. The most frequent way this is done is by example and modeling. Therefore, if you want your bundle of joy to tell the truth, you will need to make sure you do likewise, to everyone, in all situations.

Another frequent way adults miss the mark in teaching a child to tell the truth is to ask the child to lie. Saying it this blatantly probably makes no sense to you, but hear me out and it may sound familiar. To teach a child to be honest first and foremost requires that you be honest. You cannot teach a child to tell the truth by being deceptive yourself (as adults we often avoid the term lying if it refers to our own behavior). Adults teach a child to lie when they ask the child to answer a question to which the adult already knows the answer. There are thousands of examples of this. Mom finds her missing necklace in her daughter's room, and after school asks the child if she has seen it. The problem in this situation is that Mom knows the answer and deceptively pretends not to. Exactly what would you expect the child to do with this test of principles?

The child will normally use language to avoid what she doesn't want to happen — getting caught. In this example I suggest that Mom lays out the truth, "Jennifer, when you were at school I found my necklace in your room, and this is something we will need to talk about right after dinner." The message is straightforward and the odds go down, although not completely, that the child will try to lie that she doesn't know who put it in her room. If you get the age-old story that the necklace fairy must have done it to frame the innocent child, proceed directly to the sentencing phase of the trial without allowing further rebuttal or appeals. This analogy to a court process is not the most fitting because this is not court; you do not need evidence beyond a reasonable doubt. In day-to-day situations of this type, I suggest you proceed with the obvious and not call in a crime scene investigator to lift a fingerprint or obtain DNA proof. As a parent, when you are convinced of the facts, respond accordingly. You may at times be wrong, but you will have responded correctly most of the time without a protracted legalistic argument about who may have been responsible (the evil fairy defense). If you are wrong, it gives you an opportunity to model taking responsibility for a mistake.

Being Firm and Being Friendly

The tone I suggest with all parenting is to be firm and friendly. This is important with traumatized children because firmness alone is registered in the child's brain as equivalent or similar to past harsh abuse. However, being friendly without being firm often results in the child not taking you seriously. This is another of many balancing acts for the parent. Finding the best balance is going to depend on the child and the situation.

As parents, we do not always have the ability to be both firm and friendly in every situation. If you are driving to the mall and your child sitting next to you grabs the steering wheel to get you to pull into Burger Bonanza, being firm is the first priority and being friendly for the moment can be suspended. However, later on your trip it would be wise to let him know that the situation was dangerous and upsetting because you want everyone, including

CHECKLIST FOR POSITIVE DISCIPLINE

✓ Teach, don't punish; it makes a big difference.

✓ Keep your tone positive or the child is influencing you and not the other way around.

✓ Have the consequences flow from the problem behavior by using logical consequences.

✓ Stay in control of your responses and your emotions, or the child is controlling you.

✓ Practice the "new day" concept so that when the child is ready to do better, you are ready to allow improvement.

✓ Parenting is a team sport.

✓ Distinguish between the child and the behavior.

✓ Give five times more praise than criticism.

✓ Don't ask the child to lie by acting like you don't know the truth.

the child, to be safe in the car and you need his help. At this point, you can ask the child for help by never touching the controls of the car. If he agrees, give him a handshake and a smile. If he does not agree, you can convey to him that he will need to think about it more and make an agreement with you if he wants to come along on future trips.

Giving a firm and friendly message in most situations establishes a tone of self-control, safety, caring for the child, and being in control of the situation. These are all essential messages for the child to pick up from you.

A nine-year-old boy with a bit of a speech problem loved to argue and completed his closing argument to the jury (staff) with, "I waste my case." [Just what I was thinking.]

Chapter

4

Addressing Violence

In this chapter, I will do two things. The first is to consider violence as one of the most serious issues facing the adults who are trying to help a troubled child and offer some thoughts on what to do about violence coming from children. The second part of the chapter will switch gears and talk about the therapeutic value in physical interventions with violent children. These are two very complex issues to combine into one chapter, so, although I will touch on many issues, of necessity this chapter will not be a comprehensive treatment of violence. At the same time, I do not believe someone can work with one or more very difficult children without running into the need to understand and address violent behavior from the child.

Our starting place is an overview of violence in our society in order to establish a backdrop within which we enculturate our young people. After looking at violence in general, we will move to violence coming from children.

What Do We Know about Violence?

The quick answer to the above question is that our society knows all too much about violence, or I should say, knows too much about the consequences of violence that we find all around us. Because it is repeated in the mainstream media so often, most people know that violence is a serious problem in the United States. We are confronted with the fact that it is more of a safety risk for a tourist to come to America than to most countries of the world. We know that our rates of child abuse are far higher than any of the other developed countries of the world. We also know that the rates of gun violence in America dwarf rates in any established and stable country in the world. One only has to look at the modern American culture to see that violence seeps into every aspect of our culture — our families, our foreign policy, our schools, our entertainment, our sports, and our post offices, where the term "going postal" now has obtained a generally used meaning to snap and respond in a violent rage.

There are many startling statistics that can symbolize the violence problem in America, but I will mention two. The prevalence of criminal violent acts among teenagers in America is so common, particularly among males, that the majority of teens commit a violent act before age 18. Yes, this means that for male teens in America today it is normal, or better said, normative, to commit violent criminal acts (Verhaagen, 2003). The second startling statistic is that included in our nation's astronomical rate of homicides: 1 out of every 30 murders in America is a parent killing his or her own child! That equates to parents killing 550 of their own children per year. There isn't much more that needs to be said about that statistic.

But is our culture as violent as some would have us believe? My answer is that our culture is more violent than most of us can imagine. This is particularly true when violence means more than murders and aggressive crime. Violence is much more than criminal assaults, it also comes into play with intimidation, discrimination, classism, poverty, hate crimes, harassment, property crimes, bullying, and a host of realities all too common in our culture.

Some sociologists and researchers strive to set the record straight and point out that despite the media reports of school shootings in the last few years, such school shootings have actually statistically gone down during this period while media coverage has increased. They also point out that youth violence has statistically been dropping over the last decade (Satcher, 2001). Isn't this good news? Wait just a minute before you answer.

Safety in school has become a national priority over the last few years. We know this because the Secret Service has been asked to help not only keep the President safe, but also help keep our children safe in our schools. While it is true that deaths due to school shootings, such as occurred at Columbine High School in Colorado, have gone down over the last ten years, it is also true that over 3,500 children per year are expelled from schools for carrying a firearm. There are over 250,000 serious violent crimes in our schools each year. With a spotlight on violence in schools, last year 7,000,000 incidents of bullying were identified in American schools (Sprague, 2003). Does that sound like school violence is less of a problem than the media makes it out to be?

Let's look at the overall crime rate. Experts tell us that from 1983 to 1993 there was an explosion in violent crime among children in America. This fact has never been fully understood, but since 1993 the violent crime rate has actually gone down among children. But just as with school violence, let's look a bit closer. The statistics often being quoted are rates of criminal arrests and convictions. Are arrests a good measure of the crime rate among children? Formal arrests are one measure, but not a very good one. Most youths involved in violent crimes are never arrested (Loeber, Farrington & Waschbusch, 1998; Snyder & Sickmund, 1999). Arrests and crime rates are directly affected by law enforcement resources, community priorities, and legislative and legal decisions as to what to formally pursue and what to ignore.

Another method for determining the crime rate is to sample young people and ask them if they have been involved in crime or violent acts. Although this method of determining the crime rate also has flaws, there is considerable research that self-reports of children are as reliable, if not more so, than those of adults (Eisen, Donald, Ware & Brook, 1980; Maylath, 1990; VanAntwerp, 1995). When adolescents are asked about involvement with violence and aggressive crimes, the picture is very different than national arrest rates. Self-reports indicate that there has been no decrease in violent or criminal acts over the last ten years, although there has been a decrease in the children caught and prosecuted (Satcher, 2001). In the first comprehensive report from the Surgeon General on violence, the following conclusion was reached: "The best available evidence from multiple sources indicates that youth violence is an ongoing national problem, albeit one that is largely hidden from public view" (Satcher, 2001).

What is not hidden from public view is our society's fascination with violence in our entertainment industry. The celebrity status of serial killers in America is only overshadowed by athletes and movie stars who display antisocial behavior. Hollywood indulges our appetite for violence as does television. Although there is still an attempt to say that the impact of violent movies, television, video games and music is only short-term and has no lasting effect on children, I do not find this argument logical or compelling. A decade ago, research was showing that exposure to media violence desensitizes children and youth to violent acts and also results in individuals more likely to commit violent acts (Hughes & Hasbrouck, 1996; Lieberman, 1994). With the exception of research studies commissioned by the Motion Picture Association of America, reputable scientific studies since have shown a very similar impact of exposure to depictions of violence. The Surgeon General's 2001 report on Youth Violence says, "In sum, a diverse body of research provides strong evidence that exposure to violence in the media can increase children's aggressive behavior in the short term. Some studies suggest that long-term effects exist, and there are strong theoretical reasons why this is the case... Research to date justifies sustained efforts to curb the adverse effects of media violence on youths" (Satcher, 2001).

What Violence Looks Like with Difficult Children

I began this chapter with a societal view of violence to give a context within which we as parents are trying to move our own children away from violent acts. However, as a parent, it is not the overall crime rate that you are confronted with as much as violent acts in your family from a raging child. It is common for infants and very young children to express themselves in extreme ways: they scream, their little faces turn red, they can bow their backs and thrash around, and the cause could be anything that is going differently than the child would like it to. We don't call this violence because it is normal for infants to express themselves in this way. Even though expressive tantrums for infants are normal, the reactions can measure pretty high on the Richter Scale.

When children grow older, it progressively becomes less normal for the child to continue to rage about small, medium or large things, and to rage multiple times per day. At some point, parents are confronted with the fact that something is wrong with their child's ability to handle the events, changes, stresses and disappointments of daily living.

In the next section we will consider the biological base of violence in the brain. Developmentally there are some children who do not move beyond the emotional responses of infancy, which include disproportionate reactivity to events around them. The most common reasons children overreact to stresses in life are: significant communication disorders that produce an inability to communicate other than with extreme behavior, children who have learned to overreact from the modeling of parents, and the most frequent cause which is the presence of significant trauma in the early years of the child's life. While all three of these conditions could be involved, they all have separate roads to improvement.

Communication disorders can leave the child unable to interact with the world effectively and produce frustration that can come out in violent rages. These disorders, such as autism, can be

71

improved with a variety of proven therapies and training for care providers. Poor modeling from parents can be improved with consistent work to model and teach the child more effective ways to handle challenges in life. Significant trauma in a child's life will produce patterns of negative behavior that will often need effective trauma treatment to improve.

Violence from children can take many concerning forms. There are overt acts and there are also covert violent acts, which are just as concerning for parents. Overt acts can include significant tantrums that involve the destruction of property, hitting, spitting, kicking, biting, throwing objects, violent threats, hurtful language, and self-abuse. Covert acts could include fire setting, writing threatening messages, various acts of sabotage around the house, eliminating in places other than the toilet, harming pets or making threats of harm when the parents are not watching. Parents often ask if what they are running into with their difficult child is normal. As we saw with violence among teens, just because behavior may be normative (occurs with a high percentage of the population) does not mean it is healthy or not a problem. All of the above examples of overt and covert violence are unhealthy, although they frequently occur with many difficult children.

After the family setting, the next location where violence can become an issue is in schools. Due to the highly publicized school shootings in recent years, school violence has received substantial attention. Although the evidence indicates schools are actually the safest place in our society for children, there is more we want to do to have all children and school personnel safe in schools. Schools are ideal settings for violence prevention programs that may include skill training. School violence prevention programs are readily available, such as *The Second Step Program* and *The Violence Prevention Curriculum for Adolescents* as well as others (Larson, 1994; Stephens, 1995; Walker, Colvin & Ramsey, 1995). There is no question that school shootings in suburban middle-class America have sensitized schools to warning signs of violence. One result is that safe and responsible behavior among students is now a priority in every school in the country.

The Biological Determinant of Violence

Violence can have multiple causes. It can be the result of the modeling of others. It can come from brain injury or significant psychiatric disorders such as schizophrenia. There is even a theory that a violent disposition can be passed on genetically, a possible explanation of why biological sons of violent fathers display violent traits even when they have not been raised by the biological father and have had no contact. Of these potential causes for violence, the issue we will cover is how violence can be brought on by influences to the developing brain in children.

Bruce Perry is a well-known researcher in the field of understanding the brain. He has identified what he calls the malignant combination of experiences that can produce violent patterns of behavior in young people. This combination includes:

- Lack of critical early nurturing. This can be physical and/or emotional neglect.

- Growing up in a chaotic and cognitively impoverished environment.

- Living with persistent fear and physical threats.

- Watching the strongest aggressor win power over others (Perry, 1997).

Each of the above factors has a direct effect on the developing brain. The lack of supportive nurturing is directly linked with the inability of the individual to self-soothe. Infants do not internalize the ability to calm after stress when this help does not first come from a nurturing care provider. This leaves the child either in a stressful state or anticipating a stressful event much of the day. Chaotic and impoverished environments do not provide the structure and predictability that children need to feel safe and secure. If the environment does not support cognitive development, the child will not learn how to use internal skills to understand and influence events that occur. Living with persistent fear and threats promotes the stress response of "fight or flight."

The younger the child, the more the stress is all-consuming because the child may not be able to resist, or to run away.

The last factor is to observe the pattern of the strongest aggressor coming out on top. Many children see this in the family dynamics of domestic violence where physical size and brutality rule the family. This can also be experienced when the parent physically abuses the child by dominating the child through painful physical force and power. The influence of observing the victor, the one who is the most aggressive and violent, is one of many reasons why we need to take a critical look at how violent aggressors are portrayed in movies, video games and even professional sports, at least when children are watching.

As indicated in the combination of factors that produces violence, the fact is that a direct link has been established between trauma and violence. One way to look at this is to consider that when a child is subjected to a combination of emotional and cognitive neglect, while experiencing the stress brought on by trauma, violence is often the result. This formula is based on the fact that different parts of the brain play varying roles in producing behavior. Lower parts of the brain are more primitive and control basic survival functions. When a child lives with physical and emotional threats, the results are increased reactivity or startle response, along with heightened anxiety and increased muscle tone. The mid-brain or limbic system influences behavior through impacting emotions. The higher regions of the brain allow the person to be thoughtful about goals, to make decisions and choices, and to override behavior directed by lower regions of the brain. Therefore, when the lower regions of the brain become highly developed due to traumatic stress and a primary focus on survival, while at the same time the higher regions of the brain are underdeveloped, the result is often the expression of primitive emotions and behaviors that are not regulated by thoughtful consideration. The resulting combination could be one definition of violence.

Keith Learned Violence Well

Of all the violent children I have worked with, Keith may lead the list. I first worked with him at age four. I read a report and frankly could not believe the information and questioned its accuracy. I agreed to work with him somewhat out of curiosity. It took about 48 hours in our program for us to find out that the information on this child was all too accurate. He talked, at times, in the way Anthony Hopkins in "Silence of the Lambs" talked. He attempted to hurt you when you were not paying attention and, if successful, would laugh in a way that some described as evil. An exorcism was mentioned to us more than once, but Keith was not full of a demon, he was full of the results of sadistic and violent trauma for his first 18 months. We wanted to know what produced a child like Keith, and it was a profound tragedy: beaten, sexually abused, sexually involved with both parents, given drugs, terrorized, and more — all as a baby. Both of his parents were serving long prison terms for the abuse. It is impossible to describe how hard it was to work with this child, but we all did work with him, day after day. We nearly threw up our hands on many occasions, but kept trying. His violence began to decrease, but only after nearly two years of work. Keith always comes to mind when I hear someone claim the latest short-term therapy could work with anyone. Keith is now in his 20s. He will have to guard against a predisposition to aggression throughout his life. He stays in touch because he sees us as his family. From his violent beginnings, I continue to have hope that we helped narrowly avert having another violent person on our streets, at least so far.

Violence does not always arise from an overactive nervous system. At times the opposite is true. Research has identified that among some aggressive individuals and conduct disordered young people, they actually have low levels of arousal and low reactivity. Although the cause of this pattern of low arousal is unknown, it may be caused by impairment or underdevelopment of parts of the neocortex, particularly the prefrontal lobes. Physical damage to this part of the brain, such as traumatic brain injury, has long been found to cause a significant change in the behavior and even the personality of the individual.

It is not essential for a parent to know where in the brain violence has its roots, but it may be very helpful to remember that anything that accelerates the lower brain responses of fight or flight and depresses the higher reasoning centers of the brain that impact reasoning and self-control will encourage violence. Some of the influences in our culture that do exactly this are traumatizing a child, living in a high stress environment, domestic violence of all types, and, with older teens and young adults — intoxicants (Perry, 1997). We started the chapter with a brief look at the presence of violence in our culture. This grim reality will be easier to understand when we consider the above formula and study the levels of domestic violence, child abuse, families with high levels of stress, along with the amount of substance abuse that exists in our culture. The inevitable result is a high level of violence in American society.

What Are the Ingredients to Containing Violence?

Despite the cause of violent behavior in children, the good news is that success is possible with the great majority of these children. I am often asked if our program can work with any level of severity of troubled children. Although for the most part, the answer to this question is yes, I am always quick to say that we approach working with every new child with confidence, knowing that all we can do is our best, and we shall see if our best is good enough. This is an approach that I would offer to parents, teachers, therapists, coaches and anyone reading this book. When a difficult child is referred to me, I am wise enough not to offer guarantees other than to guarantee I will do my best. There have been children in the past that I have not been successful with, and I know there will be some in the future.

There are many ingredients that go into whether an intervention helps an individual or not. Some of the ingredients are the timing, the factors that make the individual receptive or not, and whether the approach fits the individual. I have a personal list of six children out of literally thousands who I do not believe benefited from our work with them. The list used to be seven, but one of the children on the list contacted me during the last year and said her life was changed with our help, and she would be forever grateful, then asked for a loan (I'm kidding about the loan). This was very good to hear because I couldn't tell this from her response throughout her time with us.

I want to make it clear that I do not define success with challenging children as a final parting where the child breaks into tears, gives me a big hug and says, "I will never forget you," like in a Disney movie. This does happen with some children, and it helps recharge our batteries, but the more troubled children may just as often mumble, "Catch ya later, Jerk." As I frequently suggest when working with difficult children, do not lean heavily on what they say. I often notice that the most difficult children make substantial change, but will refuse to let you take any credit for it, which is just fine with me. I also believe that all of us who work with very difficult children are gardeners who sow the seeds of skills, socialization and success. However, we do not often get to participate in the harvest, which is usually many years in the future.

There are many difficult problem areas that surface when working with troubled children, and violence is one of the most frequent. Like many of the other difficult problems, such as sexual behavior and fire-starting, the best interventions involve the use of some standard principles. Three generally accepted components of successful interventions for children who have problems with violent behavior are: environmental approaches that consider all the problems and needs of those involved, comprehensive early intervention implemented at early signs of problems, and finally, direct parent training and support in parenting practices that have been proven to work (Patterson, Reid & Dishion, 1992). It is often not necessary to put the child into a special regimen specially designed for violent children; rather it is important to implement the following straightforward principles that will be further explained in Chapter 12.

- Take the time to understand this child and the roots of the violence.

- Translate the meaning of the child's behavior and develop a plan that best meets this individual child's needs and issues.

- Ensure that the child feels supported by you and other adults.

- Give the child more positive statements of effort and improvement than negative corrections (five positive for every one negative).

- Develop a team of people working on the same goals with the child; team interventions have the best outcomes.

- Come across to the child as confident in the role you play of parent, therapist, teacher, grandparent or coach.

- Don't just focus on behaviors, intervene with the whole child: feelings, thoughts, attitudes, beliefs, moral development, and goals.

- Provide an alternative to violence that works for the child.

- Separate the child from the behavior and use other aspects of positive discipline described in Chapter 3.

- Don't lock the child into old behaviors; make sure you recognize when the child improves.

- Have very clear and firm expectations of the child, regardless of how many times the child has not met your expectations.

- Get the consultation and help you need.

- Ensure adequate supervision of the child; there is no substitute for adult supervision.

- Make sure you get some time away from the child; if your batteries are low, you are both in trouble.

- View every situation as an opportunity to learn. As a student, you are expected to make some mistakes along the way.

- Do your best and don't take the outcome personally.

There are very few children who actually intend to cause serious harm to others, although many children act out and use threats. Most troubled children have an absence of internal controls and inner confidence that they will be cared for and protected from violence. Traumatized and abused children quickly learn that a good offense is the best defense. They learn to sound tough, to keep people away by threatening or being violent in unpredictable ways. Most violence in children has a purpose; learn the purpose and you have taken a major step toward a plan to address the violence. The fact is that violent children are not monsters, at least not yet. They are frightened children who feel as if they have been placed in the lion's den with no one to protect them. They predictably do what anyone would do in such a situation: they either pretend they are the meanest dog in the pack to protect themselves, or they learn to hide and fight back when no one is looking.

The children who actively confront adults in all settings get the majority of attention, but I have always believed the passive or shadow children are actually more difficult to work with. The principles mentioned above are helpful for both of these responses, which are outgrowths of the "fight or flight" response to threatening situations. But what is the threat these children are experiencing? The best answer is that the threat is in the child's mind, just like the ghost under the bed when the light is turned off. Just because the ghost is not there when the parent turns on the light, does not make it any less real when it is dark and the child is convinced it is there.

Children who act tough and threaten others are not actually looking for a fight, they are looking for reassurance that the environment is not abusive, and caretakers will have the power to face threats while maintaining safety for everyone. A great deal of violent behavior is consciously or subconsciously designed to receive this reassurance from adults. Many of the principles recommended above are designed to give the reassurance that the child is seeking. When children become violent, it is important to respond firmly and make it clear what will and will not be tolerated. This will establish the boundary the child needs to know that the adults have the situation under control. I have had young, violent children tell me after an incident, "What if my abusive dad shows up? How do I know you can keep me safe?" This statement explained why the child had become violent — to see if I could handle the situation and ensure the child's safety.

I have written before about the importance of physical touch to children including Chapter 11 in *Raising Children Who Refuse To Be Raised* entitled "Physical Touch and Parenting" (Ziegler, 2000). Touch is the first language that children learn. Violent children usually react to situations based on emotional responses, without including a thoughtful process to consider what they want to accomplish and why. The job of the adult when there is violent behavior is to have the child begin to use his or her thoughts or executive functions. If children cannot learn to think when feeling stress, they are locked into a long-term pattern of reactivity and being controlled by events around them. For young children, a very effective way to address violence and have the child begin to think about the situation is the use of a specific type of physical holding.

In recent years, there has been considerable discussion about physical interventions with children. Unfortunately, the solution has been proposed by some before the problem has been clearly identified. The solution of some risk managers, politicians, and bureaucrats is to eliminate the use of physical interventions with young, violent children. What they propose instead is to bargain with the child, offer the child an incentive to stop violence, and generally to take any steps possible to avoid a physical confrontation. Such responses to violence do not provide children with the firm boundaries they are seeking, and instead may reinforce violent behaviors. This is a complex issue, but after 30 years of working with the most violent young children, I believe the goals of those who would eliminate physical interventions with violent children are misguided, and they fail to understand the needs of these children. The following section was written for a Child Welfare League of America publication in response to an anti-holding article, "Practicing Restraint" (Kirkwood, 2003). In my response, I take the position that physical interventions can have important therapeutic benefits for violent children who are seeking reassurance when they demonstrate violent behaviors.

The Therapeutic Value of Using Physical Interventions to Address Violent Behavior in Children

A quick review of the published information on physical interventions over the last three years would seem to indicate that a fundamental and universal shift has occurred, away from the use of therapeutic restraint, as well as the use of seclusion, to address violent behavior in children. However, this is somewhat deceptive. Treatment environments have been faced with increasingly violent and assaultive children in a continuing trend that was identified a decade ago (Bath, 1992; Crespi, 1990). This challenge must be considered along with the fact that young children most often present violent behavior in treatment settings (Miller, Walker & Friedman, 1989). Unlike the impression given by recent media, the reality is that most treatment centers for young children use physical interventions to address violent behavior in a safe and effective manner. It is true that physical interventions have been the subject of substantial training to ensure that they are done according to national crisis management guidelines, but it is not true that the mental health community has abandoned physical interventions for violence.

It is important to clarify the interchangeable terms "therapeutic holding" and "physical restraint." They refer to a physical intervention where a trained adult stops a child from hurting himself or others by using approved crisis intervention holds to protect the child until the child is no longer a danger. There are a

81

variety of approved holds but all of them restrain the child from being violent and causing damage to him- or herself or others. A distinction must be made between the type of holding discussed in this article and "holding therapy," which is a physically intrusive method to produce a crisis in a child and force the child to experience physical or psychological pain. Holding therapy and other similar intrusive techniques are not sanctioned by any legitimate professional organization and, in the opinion of the author, are not therapeutic and are not valid psychological treatment.

There is increasing pressure on residential treatment programs to become restraint- and seclusion-free, but is this direction in the best interests of the children? The answer will emerge only after a dialogue of the valid points on both sides of this issue, but, to date, only one point of view has been advanced. The purpose of this article is to provide another perspective on this issue, one that has not been previously put forward.

Numerous types of interventions have been used over the years to address violent behavior among children and adolescents (Troutman, Myers, Borchardt, Kowalski & Burbrick, 1998). In settings such as psychiatric hospitals and treatment programs, two of the most frequently used interventions are therapeutic holds (also called therapeutic restraint) and giving the individual a chance to regain self-control in a seclusion or quiet room. Interventions less often used to address violent behavior are mechanical restraints and using medication for chemical restraint (Measham, 1995). Over the last ten years the latter two interventions, mechanical and chemical restraint, have been criticized as excessive and too restrictive. Mechanical and chemical restraints have declined in some programs and have been eliminated in others, particularly in non-hospital settings.

More recently, in the last three years, restraint and seclusion have been the subject of considerable controversy. Many arguments have been presented against the use of restraint and seclusion to address violent behavior in children (Wong, 1990). Most notable was an investigative series in a Connecticut newspaper, the *Hartford Courant* (Altimari, Weiss, Blint, Pointras, & Megan, 1998). This exposé of injuries and deaths reportedly caused by the use of restraint and seclusion is often credited with starting the current wave of criticism against the use of restraint and seclusion. This controversy has ranged from media coverage to policy change and new federal legislation.

The array of criticism directed at the use of restraint and seclusion has one glaring absence, a review of the therapeutic benefits of physical holds to address violence among children. Although seclusion is often used interchangeably for therapeutic restraint, the two are very different interventions bringing up very different issues. The focus of this article will not be seclusion, but rather a review of the therapeutic components of physical restraint.

Before addressing the potential therapeutic components of physical restraint, it is important to briefly consider the most frequent criticisms of using this intervention. A recent nationally published article is a good example of the criticism being directed at the use of physical restraint (Kirkwood, 2003). The article calls restraint violent, dangerous, and even potentially deadly to children. The point is made that this intervention can actually cause further trauma due to concerns such as counter-aggression by adults and repeating abuse the child has experienced in the past. Restraint is called a violent means to maintain control and "rule over" children. Rather than use physical restraint, the article recommends negotiating with the child, understanding the reasons behind the behavior and giving the child choices. Some critics have gone so far as to say a physical restraint should be avoided at all costs and any use of physical restraint is a treatment failure.

In the face of such harsh criticism, is there any defense for physical interventions such as restraining violent children? The author believes there is, but the starting point of discussing the therapeutic components of physical restraint must begin with an acknowledgment that even good interventions when done poorly, or at the wrong time, lose some or all of their therapeutic value. Rather than an indictment of all physical interventions, the criticisms outlined in the article mentioned above can serve to improve the quality of physical restraint and, for that matter, all other behavior management.

All behavior management can become ineffective, demeaning and even psychologically damaging if done poorly. It is safe to say that using a violent intervention to "rule over" children is poor behavior management. Like other types of behavior management, if physical restraint is done in a violent and dangerous way, it may be possible to replicate the past abuse of the child, at least in the child's mind. However, physical restraint should not be step one of any intervention with a child. Physical restraint should not be a shortcut to taking the time to understand the child and the reasons behind the child's behavior. Restraint is also not the opposite end of the continuum from appropriate negotiations and setting out clear and meaningful choices.

Physical restraint is properly used only when the adult is trying to understand the child and other limit setting techniques have failed to safely address the violent behavior of the child. Interventions are also not therapeutic when they are based on a power struggle or when the adult is out of control. Any behavior management approach loses its therapeutic value if used to merely control the child without supporting and understanding the child's thoughts, feelings and goals for the behavior. This is true for all behavior management interventions, such as: time-outs, logical consequences, giving choices, and negotiating as well as physical restraint. It is not necessarily the technique that makes an intervention therapeutic, it is more often the when, how, why and by whom the technique is employed that makes the difference.

If physical restraint is a legitimate part of a behavior management plan, it must have the potential of therapeutic value when used appropriately. Among nationally recognized crisis behavior management systems there are clear guidelines as to the appropriate use of physical restraint. Behavior management systems such as Crisis Prevention Institute (CPI) and Professional Assault Response Training (PART) are two well-known examples. Both outline the safe and effective use of physical interventions after crisis de-escalation techniques have been used to address the situation.

National accreditation organizations, such as the Council on Accreditation (COA) and the Joint Commission on Accreditation of Health Care Organizations (JCAHO), sanction the appropriate use of physical restraint. If any legitimate organization were to declare physical restraint a "treatment failure," an expression currently being used by opponents of physical interventions (National Technical Assistance Center for Mental Health Planning, 2002), one would expect it to come from entities that hold organizations to the highest standards of the industry, and yet all major national accrediting bodies sanction the use of physical interventions. It is difficult to find any national professional organization, such as the American Academy of Pediatrics, that does not agree with the general statement, "Restraint and seclusion, when used properly, can be lifesaving and injury sparing interventions" (American Hospital Association and National Association of Psychiatric Health Systems). In new practice parameters, the American Academy of Child and Adolescent Psychiatry says, "If less restrictive options have failed or cannot be safely applied, seclusion and restraint procedures may be required." In another part of the guidelines, under indications for the use of seclusion and restraint, when restrictive interventions are needed, physical restraint is called preferable for young children and seclusion is preferable for adolescents (Masters & Bellonci, 2002).

Here are some of the reasons why physical restraint, when done well, can be an important, effective and therapeutic intervention to address the violent behavior of children.

Physical touch can be very therapeutic to children, particularly in a crisis. Long before a child learns English, Spanish or Swahili, the first language a child learns is the language of touch. Touch is considered a basic need for all children. When a young child is frightened, the first instinct is to hold on to a trusted adult. Children who demonstrate serious acting out often do not know how to ask for what they need, yet supportive, firm, and safe physical touch can give a child a message of reassurance. If touch is poorly used, such as slapping or striking a child, the message of such a touch can be very frightening. When a young child is in a crisis situation, touch can be one of the most reassuring interventions if the touch lets the child know that the adult will ensure that the situation will be managed safely for everyone.

Emotionally defended children can become psychologically more real and available after an emotional release during a physical restraint. This dynamic is not restricted to children. It is often when our emotions overwhelm us that we open to learning something new that we have defended ourselves from. There is a parallel in psychotherapy to this dynamic when a client has a difficult but insightful experience that usually includes being catapulted beyond the individual's ability to keep out important information. For some children, it is difficult to get to this place without some form of emotional meltdown and physical intervention that often opens up defended emotions.

Children need to know the adult will ensure everyone's safety. The adult is responsible to ensure that the child cannot hurt him- or herself or others, and if other management methods fail, physical interventions are important. The adult cannot put the responsibility on a child for regaining inner control once it has been lost. The amount of time it takes for any crisis situation to be under control, during which time chaos reigns, is the amount of inner fear the child has. Children can regain their footing, but the assistance of a supportive adult can be critical.

Young children with emotional disturbances need and often seek closeness with adults, and violence is less threatening than other forms of intimacy. Behavior cannot always be taken at face value with children who experience violent rages. In fact, these children can often act counterintuitively. They can push you away when they want closeness, they can strike at you when they are beginning to care about you, and they can act in ways to receive reassuring touch by becoming aggressive and violent to themselves or others. It is important to understand why a child is acting the way she is. At times, a frightened child seeks and needs the reassurance of physical touch when she can't allow herself to ask for physical comfort. It is often with trusted adults that young children become violent, because they know they are safe and they will get the reassurance they need. If they do not find the physical reassurance they need and seek, they will often raise the level of acting out until they get it.

Physical restraint is the surest and most direct way to prevent injury and significant property damage when the child loses control. The above referenced article in *Children's Voice* (Kirkwood, 2003) begins with a description of a child doing significant damage to a car with a rock. In this example, the adults stood by and did not stop the child and the author called this a better, however, more costly intervention. This seems to defy common sense. Would any parent stand by as a child does thousands of dollars in damage to the family car? Recently, a child in our program picked up a rock, ran around a new car and heavily scratched it to the amount of $2,650 damage before an adult was able to quickly intervene. Afterward, the child felt badly for such out of control behavior and said good kids do not do such bad things. It is important to understand that kids, as well as adults, view themselves in relation to their own behavior. Abused children develop a sense of self as bad when they act badly. It only makes sense from a practical and therapeutic perspective to stop children from hurting others and doing damage they will use to feel worse about themselves. Physical interventions may be the best way to ensure this.

Traumatized children must learn that emotionally charged situations and all physical touch does not end in being used or abused. The human being has several types of memory, including factual (explicit), subjective (implicit), emotional, experiential and body memories (Ziegler, 2002). Early experiences of touch can establish a lifelong trajectory of meaning attributed to physical touch. It is common that children with emotional disturbances have difficulty with caring touch. Body memories need to be addressed while the child is still young or the child can avoid the very closeness she needs. Abused children learn that when

87

someone gets angry, someone else gets hurt, usually the child. Supportive physical restraint retrains the body not to fear touch from others.

"Will you promise that you will stop me?"

It is currently popular to talk about reducing or eliminating physical interventions with violent children. It sounds like something anyone could support, until you are responsible for the safety of a very violent child. Since working with violence is my profession, I miss the logic of avoiding physical interventions at all costs. Nan was a violent child, not only to others, but also to herself. If not stopped, she would have seriously injured herself or worse during several suicide attempts. She would also hurt others. We explained to Nan that we would not allow her to hurt herself or others, and we would do what it took to fulfill that commitment. She would try to jump off a staircase or run away into the woods in freezing weather. Each time we stopped her. She responded by trying to hurt us, but each time ended in tears and we talked about the pain of her childhood. This was about the only time she opened up. One day she said, "I know I make everyone angry with the way I act, but will you promise me something? Will you always stop me when I become hurtful?" We did promise. Nan survived her childhood and today is the mother of two children.

An intervention considered to be good parenting is likely to be good psychological treatment. Psychologists, family therapists and parent trainers would all call stopping a child from running into a busy street good supervision and effective parenting. They would also recommend that a parent prevent an older and much larger sibling from physically harming a younger sibling. It is not hard to imagine the same parenting consultants suggesting that when an angry child is heading for the family car with a baseball bat, that the bat be taken away before the damage occurs. If these parenting interventions would be basic common sense to most everyone, why would some call these same interventions unhelpful and non-therapeutic to children with serious anger problems?

Children with emotional disturbances need the assurance that adults are safely and appropriately in control of the environment. Serious acting out, such as violence, is often seeking this assurance. Most emotional problems in children have their source in chaotic, abusive and/or neglectful home environments at some point in the child's life. To be in a home where the adults are not in control of themselves or the environment is like going down the road in the back seat of a car with no one driving — it is terrifying to a child who has been there. These children often push a new environment until they find out whether the adults can safely and appropriately manage the challenges. Often, when a child has such reassurance and can rely on others for basic needs, he or she can once again get back to the task of being a child.

Treatment programs are responsible for directly addressing violent behavior and not just skillfully preventing the behavior from presenting itself during treatment only to reappear in the home or community after treatment. The argument that all physical restraints can and should be avoided at all costs may address the principle of prevention, but misses the point of treatment. In the extreme, all physical restraints could be avoided; this simply requires an adult to passively stand by and allow a child in a rage to do whatever he or she wants to do. One may call this "preventing" a restraint, but how did it address the responsibility of a treatment program to treat and extinguish serious violent and antisocial behavior? The role of prevention and treatment are quite different. Not intervening when a therapeutic response is called for is not so much prevention as it is abdicating adult responsibility. If someone needed treatment for a debilitating phobia of spiders, the symptoms could be prevented by having an insect free environment, but this would not be treating the phobia. Programs charged with treating violent behavior cannot simply ensure that the symptoms never come up in the treatment environment because they will surely resurface once the child leaves that setting. In psychological terms, treatment often requires steps such as re-exposure to stimuli, cognitive reprocessing, skill development, practice and mastery, none of which have an opportunity to happen if preventing symptoms or preventing a particular intervention at all cost is the goal.

Are therapeutic benefits guaranteed by the appropriate use of physical interventions? No intervention comes with a guarantee. However, as one side of this debate offers sensational media stories and points to abuses of physical interventions (and there have been abuses), there exists research and professional literature that has found therapeutic value in physical restraint when used properly. Restraint has been found to shorten the crisis over other interventions (Miller et al., 1989). Research studies have found physical restraint effective in reducing severely aggressive behavior, self-injurious behavior and self-stimulatory behaviors (Lamberti & Cummings, 1992; Measham, 1995; Miller et al. 1989; Rolider, Williams, Cummings & Van Houten, 1991). Physical restraint has been found helpful in treating aggression with dissociative children (Lamberti & Cummings, 1992). Physical interventions have also been recognized in the role of re-parenting children who have not been taught limit setting due to absent parenting (Fahlberg, 1991). Physical restraint has been called an effective intervention to protect the child and others from harm and prevent serious destruction of property (Stirling & McHugh, 1998).

A frequently cited criticism of restraint is that it takes away the ability of the child to learn and internalize self-control. However, research studies have found the opposite. In two studies nearly a decade apart, physical holding produced rapid gain in internal behavioral control (Miller, Walker & Friedman, 1989; Sourander, Aurela & Piha, 1997). Restraint has also been found to be helpful in developing control for some children through attachments to emotionally important adults (Cotton, 1989), and for protections and socialization (Bath, 1994; Cotton, 1993; Miller et al., 1989, Rich, 1997; Sourander, 1996). Physical restraint has been called ethically sound (Sugar, 1994) and recognized for significant therapeutic benefits (Bath, 1994).

The arguments for and against the use of various interventions such as medications, institutionalization, physically intrusive therapies, seclusion, and physical restraint are important discussions. However, children are not served when only one point of view is expressed. Many interventions, including physical restraint, can have damaging consequences when improperly used; however, at times the consequences of not using serious interventions can be even more damaging to a child. A five-point evaluation of interventions for violent behavior has previously been recommended (Ziegler, 2001): 1. Was safety ensured? 2. Was self-control internalized? 3. Was the intervention individualized and based on understanding the child? 4. Was the intervention therapeutically driven? and 5. Was the intervention effective in producing the desired result?

If we are to meet the challenge of increasing numbers of violent children in our system of care, we must carefully consider how we can best meet the short- and long-term needs of these children, while ensuring the safety of other children, their parents, and the community at large. A reasoned approach to this question would be careful consideration of all the issues, and not a singular movement to reduce or eliminate physical interventions, which have been found to be safe, ethical, effective and therapeutic.

Checklist for Working with Violence

✓ What is behind the violent behavior?

✓ Eliminate the causes of the behavior.

✓ Screen the environment for any violent themes.

✓ Develop a team to work on the child's issues in all settings.

✓ Provide a firm structure with zero tolerance for violence.

✓ Make sure the child knows you are very serious.

✓ Back up your boundary on violence with physical interventions when needed.

✓ Establish a baseline for violent behavior and work progressively to reduce the behavior.

✓ Give the child other ways to get attention.

✓ Have a crisis plan if behavior becomes dangerous.

Part II

*Understanding
the Psychological Needs
of Troubled Children*

An 11-year-old was on the phone learning about his family background from his biological father when the boy asked, "Am I Jewish?" After the call he spoke to one of the staff and said, "It turns out I am not Christian after all, I am German." [Why didn't Martin Luther figure that out?]

Chapter

5

What Traumatized Children Did Not Receive While They Were Being Mistreated

It would be difficult to find an adult or child who would not agree that child abuse is a tragedy. In the past, child abuse was in the shadows of our society, we looked the other way and hoped bad things were not happening to children in their own homes. Thanks, in part, to C. Henry Kempe, a medical doctor who made the medical profession acknowledge "child maltreatment syndrome," the problem of child abuse is out in the open. Over the last thirty years, child abuse has become one of our society's biggest concerns. However, despite the attention and media devoted to this problem, few adults fully understand the impact and true consequences of abuse.

For the past 20 years, Vincent Felitti, M.D. and colleagues have been studying the long term effects of child maltreatment. His findings may revolutionize medicine. Dr. Felitti, a specialist in internal medicine with no previous expertise in child abuse, began to study chronic medical conditions such as obesity, smoking, pulmonary disease and many other medical conditions. The results of research over time have shown that one specific cause, more than any other, accounts for poor physical, social and psychological health throughout life — child abuse. Based on the

95

results of 20 years of study with the largest sample of its kind, preventive medical practice should turn its attention to early childhood in order to prevent debilitating medical and psychological conditions that lead to such enormous problems as: drug and alcohol addition, smoking, obesity, depression, pulmonary disease, teen pregnancy, suicide attempts and premature death. This study states, "Adverse childhood experiences are the main determinant of the health and social well-being of the nation" (Felitti, Anda, Nordenberg, Williamson, Spitz, Edwards & Koss, 1998).

In America we have put considerable resources into preventing abuse, as we should. We have also developed safe places for children to be when their own homes are deemed unsafe. But too often, we take abused children out of an unsafe situation, put them into a safe foster placement, and believe we have met these children's needs as we look for another child to save. This statement is a bit simplistic, but it reflects the common thinking of our system, that when children are in a safe and loving home they should flourish. All too often this is not the case — because you can take the child out of the abuse, but you can't take the abuse out of the child.

My intention is not to criticize our system of care. There are many thousands of wonderful families who open their homes and hearts to be foster and adoptive parents. There are also thousands of caseworkers who struggle with large caseloads and few resources to do the best they can. But all of us in the system of care need to understand what traumatized children truly need, if we are going to repair their damaged lives and give them a fighting chance for a successful future. With all due respect to the Beatles, love is not all you need, or should I say love is not all traumatized children need — as most foster and adoptive parents have learned. Most of us have loved someone in our lives, only to have our love rejected. Our love had little positive impact on the other person if the love was unwanted and not valued. As foster and adoptive parents, we can love a child all we want, but it has little positive impact on the child if the love is rejected and viewed by the child as having little value.

If love is not enough, then what is enough? Love is a necessary condition to reaching a traumatized and abused child, but it is not a sufficient condition. We must love these children even when they reject us. The experience of continually loving someone who continually rejects us is either great practice in unconditional love, or heartache and depression — we get to decide. It does not feel very good to have our caring continually rejected, but it is great practice of the highest form of loving another person. When I say we must love these children, I mean our love must be real, it cannot be professional love or pretend love. When children have lived without love, it is like living in a desert where your thirst is never quenched. Such a child can tell the difference between a mirage and real water.

As caring adults who reach out to abused children, we all believe we have something to offer the child, and we intend to give our gifts to the child. What is difficult to prepare for is how completely we will probably be rejected by the child. We cannot prepare for this because, until it happens, there is no way to understand what it is like. We can tell a teen to be prepared and not take it too hard when he falls in love with someone and is rejected. But our words will mean little when this actually happens. He probably will not look at you, smile and say, "Oh, this is what you meant; thanks, I feel better already." Most of us are that teen the first few times we love a child coming into our home, and the child throws our love into the trash or back into our face. Even if we understand what is happening, it does not feel good, this time or anytime.

Abused children generally do not have experience with love. The concept just does not make sense. Let's see, love is when someone else's needs are more important than my own; or love is wanting the best for the other person (they would understand "love is never having to say your sorry," but I never understood that one). Abused children know about being used, they know about meeting the needs of self-centered parents; but why would anyone give up self-gratification to make sure someone else is happy? This is way beyond their experience and makes little logical sense. Therefore, when you come along with your caring and your attempts to help the child, the child is no fool; she knows you want something and probably at her expense.

We have all misjudged people in our lives who we initially did not trust because we underestimated them. During the time we did not trust them, it made no difference how trustworthy the person was, it was lost on us because of our mindset. Abused children live in a world where no one can be trusted. These children have experienced firsthand what happens when you are vulnerable to someone, with terrible consequences. They will do anything to avoid such an experience in the future.

Although love is a necessary for abused children, we must understand that our love will seldom be accepted anytime soon, if at all, by the child. Even so, the love must continue or the first condition of meeting the child's needs will be lost. There are a number of other needs that traumatized children have in order to be successful in life. Let's take a look at some of these needs.

To Be Understood

Abused children need and deserve to be cared for by parents, teachers and supportive adults who understand them. It is often difficult to comprehend the abuse the child has gone through; but one thing is clear, the child's needs did not come first in an abusive home. If our home or our help is to meet the needs of the child, then we must first and foremost understand what the child's external and internal experience has been in the past, and probably continues to be in the present. Many foster and adoptive families expect the child to adapt to new family rules and routines. Adjusting to the family will require many adjustments for the child. However, what the child needs is for the family to adjust first by making room for the child, and finding ways to meet the child half or three quarters of the way.

Michelle Let Me Know When I Was Right

A mistake adults make is to believe troubled children will tell them in words what they are going through. A child will tell you all right, but not the way most adults do. We need to go to them and tell them what we see. Michelle was an example. She would rage and become hurtful to herself and anyone around her at predictable times — for example when she had contact with her mother or her grandmother. On a number of occasions, I had to stop her violence with a therapeutic hold. I told her I understood that she was very angry at her family (and she had reason to be). Her response was, "Go to hell," and she would intensify her rage. After she wore herself out, she always sobbed like a toddler. She knew I understood her rage, and she let me know this by screaming at me. This raw and very honest intimacy she gave me let me know we were connecting. As with Michelle, it is our job as adults to understand the communication the child gives us.

A complete assessment of the child's needs, problems and contributing factors to her feelings and behaviors is an important aspect of understanding the child and then ensuring that the child's experiences are understood. With the most difficult children, the evaluation can be daunting. However, it is unlikely that you can come up with solutions until you have a good idea of the parameters of the problem. Dr. Ron Federici points out that there are nine aspects to a comprehensive assessment to best understand the difficult child: 1. A comprehensive developmental pediatric evaluation, 2. A thorough audiological and visual exam, 3. A pediatric neurology evaluation, 4. Genetic studies, 5. A neuropsychological evaluation, 6. Speech and language evaluation, including auditory processing, 7. Educational evaluation, 8. Physical and occupational therapy evaluation, and 9. Family therapy assessment (Federici, 2003).

The child will almost always be unable to tell parents what is happening inside of him. The child will also be unable to give parents a list of his most urgent psychological needs. It is the job of the parent to identify these needs, with the help of other adults working with the child, and to come up with a plan to meet these needs.

Safety and Predictability

The first need of all children, particularly traumatized children, is to feel safe and secure. Safety is a basic need and often lacking in the home or homes of difficult children. In *Raising Children Who Refuse To Be Raised*, I went into detail identifying basic needs of children for both parents (p. 34-39) and therapists (p. 14-19), which I will not repeat here. It is not hard to see why safety is the first basic psychological need of children. Traumatized children will be more hypersensitive to threats to safety. If the environment is experienced by a child as unsafe, there will not be a possibility of healing from past abuse, of learning prosocial skills, or of being able to think and act as a child. With this being the case, the environment must be very safe, predictable and secure, and extra care must be extended to ensure that the child actually experiences the safety that exists in the setting.

Belonging Somewhere

Everyone needs to belong. Humans are social creatures, and we live or die based upon our ability to belong to a social unit. While some animals are able to fend for themselves soon after birth, humans depend on their care providers at least until age 25 (at least it seems like it; sometimes it is sooner). Actually, a successful human needs connection to others throughout life. The need to belong is related to the reality that the world is a difficult and scary place. It is less so if we are a part of a unit: a family, a team, a tribe, a gang, a club or hundreds of other groups that give us more security and confidence to function in life. Even the most secure people will quickly lose much of their confidence if they lose a significant other or they are ostracized or shunned by their family or church group. Our connections give us the support and the inner belief that we can negotiate the hazards of living because we have support, protection in numbers, and others to go to when times are bad.

For difficult children, the need to belong is even more critical than for others; but the child will work hard to disguise this need. Troubled children will act tough, they will verbalize they need no one in life, and they often will reject the connection offered by caring adults. I have written before about the rule of opposites, meaning troubled children often verbalize the opposite of what is closer to the truth for them. Regarding belonging, the more the child protests that she does not need nor want anyone, the more important this need may be for the child. When I work with families, it is important that they learn this rule of opposites quickly so they have a better chance to understand the child's real message. The children who protest the most about family gatherings or events are precisely the children who need such events in their lives.

Traumatized children need to belong, but they also need to be themselves, not just our version of who they should be. While it is important to make room in your family, your classroom or your soccer team for a child who has a strong need to belong, it is important not to misunderstand what belonging means. In my opinion, there is a difference between belonging to a family and a family "claiming" a child. The term claiming is mentioned frequently in adoption circles, but it is a term I do not use. I have no problem with an adoptive family taking a young child into their home and having the child become a full member of the family. As a term, claiming sends a message of ownership. In our culture we do talk about *my* husband or *my* daughter; however, when this reference carries with it ownership rather than a statement of connection, I am less comfortable. Adoptive parents are often encouraged to "claim" their new child. Again, I have no problem with a lifelong commitment, if that is what is meant by claiming; but when ownership is the tone, there will be problems with troubled children. We have spoken previously of the hypersensitivity of traumatized children to agendas from adults. If the goal of the adoptive parents is to claim the child as their own, the difficult child will resist such an attempt. The harder the family claims the child, the more resistance the parents can expect.

Don't Make Promises You Can't Keep

In our Wednesday therapy group, the topic was adoption. I asked the children how many had been adopted before and five raised their hands. I ask if anyone had been adopted more than once and three raised their hands. I asked the three children if I could ask them some questions about adoption and videotape their answers, they agreed. In the middle of the interview I asked, "What should I tell adoptive parents never to say to the child?" The answer was agreed to by all three children, "Don't tell us this is our forever family, because we have heard it before and it isn't true." This and other promises were mentioned by the experienced adopted children as what not to tell an adopted child. Don't make promises that you can't keep. I go a step further and suggest you not make promises at all; troubled children don't believe the promise, and even if you keep it, they find a reason to tell themselves you didn't.

There is a difference in my mind between belonging in a family and being claimed by the family. The difference is room for the child to decide. If an adult tells a troubled child who he must be close to and who he must stay away from, there will be predictable trouble. It isn't always that the child is non-compliant, although there is plenty of that among these children, but the child resists the agendas of adults because he has learned it is safer for him to do so. This type of thinking comes from the experience of being used and abused by one or any number of adults. I suggest families, classrooms, clubs or other affiliated groups make room for the child, and allow the child some space to first hang around the fringes before joining in. You may need to accept that she is verbalizing that she does not like the group because it is made up of losers and freaks. This is a good time to ignore the words and watch the energy and behavior of the child.

Among the Basic Psychological Needs, Don't Forget Touch

Not only is being touched a basic psychological need of children, it is also one of the basic physical needs. The area of touch is perhaps the most misunderstood psychological need for troubled children. The problem is that the child pushes adults away and many adults are repulsed and less than excited about touching the child, for good reason. Who is in a hurry to get close to someone who may hurt you, or who goes out of their way to be repulsive? If the adult and the child agree to keep a distance, this mutual agreement is a formula for disaster.

I am not the first to point out the element in our society that is focused on risk management, liability insurance, and avoiding the attention of an overpopulation of attorneys with not enough work to go around. There is little we can do in life without bowing to the liability industry: driving our cars, inviting people to our homes, running our businesses, playing sports or nearly anything we do — including getting out of bed in the morning. Raising a difficult and troubled child is one of the top items on the liability scale. These kids can become violent, they destroy the family's property or the property of others in the community. These kids hurt others and, at times, they provoke adults to hurt them. They may also accuse you of abusing them. All of these qualities of troubled children make an insurance agent lose sleep. The logical result of the liability posed by difficult children is to suggest to parents to avoid touch with these children. After all, the child will usually reject your touch, and if you use physical interventions to modify the child's dangerous behaviors, you may be attacked.

We cannot parent a difficult child by listening to risk managers. Of all the psychological needs of children, I am most concerned that these children are not touched enough. Speaking from twenty years of parenting these children in my home, there are many more reasons to not touch troubled children than to touch them. Some of these reasons come from foster parent licensing authorities who don't want to increase the risks. Some of the reasons are the preferences of parents who mistakenly accept the child's protests about being touched. The latest assault on providing difficult children with the basic need of touch is a mistaken (in my opinion) national movement to eliminate physical touch in dealing with violence from young children. I addressed this issue in some detail in Chapter 4. I spend considerable time trying to have well-meaning but misguided child advocates understand that reducing the amount of touch will move us further away from our goal, not nearer to it.

Help to Climb Out of the Pit

It is not fun to be a traumatized child who makes the lives of others difficult. These children demonstrate to others the behaviors that provide us with a hint of what it is like to live inside their skin. Part of the child's thinking is that no one is going to like or be interested in him or her, so it is a good idea to reject others before they reject you. It is very common for these children come up with extreme ways to push people away because of fear. Wise adults will notice this extreme behavior and not be fooled by it. The rule of opposites would say that children who repeatedly make a big deal out of pushing people away, may actually have an equally strong desire to be close to others. These children attempt to hide this desire from people around them and perhaps try to convince themselves they really don't care.

Children who have been mistreated by others often have no idea how to make their lives any different. They mistakenly believe they know how to make their lives better, but when they steal what they want or lie to achieve something, their lives only get worse. These children live in a deep pit with little light to see clearly, no ladder to climb out, and only the ability to express in a loud fashion how bad their lives are. As a therapist and parent, I must admit to myself (and sometimes to the child) that I agree, her life looks pretty bad from the outside, and I can only imagine what it must feel like from the inside. At this point, the child often has some less than profound expletive to thank me for my insight — but I have let the child know that I see the trap in which she is caught.

The child needs someone who knows how to help him get out of the pit. Most adults in the child's life have done what seems reasonable, but is actually incredibly unhelpful, and that is to let the child wallow in his own quick sand. These adults criticize the child for not trying in school, they point out that the child has no friends because of the way he acts, and when the child rejects them the parent says, "Fine, be miserable if that is what you want." News flash to all adults: despite what they say, most children do not like to be miserable!

Many children have become familiar with the state of being miserable, and they may act or say things to have you believe they want to lose at the game of life. But I would ask you this, if you told the child you would give him a crisp $100 bill if he could beat you at the child's choice of any video game, do you think the child would be interested? My point is that these children look at situations in life as playing a game where the deck is always stacked against them. They don't know the rules, they don't have the skills they need, and when they lose (and they believe losing is inevitable) it will hurt again. Does that sound like a game you would be interested in playing?

Our role as helping adults is to reverse this process and help the child out of the pit they are in. First we shine a light in (give them some ideas about their situation), then we put down a ladder (show them a way out), and then we don't wait for them to make the first move, we climb into the pit with them and demonstrate the way out (hang in there with the child and ignore all the protests, ugly words and actions, and continue to look through the rough exterior at the vulnerable child within). As all of us who have gone through this process have learned, we seldom get a big hug and kiss for our efforts. It is more common to get spit on, cursed at, and have your family lineage questioned (you know, when they call you a son of a jackal). If I told you not to start the process of helping one of these children if you are hoping for a plaque or recognition for your efforts, you would say, "Not me, I know better." But how many adults give up on a child just because the first 100 attempts failed and the child told them just where to put their love and caring? Remember, you are a sower who plants the seeds; there are no guarantees that you will share in the harvest, which will take quite some time. Just because a nut tree will not have fruit for seven growing seasons is a poor reason not to plant one.

A Chance to Express What Is Inside

What have troubled children heard from adults all their lives? Stop being loud. Why are you crying again? Do you have any feelings other than anger? Stop pounding on the wall. If you slam the door again, I will make you buy a new one. A smart child would get the impression that adults do not want to hear about their pain, their anger, or their frustration with failing at everything they do except driving adults crazy. Oftentimes this impression is very close to the truth. For a variety of reasons, language arts class is not a good place to express how angry people make you. During the church sermon is not the best time to say out loud how bored you are, even when it is the most honest thing the child has said all week. A major part of growing up and learning to be a big person is, let's face it, learning how to shut up and live with things we do not like. When you are a child, who seems to naturally break every possible rule, you hear from adults often to not express what you are thinking and feeling. While teaching children when and how to express themselves, we also need to hear the child's real feelings and not just tell them they shouldn't feel that way.

We all need to express to someone what is going on inside of us. Troubled children have a need far greater than others. However, they do not tap you on the shoulder and ask to spend a little quality time getting suggestions from you on better handling their strong feelings. Expressing thoughts and feelings successfully is another game they do not know how to play and they generally lose. As the adult you must help the child express what is going on inside. Step number one is to allow the child to express what she feels and thinks; step two is to let the child know that you are listening, and that what is going on with him matters to you. It is not until step three that you help the child express important issues in an acceptable way. Many parents reverse the order of these three steps, and the result does not work for either the child or the adult. If you have a very expressive (in all the wrong ways) child in your home, step one is underway and you can move to ensuring that the child knows you are listening, and her experience matters to you. It is important that you really hear the child, which often means that you listen deeper than what his or her words are saying.

Helping the child express what is inside can take many forms. Don't require the child to use certain words or use words at all in the beginning. Children express themselves much more honestly with methods other than words. Expressions can take the form of art, music, sports, hobbies, and play. It is not a coincidence that experienced child therapists have been trained in using art, music, activities, clay and play as means to uncover what is really going on inside a child. These are the comfortable tools children use to be expressive. Before we ask them to learn our language, we must take the time to learn theirs.

To Have Fun

The principle job of a child is to learn and to enjoy the process. In other words, a child's job is to play. However, the ability to enjoy life and be playful is one of the first things to disappear when a child is traumatized. Certainly the abuse is not fun, and the results of abuse, such as increased worry and anxiety, tend to add a layer of heaviness to all the activities in a child's life. In our schools we tend to think of recess as a reward for doing school work or a time to take a break before the real work begins again. However, recess is a critical aspect of school in building play into the child's school day, as well as helping the child learn all the social skills needed to get along with others. For many traumatized children, recess is the most difficult time of the day.

We cannot leave the child to find the way to fun and enjoyment on his or her own. These children do not see the point of having fun. When you look at it in a utilitarian way, there are limited reasons to have fun in life. The primary role of having fun is enjoyment, not to get something productive out of it (although we have done our best to find productive reasons for exercise and hobbies). We must help traumatized child learn to have fun. Play for play's sake may be natural for most children, but not after trauma. You will need to create opportunities for the child to have fun and to enjoy activities. Even when traumatized children have the opportunities, they often turn play into work and having fun into a negative experience. This is the same dynamic that traumatized children bring to many activities in life. What they need from us is modeling (do you have fun in your life?), opportunities, and help to learn what fun and enjoyment are all about.

Patience from Someone Who Will Travel a Rocky Road with Them

It is a given that helping a troubled child will be difficult. For staff who work with children in my programs, I look for the caring of a Mother Teresa and the firmness of a General Patton. One quality without the other will not work with these children. Mother Teresa was an inspiration to millions because she opened homes for the hungry, the dying and the destitute. However, she did not go around the world opening treatment centers for the non-compliant, the fire-setters or the conduct disordered. For these issues, an additional set of skills and approaches is important. But a trait both Mother Teresa and General Patton shared was patience. Patience is one of the psychological needs of difficult children, to have an adult with the superhuman patience to withstand the gale force winds and the biting cold that often comes from these children, and is usually directed at any adult who shows interest in them.

Patiently meeting each one of the needs discussed in this chapter will place demands on the adults and the environment the child is in. The goal is not to give the child everything she wants, nor is it to meet her needs over everyone else's. The goal is to show the child there is a place where she can, perhaps for the first time, get what she needs, and with a little investment on her part, she can also get some of what she wants. The parent will also need to demonstrate to the child that you will not give up on him.

Troubled children, whose psychological needs are generally not met, learn that they must become aggressive and demanding in pursuit of what they need and want, or they will come up empty-handed. It all begins with the child experiencing a world that does not understand and does not provide what he or she really needs. If they learn their needs are not met, these children become desperate and aggressively focused on controlling others and demanding that they get what they want. This dynamic, particularly when it relates to the need of safety, is what robs the abused child of her childhood years. Most badly abused children are unable to be carefree children with a curious interest in people and experiences around them. The trauma they have lived through creates fear of new experiences and a dread of what adults might do to them next.

It is a long road for troubled children to get past the fear of everyday living and to regain the fun and discovery of childhood; most will be unable to travel this road without a guide. The demands on the guide will be great, but the rewards for the child are immeasurable.

Seeing Strengths When They Look in the Mirror

The last two psychological needs are a bit more intangible than those listed above, but are also important to troubled children. The first is to begin to see some value within themselves. This can only happen when we look in the mirror and notice at least something in ourselves that we or others like or value. Because traumatized individuals lose much of their ability to self-reflect, it will first require that others point out their strengths.

While it is a need we all have to value ourselves and see our positive qualities, this is the top rung of the ladder for traumatized individuals to reach. It takes a very long time and many will not reach this rung, but it is no less of a need. A child's behavior is heavily influenced by self-perception and the resulting emotions that are generated. Difficult children by definition have multiple behavior problems that need to be changed if they are going to have any success in life. If we are to help these children change aggressive, destructive and negative behaviors, we must help them overcome the negative self-perception that has resulted from the trauma in their past.

A fully functioning person is a complex weave of fibers that all play their roles in creating the whole person. If some fibers are weak or others are not present, the weave can begin to unravel. Helping a troubled child requires that we pay attention to all aspects of the child's external and internal life. Although doable, parenting these children is the most difficult job any of us will ever attempt, and we cannot go into it expecting to have our needs met.

Seeing Hope in Your Face When You Look at Them

Having a negative self-perception robs the child of any confidence and hope for the future. Like so many of the other needs that we have covered, the child must get this hope from the outside. From the moment a newborn first opens his eyes and sees the world, the child learns to look first at the human face. Children generally first connect with the face of their mothers and within a short time can distinguish the mother's face from others. Throughout the developmental years, the child continues to look in the face of care providers to see if things are good or bad. The child does not have verbal language for many months, but communication is handled through reading the look on mommy's face.

We must ask what the message is that troubled children read in our faces. Do they see repeated disapproval, frustration, or even disgust? Trust me, I understand how hard it is to communicate confidence that this struggling child standing in front of you will be able to meet the most basic request from you. I struggle with this every day. But if the children do not see hope in our faces, where will the hope come from that lets them know there is something inside of them that can change the negative patterns that seem to control them? When I mentioned that these children must look in the mirror and see that they have strengths, the most frequent mirror they look into is your face. What is the reflection they see coming back from you?

With each of the nine psychological needs covered above, the child will neither ask for what they need nor necessarily thank you when the need is met. Troubled children are like an infant who does not ask her mother to change her diaper to feel more comfortable, she screams like there will be no tomorrow! The goal is to be noticed and to get maximum attention, hoping the adult will figure out what is needed. The arrested development of traumatized children produces this same dynamic where they do not ask for what they need, they act in ways to get maximum attention, usually negative, hoping the adult will figure out what they truly need. It is our job to get beyond the content of the outburst and determine what the child really needs at that moment, and what is needed over the long-term for success in life.

THE UNMET NEEDS OF TRAUMATIZED CHILDREN

✓ The need for love - the majority of traumatized children did not receive love and therefore don't understand their own need for love.

✓ The need to be understood.

✓ Safety and predictability.

✓ Feeling like he or she belongs.

✓ Supportive and reassuring physical touch.

✓ Someone to help them move forward when they find themselves stuck.

✓ An opportunity to express what is inside, even if it is not pleasant.

✓ Learn to have fun.

✓ Patience from adults who will be there for them.

✓ Seeing personal strengths when looking in the mirror.

✓ Seeing hope in the faces of adults in their lives.

In a class on morality, a question came up about the Resurrecti
man with serious sexual acting out problems approached me w
found in my Bible where it says to hope in the Re-erection." [Afte
more interest in Christianity.]

Chapter

6

The Pervasive Impact of Tr;
on a Child's Developmei

Many adults, including teachers, thera
adoptive parents, probation officers, police offic
judges have learned to ask if the background of
life included significant child abuse. They
because the presence of abuse answers many oth
the individual's struggles in life. In most ca
forgone conclusion that troubled individuals
history. For example, a large majority of adults
arrive at a mental health center or counselor';
abused at a young age. The results of trauma h;
impact that first affect childhood from several p

It is true that every experience in life is
human brain and, therefore, has an impact on th
events are processed as enjoyable, some are ne
are unpleasant, and then there are the ex
registered in the brain as threats to survival. E
either life threatening or are perceived by the
what we refer to as traumatic memories. The
put a "bookmark" on a memory that can quick

ow being found that the brain can also categorize memories
·e not to be recalled later. Let's begin with the former.

e know a great deal about how to enhance the memory of
duals. There are training programs and courses that have
ods to do this. There are even examples of people who have
d themselves to successfully recall enormous amounts of
nation, such as memorizing the Bible. Every student has
·d hard to improve their memory of facts in order to
ete an assignment or do well on an exam. It is important to
on that memorization of facts, such as remembering the
sburg Address, is only one type of memory — factual or
it memory. Some memories are so positive or impactful that
n't need to train ourselves to remember them. For example, I
aber where I was when Neil Armstrong took the first step on
oon, and so do millions of other Americans. Sometimes very
ve events are so impactful they are also vividly remembered.
events might include President Kennedy being shot and, for
Americans, hearing the news about the attack on Pearl
or. More recent events of this type might be the Challenger
sion and, for most everyone, the attack on the World Trade
r and Pentagon. Other events become important to us due to
personal significance. The smart husband will remember not
is wife's birthday and their anniversary, but also a host of
s so he is ready for the important test, "Honey, do you
ober..." The right answer is, "Oh yes, how could I ever
?"

r many years there has been the belief by many who work
he victims of trauma that the brain has the ability to block
collections, often called repressed memories. For example, it
amon for individuals in a serious accident to remember every
of their day leading up to the accident, but be unable to
anything about the accident itself. On the surface, this has
made logical sense. Doesn't the brain know important from
oortant events; and doesn't the brain make sure it remembers
aportant parts of our lives? The answer appears to be yes,

and, in fact, some important events appear to get very special treatment indeed.

Despite years of legal challenges, assertions by a few researchers, and a national network of accused abusers that claim there is no such thing as repressed memories, recent research appears to support the fact that the brain has this ability. For those of us who have worked with trauma survivors for years, this comes as no surprise. Why do some traumatized individuals recall almost nothing about their abusive childhoods? Why do some rape victims have difficulty remembering any details of such a horrible experience? Dr. Michael Anderson, a psychology professor at the University of Oregon, along with John Gabriel of Stanford University, have recently conducted research to show that a person can tell the brain to ignore some things that may otherwise be remembered and to recall other things the brain may not have remembered. These researchers indicate that selective memory appears to be a function of the prefrontal cortex and the hippocampus. If the body has the ability to shut down consciousness when faced with overwhelming pain, as in physical shock, why wouldn't it also be able to shut down during and after trauma in a process that could be called psychological shock?

The above example of the impact of trauma on the brain is only one of the intersecting factors that result in traumatic experiences profoundly changing not only memory, but potentially the individual's personality and perspective on self, other people and the world at large. To consider how trauma affects the developing child, we will discuss the process of attachment as well as other impacts on the brain, above and beyond memory.

Trauma and Attachment

Perhaps the cruelest impact of trauma on a child is the resulting effect on attachment. Designed as an instinctual method of survival, children who are traumatized very early in life and go through the pain of abuse, develop adaptive responses to trauma that in the long-run prevent them from finding any real success in life. As social beings, we cannot call ourselves a success without strong social relationships that support us in our pain and join us in our pleasure, our grief and our joy. Attachment and the ability to develop profoundly significant connections with others is a prerequisite to success in life.

Attachment is essential from a big picture point-of-view, where we need others in our lives on every level to feel like we belong and are connected. Attachment is also very practical and affects the personality of individuals, which in turn has a major influence on how we respond to situations and decisions we face each and every day. John Bowlby, an English physician and psychoanalyst, originally developed attachment theory in his work on the reactions of grief and loss in children. His research led to how and why humans attach in our early years.

In psychology we use the term theory not in the scientific usage of something that has not been proven, because if this was the meaning of theory, then attachment theory has been proven to be a true and accurate explanation of human behavior based on decades of research and study. The term theory is used more as a model or paradigm that explains aspects of human behavior and experience. Bowlby asserted that our early connections in life explain the way we view the world, which he referred to as our "inner working models." He also pointed out that our emotional responses to events and situations we encounter, which he referred to as "set points," are explained by the level of attachment experience we have, particularly in our early years (Bowlby, 1982). Stated briefly, the goal of all therapeutic interventions related to attachment problems is to change the way an individual perceives the world, and how he or she feels about the experiences life provides.

Repeated research with children has shown that attachment is a key factor in a successfully functioning child, adolescent and adult. Attachment has been associated with more competent toddlers, preschoolers, and students of all ages (Belski, 1988). We will discuss in Chapter 12 the importance of success in school as a predictor of later functioning. Attachment skills, or the lack of, are often passed down from mother to child. Research has shown a direct link between the quality of attachment with her baby and the quality of attachment the mother had with her own mother (Lewis, 1984). In this same research, Lewis found that a secure attachment for a child increased the child's competence in peer relationships, resulting in a more positive disposition and higher levels of empathy. Regarding traits we all would prefer in young children, research has found that a secure attachment resulted in more enthusiasm, more persistence, and more cooperation (Matos, Arend & Sroufe, 1978). In the big picture of human success and failure, the role attachment plays is primary. More on the importance of attachment can be found in Chapter 11.

Trauma and Brain Development

I will only briefly address trauma and brain development since this is the topic of *Traumatic Experience and the Brain* (Ziegler, 2002). However, this discussion would not be complete without some reference to the significant ways that trauma has an impact on the developing brain of a child.

There has been an explosion of new information on the human brain over the last fifteen years. As our technology has improved, such as the use of positron emissions tomagraphy (PET scans) and functional magnetic resonance imaging (fMRI), we have been able to study how the brain works in ways never before imagined. This has led to an avalanche of scientific research and exciting, although difficult to understand, professional literature on the brain — how it develops and how it works. These advancements have helped in many areas of science, but perhaps have been most helpful in understanding the mental and emotional problems that people develop. This is especially true for children who have been traumatized.

The word trauma can refer to a wide variety of negative experiences — accidents, painful medical procedures, or life-changing emotional events; but by far the most common traumatic experience is some form of abuse, such as physical or sexual abuse or serious neglect. Because of the impact of trauma on the developing brain, advancements in understanding brain functioning have opened new doors to understanding children in our foster and adoptive homes.

As a psychologist, I am just like you; I don't have time to get lost in complicated medical and neurological explanations. I just need to know the answer to one important question, "So what?" What should I know and what should I do differently based upon all these new studies and all this new scientific information on the brain? I have spent several years asking this question, and I now share some of the answers I have found, particularly with parents who can use the information to help their children.

The human brain is the most complex organism in the known universe. It is comprised of 1,000 billion individual brain cells, called neurons, that develop 1,000 trillion connections with each other. An infant at birth has a brain that is only 25% developed, which enables the child to adapt to a wide range of environments.

The brain of a child who is cared for by a loving family will adapt very differently than a child who has a drug-addicted mother in a home where domestic violence is common. We have learned from recent research that positive and negative experiences not only are stored in the memory areas of the brain, but experiences also sculpt the developing brain and determine how it will process all new information. This process goes on at every age, even before birth. Just because a child does not have conscious memory of an event (explicit memory) does not mean the brain does not remember (implicit memory). "So what?" Well, this helps us see that the earliest experiences of a child will not only be carved in the brain's memory, but the brain itself will develop differently because of the environment.

The brain develops in predictable ways based on experiences. A loving supportive environment produces larger, more well-developed brain structures that will help the child be smarter, more inquisitive, and feel safer — allowing the brain to put less energy into self-protection. If the child comes into a world with trauma of any kind, the higher regions of the brain grow smaller, affecting the child's ability to learn and fully understand the world other than how to survive by being ever-vigilant to possible harm.

The brain has many complex components, but basically it can be divided into four areas. The brainstem is at the base of the brain and handles the less glamorous but essential functions, such as breathing, heart rate, blood pressure, temperature regulation and respiration. The diencephalon includes several parts of the brain and controls motor regulation, such as walking and balance, as well as appetite, sleep patterns, and the memory to ride a bike even after years of no practice. The limbic system controls emotions, perceptions, attachment and sexual behavior. Much of what happens in the limbic system is automatic and not affected by reasoning. It is therefore the limbic system that beer advertisers target, and why the overexposed 2004 Super Bowl half-time show will be remembered by some more than the game itself. The limbic system is fundamentally impacted by trauma. All memories of trauma are processed and stored in the limbic system. These memories are, for the most part, unavailable for conscious recall. The last and highest region of the brain is the neocortex. This is the largest part of the brain and controls the personality, goals, decisions, and what makes a person a success or a failure in life. The difference in the overall functioning of the brains of Adolf Hitler and Mother Teresa was minor, but the neocortex produced very different people and a very different result. "So what?" Traumatized children operate from the limbic system and don't understand why they act as they do. The goal is to provide safety for these children, so they can operate and develop the higher regions of their brain. Higher brain activities are called executive functions and include: decision making, learning from the past, developing values, and forming a personality others care to be around. More executive functions are listed in Chapter 7.

MORE ANSWERS TO "SO WHAT?"

✓ Consider all problem behavior within the context of survival to understand "why he keeps doing that."

✓ Repetition is important because with every positive experience, the impact is stronger on the brain.

✓ Traumatized children expect the worst and focus on the negative. If you understand this, you will be better prepared for it.

✓ Childhood neglect in the long-term is the most damaging trauma. The child must not have basic needs threatened in any way or survival will be all he thinks about.

✓ Do not allow radical therapies for traumatized children. "Holding Therapy," "Rage Reduction," and other desperate approaches trigger the trauma memories in the limbic system and make matters worse.

✓ When abuse occurred, the brain was focused on survival, not learning. The development the child missed due to abuse will need extra attention.

✓ Trauma will often lower IQ scores below true ability. Retest when their environment is helping them heal and watch the scores go up.

> ✓ The goal in healing trauma is not to keep the child calm. The goal is help the child, when agitated, learn skills to reduce the agitation. This repeated stress/ relax cycle is what most helps the child.
>
> ✓ Promote play with traumatized children. Play is very healing to the brain and the emotions.
>
> ✓ Don't give up hope! The brain is capable of healing in ways we do not yet understand. Healing takes a long time and the child may not get there while still in your home, but every positive experience makes a difference.

The primary job of the brain is survival. If survival is threatened, the rest of the brain shuts down except for functions that help self-protection. The brain adapts throughout life, but the strongest adaptation is within the first two years of life. "So what?" Early nurturing care for a child makes a lasting difference as does early abuse of a child. However, the brain continues to adapt to the environment, so ingrained patterns can be changed with consistent positive experiences.

The brain is made up of networks of neurons (brain cells) that communicate with each other. If mommy is a caring, loving, nurturing provider for the infant, a strong neuro-network develops that says "mommy is good." If mommy is self-absorbed, unresponsive to the child's needs when she cries and physically abusive to the child, an even stronger neuro-network develops that says "mommy is to be avoided" in order to support survival. "So what?" To an abused child, mommy can be any adult in the role of care provider, which may include foster parent, adoptive parent, teacher, grandparent, etc. The reason attachment is a common problem with many abused children and children in a foster or adoptive home should be clear. The goal must be to develop new neuro-networks that promote safety, predictability, caring, and the child's physical and emotional needs getting met. Remember, the brain literally changes with every experience. It will continue to adapt in your positive, nurturing home regardless of how serious past abuse has been. Yes, Virginia, there is hope!

Issues in Trauma Therapy

In the next chapter we will go over in detail the essential steps of trauma therapy. However, there are a number of general points to address that will set the stage for what will come next.

Three of the most typical causes of mental health and criminal justice problems in America are: 1. Personal emptiness, depression and the inability to find inner strength when life gets challenging, 2. Disconnection from others or the inability to know how to get the closeness we deeply desire, and 3. Violent behavior or the unregulated lashing out at others for a perceived injustice. Violence is enhanced by activation of primitive brainstem functions, such as respiration, heart rate and blood pressure — while at the same time decreasing higher brain functions, such as thoughtful reasoning ability. It is no coincidence that these same three issues have been called the "Trauma Trilogy" and some of the most frequent results of significant trauma (Perry, 1995).

It is common for a traumatized individual to act as if he is still in a threatening situation. The threat is real, not necessarily on the outside, but on the inside in their neurological processing of events. One damaging effect of trauma is to align the awareness of the individual with stimuli related to past stress. The result is to under-react or be unresponsive to non-threatening situations, which are viewed as unimportant; but at the same time overreact to perceived threats, which are viewed as all-important (van der Kolk, 1999).

The traumatized child is often in the state of low-level fear, hyper-arousal and/or dissociation (spacing out) to avoid the stress he finds ever-present in his environment. Hyper-arousal is produced by poor internal regulation and hypersensitivity to stress. Symptoms can include hypervigilance and mood, attention and sleep disruption. Recent research is providing a possible clue why sleep disorders are the frequent result of trauma. It may be that ample deep sleep is one way that we erase the stress of our lives. When trauma affects sleep, we may be unable to wipe the stress slate clean and long-term problematic sleep patterns develop.

The absence of empathy for others is a common characteristic of traumatized individuals. Trauma can produce an emotional blindness or inability to understand the experience of others. In the excellent text, *Traumatic Stress*, van der Kolk and colleagues identified a number of important effects brought about by traumatic experiences (van der Kolk, McFarlane & Weisaeth, 1996):

- The loss of self-regulation — regardless of the emotions or behaviors, the child needs someone to help him keep from spinning out of control in either a hyper or depressed direction.

- The inability to use feelings as a guide — we often "get a feel for the situation" or "feel our way through," but this process is often not available to traumatized individuals.

- Trauma often produces self-directed aggression, and the younger the individual at the time of the trauma, the more self-abuse takes place.

- Stress can cause a reduction in blood to speech centers of the — the result may play a role in the child's inability to let others know how he or she is feeling during stress.

- Children often have arrested emotional development around the age of the initial trauma — it is not unusual to have an older child act many years younger when under stress.

- Traumatized children tend to lose the ability to play. The two primary jobs of a child are to learn and to play. Trauma can have a devastating impact on both the ability to learn and the ability to play and enjoy life.

- The most far-reaching traumatic effects are associated with neglect — don't assume, because a child has not been brutalized, either physically or sexually, that she has not been profoundly affected by events early in life. Living with chronic neglect signals to the brain that survival is continually threatened and can have a stronger impact than any other type of trauma.

How Trauma Affects Perception

Perception encompasses how we understand ourselves and the world around us. Perception involves a process of consideration. We take in information and we think about it. We also add our feelings and past experiences to help us process the meaning of events. It is easy to see how perception is fundamentally altered by trauma. How perception is changed by traumatic experience is the subject of several chapters in *Traumatic Experience and the Brain* (Ziegler, 2002). I will refer to these chapters for the details as well as implications for treatment interventions. Let's begin with a brief overview of trauma and perception.

Perception can be divided into three primary categories based upon the focus of our attention. The three are: perception of the self, perception of others, and a general perception of the world as we understand it at our developmental level.

In children, perceptions of self are radically changed by trauma. The instability of the forming sense of self is a primary reason why the impact is so strong. When we are not sure who we are or our value to others, the painful (physical and/or emotional) experience of being used, abused or ignored makes a very strong case for our value being very low to the abusive person. If this person is a parent (mothers are the most frequent perpetrators of child abuse, mostly due to neglect) or someone of great importance to us, the result is a devastated self-image.

When a child is treated very badly by someone who is relied upon to meet basic needs and ensure the child's very survival, the result is not just a damaged ego structure, but a foundation of negative self-worth. The child internalizes that he has no worth and is therefore worthless. If you think of many difficult children you have worked with, you will quickly remember children who acted in ways that any self-respecting person would avoid. They make themselves unattractive, they seek reactions of disgust from others, and they are the first to be self-denigrating. When the child does not respect himself or herself, there are few limits to the child's behavior, regardless of the negative outcome.

Carla Could Cut Loose

After being removed from her home due to abuse, and then removed from her relatives home due to sexual abuse, Carla bounced through several foster homes before coming to our program at age 11. Issues of control and rage were daily events in the beginning. There appeared to be no limits to her extreme behaviors when raging, and the more disgusting the better. She had all the familiar unpleasant behaviors: foul language, spitting at adults, hitting and kicking, and saying purposely hurtful things. To this list of unpleasantries, Carla added several others. She would urinate wherever and whenever she was unhappy. If not stopped, she would take off all her clothes in order to upset others. Carla eventually made good progress in our program, but initially she had no internal self-respect and it showed. She reflected to others what she felt on the inside, all resulting from her degrading familial abuse.

The traumatized child develops perceptions of others based on four possibilities, each of which is a reaction to the early betrayal of trauma. The word betrayal is used because even if the trauma was not physical or sexual abuse, or some type of serious neglect, any type of trauma is exactly what the child must rely on the parent to protect him or her from. Even the trauma of accidents or medical procedures involves some level of the child's brain processing betrayal by the care provider. When the person the child must rely upon betrays or lets the child down, she learns to place others into four categories.

Physical Threat — the first category is any person who is perceived as a physical threat. It does not take much for an abused child to put someone in this category. The child's brain is signaling that survival may be threatened, autonomic and hormonal changes take place, while fight or flight survival mechanisms are initiated.

Unless you want a cornered badger on your hands, or a child that avoids you in any way possible, do your best not to be perceived as a survival threat to a troubled child.

Interpersonal Threat — the second category is someone who is viewed as an interpersonal threat. Such a person is viewed as a stumbling block for the child to get what he wants. Anyone who has expectations, sets rules, requires compliance and in any way impedes the child from taking over the environment is a threat to the child's control, and must be worked around or worked with (you want the latter).

Easy Mark — category three is a person who is an easy mark. In the same way grifters and con-artists size up people for their gullibility or their inability to say no, traumatized children do this with "weak" adults all around them. The child is often not correct in perceiving someone as weak. This perception may come from the adult reaching out and trying to show interest and caring to the child. However, such loving motivations are lost on the child who has only minutes to size up the enemy, and all adults are some type of enemy until they have been defeated.

Irrelevant — the final category are adults who are deemed as irrelevant. Even the adult viewed as an easy mark gets some of the child's attention — if for no other reason than to take advantage of the person and get what the child can while the getting is good. The irrelevant adult gets no notice. Irrelevant adults are all the big people walking around on the planet taking up space, as far as the child is concerned. You know instantly if a child has you in this category, you will be ignored regardless of what you say or do.

All of these categories are negative because to the traumatized child all adults are either dangerous, a roadblock, suckers, or not worth the effort to manipulate. Faced with such a choice of categories, I recommend that you avoid the first, third and fourth categories and land squarely on door number 2. None of us wants to be an interpersonal threat, but the fact is that we have no chance to impact the life of a difficult child unless we are perceived as someone he or she will need to listen to, work around, struggle with or try their best to fool. This is the only category that allows positive therapeutic benefits coming from the interpersonal struggle and the potential of a real relationship with the child.

True relationships can be defined as interpersonal connections where no one is either used or abused. As in the world of business and sales, a first impression is very important. You must let the child know that you are not a safety threat, you cannot be easily taken advantage of, and you will not be ignored. If successful, you are now an interpersonal threat the child must struggle with. It is the struggle that provides the potential seeds of a relationship. Good signs that you are on the right track are seen when troubled children respond to you with irritability, hostility, challenging behaviors and words, and attempts to manipulate. So now that you know that all these negative behaviors may actually be good signs that you are on the right track, don't you feel better already?

Perceptions of the world break down to some primitive goals: survival, immediacy and avoiding neglect. Each of these goals fits squarely into the attitude and behavior of most difficult children to push others out of the way, get to the front of the line, and grab what they can get. Survival instincts have surfaced and tell these children to grab what they need, because no one else will care for them. The only point in time to these children is right now.

Delaying gratification is for fools; get what you can while it is available. If you offer this child a dollar bill today, or he can wait and get five tomorrow, there is no real decision — he wants it now. This is not a decision that relates to math; the child knows five is more than one; this decision relates to trust. I can't trust that you are going to give me anything tomorrow, so I am going to get what I can right now! These children don't have a half-empty cup, their cup has a hole in the bottom. Neglect and scarcity, regardless of the facts, are what the child experiences. In Disneyland the rides are too short, and Christmas morning is over too fast, and by the way, "where is the present I really wanted this Christmas?" Most adults look at these children and are confounded by the lack of logic used by the child. But look at the same situation through the lens of scarcity, and any feast has its limits and downside.

THE EFFECTS OF TRAUMA ON CHILDREN

✓ Traumatic memory brings past events into the present.

✓ There is new evidence to support the process of repressed memories from childhood abuse.

✓ The impact on attachment can lock the child into failure throughout life.

✓ Trauma puts an indelible mark on the brain, but research about the brain's adaptability is encouraging.

✓ Depression, isolation and violence are common outcomes of abuse and trauma.

✓ Trauma alters perceptions that hinder the person's ability to correctly understand people and events.

✓ Trauma often creates a war zone between the child and everyone else; we must get the attention of the child, and then gain respect if a true relationship has a chance to develop.

New to the program, the four-year-old girl was having her eighth tantrum of the day when one of the boys quipped, "We have a new radio station at Jasper Mountain — Kelli point three, all Kelli, all of the time." [Playing today's hits and yesterday's favorites.]

Chapter

7

General Considerations of Trauma Therapy

A discussion of healing the effects of trauma are synonymous with the healing of post traumatic stress disorder. Not everyone who encounters a traumatic experience develops PTSD. Some people get through a serious car accident and count themselves lucky and go on with their life. Some soldiers go into battle and return from war perhaps more sober, but for the most part ready to leave war behind and return to civilian life. There are even abused children who do not develop symptoms of post traumatic stress disorder, although most children experience at least some symptoms following abuse. However, for many individuals the experience of trauma alters their lives for a long time, or possibly for the rest of their lives. With approximately 5,000,000 new cases of childhood trauma occurring each year (Perry, 1995), there are thousands of children who need outside help to be able to go on with the rest of their lives as normally as possible.

Since trauma affects the whole person, the best strategies for healing will impact the person's mind, body and spirit. For abused children the physical scars, if there are any, generally heal easily and significantly faster than the emotional or spiritual scars. Before we move into a detailed discussion of the ten essential steps of trauma treatment in the next chapter, there are some general aspects of the healing process that will be covered here.

Due to the nature of trauma, where the experience signals an intense threat of survival to the brain of the child, the most typical result is the brain processing future experience through past traumatic memories. The brain does this to accomplish its primary goal of facilitating survival. If the child narrowly escaped death, in the opinion of the brain's limbic system, it is essential to be vigilant in case the threat returns. This is a natural and healthy process. There are many examples of this neuro-processing aiding the individual's survival. If a teen makes the error in judgment to drive too fast in a car and has an accident, the odds are very good that the individual's brain will recall the experience the next time another decision is made concerning speed. But the default setting by which the brain processes new information through old trauma memories also produces far too many false positives (believing there to be a threat when there is none). For example, after a car accident the individual may demonstrate symptoms riding in a car at a safe speed or perhaps even looking at a car. Symptoms of stress occur because the brain becomes fixated or stuck on recollections of past traumatic experiences.

Why Does She React so Strongly to Women?

It is often difficult to immediately see why, but many abused children act differently with different people. It is helpful to observe for differences, and compare what you find with information about the child's past. Many children treat mother figures poorly and with little respect. This may come from a neglectful mother, or a mother unable to protect the child from an abusive partner. Other children are angry or fearful of males, perhaps coming from past abuse or observing domestic violence. Considering such different reactions can help anticipate a child's behavior. It may also help when considering the gender of a therapist or a teacher.

It is not hard to see that an experience such as being physically abused by dad or neglected by mom can become a problem where the child fears all men, or does not trust any woman because of the recollections of the trauma experience. The general goal of healing is to help the individual overcome the tendency to organize his or her life around a past negative experience, regardless of how significant it was.

Another way of stating the general goal of trauma therapy is helping the individual live in the present and keep the previous trauma in the past. As anyone who has worked with seriously traumatized individuals knows, this is not easy. Today I went to the movie theater and saw *Mystic River*, a movie by Clint Eastwood and starring Sean Penn and Tim Robbins. In the film, which I predict will be remembered as one of Eastwood's best works, Robbins plays the role of an adult who was abducted as a boy, abused for four days by two men, and was able to eventually escape. However, he grows to adulthood and remains haunted every day by the experience. In a memorable scene, he explains that his body returned from being abducted, but the person he used to be was never seen again. It is a compelling depiction of PTSD, and the observant viewer will see the effects of past trauma in several characters in the story. It would not surprise me to learn that the author had some personal experience to be able to tell this absorbing story.

If the general goal is to help the individual really live in the present and not in the past, three conditions will help: 1. Develop control over emotional responses to events and, in particular, decondition anxiety, 2. Reframe the cognitive process to remember that the bad experience was in the past, not in the present, and 3. The past trauma must be integrated into the self-concept and not take over the self-image of the person (van der Kolk, 1996).

There is an old adage that says, "Time heals all wounds." Once as a teenager, my three brothers and I all forgot my mother's birthday the same year. The response from my mother put an indelible mark on all our brains, and that has never happened again. Fortunately, time has healed my mother's wound, and she has forgotten this event (that is until she reads this chapter). Time does heal some wounds, but appears not to heal some trauma. It appears that time does not heal significant trauma because the brain incorporates the negative experience in its understanding of new events. Particularly for children, the healing of significant trauma appears not to occur over time <u>unless</u> there has been some helpful external intervention (Terr, 1993). For this reason, it is generally a sound idea to provide some level of professional treatment for every child who has experienced significant trauma (Sgroi, 1989).

Frequent Symptoms of Trauma

As in physical medicine, treatment of trauma must usually target the symptoms creating a problem for the individual. Everyone does not act the same following trauma, but the following are frequent symptoms.

- Fear is the product of the individual's survival needs being threatened and the continuing concern that it could happen again.

- Anxiety is the apprehension that at any moment the traumatic experience could return, and you need to be ready to fight it or run from it.

- Depression and sadness are the result of the individual having a high level of concern and energy, but unable to put the energy into any external actions to reduce the anxiety — thus resulting in an internal feeling of helplessness and vulnerability.

- Anger/Hostility in part is the fight dimension of fight or flight. It is also the frequent result of the individual feeling trapped and projecting ill-intent onto others.

- Self-destructiveness comes from internalizing responsibility for being the problem in every situation. The child believes that she would be loved like other children if it were not for the fact that she is a bad person. Self-harm can also be the result of the child continuing the abuse she has previously experienced.

- Sleep Disturbance occurs when the brain cannot reduce tension and stress enough to enter into deep sleep, which is required for physical healing and a reduction of the impact of negative experiences.

- Somatic Complaints are common because a traumatized child is accustomed to hurting, and often is either over sensitive to pain and focused on what is going wrong inside, or the opposite, being insensitive to pain and not allowing the body to really feel either pain or pleasure.

- Eating Disorders are sometimes a symptom because healthy eating habits are a major way we care for ourselves. Individuals who do not care for themselves sometimes use eating to cause damage or to symbolically represent their lack of self-caring and self-love.

- Self-esteem Issues are most often a reflection of what the child has learned from others about his or her own value. Abused children take in the negative messages of abuse and neglect, and they miss out on the confidence-building message of parental love and belief in the child's value and worth.

- Poor Interpersonal Relationships are frequent because first, the child never knows when the next abuser will show up and therefore does not trust others. Second, loving another person requires some level of self-love. It is extremely hard to love or value another person when you do not love and value yourself.

- Dissociation is one end of the fight or flight continuum where the child is unable to physically get away, so she mentally flees the situation. Some level of dissociation is frequent with all trauma survivors, but is most common among females and young children.

- Isolation is the result of being in a cold world without the support and protection needed for safety, much less to get ahead and have a successful life. The most frequent experience of abused children is they believe only they have been singled out for abusive treatment and, therefore, they are alone in the world.

- Guilt and shame can occur when the child internalizes messages from adults that he is, in part, responsible for the trauma. If he was a better child he would not have been beaten by the alcoholic father, or if she were not so attractive she would not have been molested by Uncle George.

- Lack of Trust comes from the experience of being unable to rely on adults for necessities or for anything the child wants. Trust problems are usually generalized to all adults, and often all peers as well.

- Pseudo-maturity combined with delayed development is a frequently occurring combination in which the child physically matures or acts older than his or her age but is actually underdeveloped in most areas (Sgroi, 1989).

- Hypervigilance is the result of unending anxiety, particularly in settings similar to past trauma or settings that are not familiar.

- Elevated Startle Response includes hyper behavior, increased autonomic arousal, and being on edge. The child is poised to jump at loud noises, unanticipated events and surprises, or most anything that happens around him.

- Aggressive/Controlling behaviors are the hallmark of traumatized children. Control must be achieved in order to ensure safety because the child has learned from past experience she cannot rely on adults. The control can be aggressive or it can be covert or passive aggressive, whichever is more successful at establishing the child's control over the environment.

- Learning Problems arise when the child is overly focused on survival and misses the developmental learning periods for basic skills. The traumatized child must prioritize learning into two categories: first, what will aid survival, which is priority #1 and critically important, and second, everything else, which is not important.

- Flashbacks and Intrusive Memories are frequent results of the brain continuing to process past experiences by comparing them with new experiences. Often the lines of past and present become blurred or may disappear entirely, such as in an intrusive memory or flashback.

This is a long, but still incomplete list of potential symptoms of previous trauma. The goal of treatment will be to help the individual reduce these negative symptoms, allow him or her to live in the present, and move forward without the ball and chain of the past.

What Research Tells Us about Trauma Therapy

Research on trauma over many years has consistently shown the same themes: the child should receive help to recover from abuse, the help needs to be provided at the right time, and the treatment must be provided in the right way. Unlike other mental health interventions that may, at worst, be ineffective, trauma therapy can be directly harmful to the child if not done properly.

The research on working with traumatized individuals began with adults, in particular adults after wartime experiences. As the base of trauma research has developed over the last fifty years, we are learning that much of what occurs to adults after trauma also occurs to children. Here are some of the themes of research on trauma therapy, and what we should keep in mind to avoid doing damage and to assist trauma survivors in the healing process.

It is generally recognized that an essential and delicate component of treatment is to re-expose the individual to the thoughts, feelings and associations of the trauma. It is obviously delicate to put a traumatized individual in a situation that will bring back the fears and negative memories of a life-threatening event, unless proper precautions are taken. If re-exposure is done poorly, the individual could be re-traumatized or simply dissociate and psychologically flee from the experience. Dissociation during treatment would have no therapeutic value and would harm any therapeutic trust that has been developed. I will discuss in some detail the process of re-exposure in the next chapter. However, research on adults and children has been consistently clear that to heal the individual from many of the symptoms related to past trauma, the individual must face the past, and then put it in a new perspective. A few of the researchers who have identified the need for re-exposure are: Baudewyns, Hyer, Woods, Harrison & McCranie, 1990; Blake, 1993; Cooper & Clum, 1989; Foa, Rothbaum, Riggs & Murdock, 1991; Foa, Steketee & Rothbaum, 1989; Keane, Fairbank, Caddell & Zimering, 1989; Peniston, 1986.

When re-exposure to trauma is effectively and carefully done, research has found that intrusive recall, flashbacks and overall anxiety can be reduced (Brom, Kleber & Defares, 1989). Other research indicates that important therapeutic components must be combined with re-exposure. A supportive therapeutic relationship in which the client experiences safety has been found to be important (van der Kolk, McFarlane & Weisaeth, 1996). Additional components of treatment should be an educational and cognitive reprocessing (LaGreca, Vemberg, Silverman & Prinstein, 1996; Resick & Schnicke, 1992).

Trauma Therapy 101

In an attempt to demystify a complex process, the following conceptualization of trauma therapy, while somewhat oversimplified, provides a general framework.

The first step of any therapy with children is to ensure that the process is not only safe, but the child internally experiences the process as safe. Therefore, trauma therapy could be put into a "SAFE Model": Stabilize, Assess, Facilitate the recovery process and Environmental interventions.

Due to the nature of trauma, it is essential to ensure that no active trauma is still occurring. This may, at times, be more difficult to determine than you may anticipate. If anyone in the child's life is producing a threat in physical or emotional ways, the child will not let down defenses that have been developed for protection. It may not just be adults that could be perceived as potential abusers by the child. If the child encounters a bully at school or in the neighborhood, the child will not feel safe enough to begin the long road to reducing hypervigilance and anxiety — both developed as a response to former trauma.

Stabilization is the first step in the process. This step attempts to return the child's world to a safe, predictable environment where the child has no external factors producing anxiety. There are several practical steps that can be taken to help stabilize the child.

- *Enhance predictability* by increasing adherence to routine, schedule and regimentation.

- If the child has been recently traumatized, adults must *eliminate their own displays of concern and emotional responses* (tears, depression, worry, anxiety or anger) to what has happened. These emotional outbursts can result in mixed signals to the child that something bad has happened and possibly the parent is angry at the child.

- *The child's world must be returned to what it was before* the trauma as soon as possible.

- *Increased attention to routine and schedule* involves holding the child tightly accountable to rules. This is often the opposite of what adults want to do, but holding the child to rules gives the child a sense of structure.

- Work to put the *attention of the child on the present*. This can be done with activities, spending quality time with positive adult figures, and having an active, involved setting for the child where the present is more compelling than the past.

Once stabilized, and there is confirmation no traumatic experiences are currently taking place, the assessment phase of the process can begin. Since trauma is an internal experience, and no two individuals respond the same to an event, the assessment of the trauma must be very individualized to the child. Several steps may help in the assessment process.

- Obtain *information on the child's history* before the trauma. What did the child like to do, what personality traits stood out, and what motivated the child?

- Seek as much *factual information on the trauma* as possible. This may involve speaking to knowledgeable adults, obtaining police reports or file information.

- Always make the assumption *there is more to the traumatic events than is presently known*. Most abuse has been going on for some time before coming to the attention of someone who did something about it.

- *Compare the perceptions of the child regarding the trauma with the known facts*. At times, the child may believe that something has happened that is quite different than the facts.

- *Don't rely on the memories of the child for factual accuracy*. But also don't ignore those memories, since what is important in trauma therapy is what was going on inside the child, not necessarily what was going on outside the child.

The active therapy process begins in the third stage of facilitating the recovery process. There are several goals for this phase of the process.

Facilitating The Recovery Process

1. Establish safety.

2. Work toward a supportive relationship with the child.

3. Provide the child with a sense of some control over the process by giving the child choices of when, where, and what you do together.

4. Encourage expression of all types: feelings, thoughts, anger, sharing dreams, art, movement, etc.

5. Encourage the child to think about events and about himself or herself. The more the child can move to a cognitive level, the better chance he or she will have to understand feelings going on inside.

6. Put the trauma in the context of what did and what did not happen.

7. Find ways to externalize what is inside the child.

I want to elaborate on both goal #5 and #7. Because so much of the trauma process is sensory and linked to the limbic or emotional center of the brain, goal #5 of trauma therapy is to involve the reasoning centers of the brain to increase the role of executive functions. The term executive functions has greatly increased in usage in recent years. This term helps identify why very smart children, at times, make very poor choices. Raw intelligence is of less value to the individual than how the mind processes information and acts upon it.

Executive Functions - Primarily Mental Functions

✓ Cause and Effect Reasoning

✓ Goal Setting

✓ Planning to Meet Goals

✓ Strategic Thinking

✓ Moral/Ethical Reasoning

✓ Correctly Interpreting Situations — Understanding communications that are abstract, indirect, ironic, sarcastic, or the use of metaphor or figures of speech.

✓ Using Past Experience to Promote Current and Future Success

✓ Linking New Information with Past Experience

✓ Organized Logical Thinking

✓ Self-evaluation and Insight

✓ Assimilating New Information Efficiently

✓ Implementation of Goal-directed Activities

If the child were a corporation, we could compare the neocortex of the brain to the chief executive officer of the company, or where the executive decisions are made. A child who does not make decisions in the reasoning centers of the brain quite literally has no one in charge of the corporation or of the whole individual. Emotions come flying out, behaviors are erratic and not purposeful, choices vary by the minute, there are no goals, no direction, and no planning to improve on deficiencies. In a sense, many traumatized children are on autopilot set at the factory (unfortunately, in this case the factory is the original abusive environment). One major goal of trauma therapy is to work to put the neocortex of the child's brain back in its rightful position of directing and making thoughtful decisions. The higher regions of the brain control the executive functions that can help the child overcome many of the symptoms of trauma.

Executive Functions - Primarily Emotional & Affect Regulation and Behavioral Functions

✓ Allostasis — The ability to reach heightened emotional arousal and then return to a calm state.

✓ Anger Control

✓ Intimacy Disinhibition — Being vulnerable to others

✓ Delaying Gratification

✓ Behavioral Self-regulation

✓ Altering Behavior to Fit the Situation

✓ Self-directed Focus of Attention — Sustained effort, Filtering out distractions, Dividing attention

✓ Expressing Complex Thoughts and Ideas

✓ Deciding Upon Appropriate Social Responses

✓ Adjusting Behavior Based on Feedback

✓ Problem solving

✓ Flexibility

The child has no experience nor means by which to internally process trauma. The child needs an adult to help do this. But the child is the one who has the internal traumatic experience, and to help you must get to the internal feelings and perceptions of the child. I have found it helpful to symbolically represent issues the child is facing, or you believe the child is facing, with some tangible object that the child can see, touch and discuss. For example, if you believe he is lost in confusing feelings inside, you might have him pick a boy doll and have him put the doll in a dark shoe box and talk about what it will take for him to get out of this dark, lonely place.

There are many ways to achieve the goals of this part of the process. Here are some I have found helpful:

- Do not take away self-protections the child needs.

- Reflect to the child that you are interested in and beginning to understand the child's inner world.

- Take your lead from the child as to how far and how fast to proceed.

- Use expressive mediums preferred by the child such as art, play, movement, puppets, metaphors and narratives.

- Explore the child's world including, but not limited to, the trauma.

- Start and stop your work with some form of ritual, such as lighting a candle, or bringing out the child's favorite stuffed animal.

- Provide a reality check for the child along the way.

- Allow the child to learn to depend on you, some dependency might come first before encouraging independence.

- Teach the child methods of self-regulation and appropriate thoughts, feelings and behavior.

- Highlight the child's successes in little things along the way.

- Teach the child skills that are needed, such as making a friend, asking for help, expressing feelings.

- Repeat important steps in order to give the child practice and to facilitate mastery of the steps in the process.

- Be aware of any signs of dissociation, and work to decrease it; therapy is not happening during dissociation.

- Expect the child to self-protect by being aggressive, not wanting to speak to you, being invasive, or trying to control you. Don't let the child control you, but you can allow him or her control over some aspects of the process.

- Work with the child's thoughts and perceptions and provide new ways to look at things. Modify some of the child's negative reactions using cognitive behavioral interventions.

- Give the child the opportunity to decide how the trauma story is going to end; the child may not be able to change the past, but the abuser does not get the last word.

The last step in the process is to build in environmental interventions. As good as any adult may be in helping the child, the child's environment will produce the greatest healing. Home is only one of the places where the child will need help and support. It is helpful to develop a team of adults working together to accomplish this step. Involve parents, a therapist, school staff, a youth pastor, a caseworker, a big brother, a soccer coach, a grandparent or any involved adult. The job of the therapist is to provide the team with a sense of the inner world of the child. I find it helpful for the team to meet frequently (perhaps monthly) early in the process, and less frequently as the environmental plan for the child is showing signs of improvement.

My final comment on trauma therapy 101 is a suggestion that four types of interventions be included in the plan for the child — individual therapy for the child, group therapy, coaching for the family, and environmental interventions at school, church, extended family and other parts of the child's world.

With a better understanding of the impact of trauma, we are now in a position to take a detailed step-by-step look in the next chapter at how to help the traumatized child.

A frustrated young lady was sitting in class struggling with a difficult assignment. Finally she reached her limit and yelled at the teacher, "You are a bitch! Yes, that's right, you are a female dog and you are barking up the wrong tree!" [I beg your pardon?]

Chapter

8

Ten Steps of Trauma Treatment

In the previous chapter trauma was explained as a causal source of much of the difficulty experienced by children who manifest problematic behaviors. The statistics are staggering when it comes to the prevalence of trauma among children. Some of the 5 million newly traumatized children each year find their way back to a healthy life, while many others do not. One of the primary factors that separates the resilient children from those who are not is the support system experienced by the child. This support system is usually made up of parents, grandparents, teachers, siblings, peers and perhaps a therapist or caseworker who is there to help the child and the family cope with the aftermath of trauma. This chapter involves a detailed look at the therapeutic process often orchestrated by the therapist.

In *Traumatic Experience and the Brain* (Ziegler, 2002), I ended the book with an overview of the ten necessary steps of trauma treatment. I have been asked repeatedly since to go into these ten steps in more detail. I will do so in the following pages. I want to start by restating that while there is a general road map that is important in trauma treatment, the approach and the methods used by the therapist must be individualized. Only when a therapist comfortably integrates a therapeutic model within his or her own personality and experience is the outcome successful. I will mention the what, why, who and when of trauma therapy, but the how to get there will be left up to the individual therapist.

Step 1: Establishing Safety, Trust and Exploration

In the same way that trauma disrupts the learning process for children by distracting their attention and focus to survival issues, successful treatment requires first that safety be established. The prime directive of the brain is to ensure survival. The instincts of the traumatized person will focus on self-protection and avoiding any perceived threat. This is the principal reason that hypervigilance is a universal experience of traumatized individuals. For example, after being in a serious automobile accident, getting into a vehicle to go somewhere will from then on take on a new meaning with the associated concern and hesitancy. It is possible for someone to work through a traumatic experience, but not if the individual believes that he or she remains in a state of threat.

It is not enough that the individual is safe, he or she must experience safety. These two states can be very different. It is frequently the case that an abused child is safe in a new foster home, but it is probable that the child will not experience the safety for some time. During this initial period, the focus of the environment needs to be on predictability and eliminating reminders of trauma, because treatment and healing will not happen until the solid base of safety is established and experienced by the child. One of the best ways to build in predictability is to organize the child's world into events that can be anticipated by the child like clockwork. It seems boring to go to bed and get up at the same time, eat at a predictable hour, take a bath on the same nights, and know on Tuesday what is going to happen on Thursday. However, as boring as a set routine may seem, this level of predictability is the cornerstone of healing for the traumatized child.

I have come to understand that any time a child is having a difficult emotional or behavior period, the best response is to provide the child with more structure. It is important to ignore the child's protests. It is even more important to see if, despite the usual complaints about the structure, the child settles down and begins to improve functioning. I have found a very similar dynamic with both traumatized adults and children.

Treatment must first be built on the child experiencing safety, and then the child's next need will be for security. As with safety, the best approach to provide security is the predictability of the environment. If the child knows what to expect, she will begin over time to reduce the stress she experiences throughout the day.

Security also has an element of being able to impact one's world. Because a traumatized child can be very controlling, I find it helpful to give the child aspects of her world she has control over. Attempting to control others can be a cry for help, just as much as excessive tears, tantruming, or other behaviors such as being afraid to go to school.

This first step of trauma treatment must be pervasive throughout the child's world. There are elements that will be important to implement in the home, and there are elements that a therapist will want to use in spending time with the child.

I believe it is a good idea to have some form of predictable start and finish to your therapeutic time with the child — said another way, some form of beginning and ending "ritual." I have asked the child to bring a favorite stuffed animal into my office, and when the stuffed animal is sitting with us, we work together, and when the stuffed animal says it is time to finish, we do. Or you could have the child light a candle (not good for children with fire issues) to open or close the session. These are ways to help the child predict what is about to happen in both starting a stopping therapeutic time with you.

Always ensure stability for the child before going further. Someone who has been traumatized is always on high alert status. The only way to get beyond the individual's defenses that come up with perceived threat, is to first eliminate any sense of external threat. Two of the most effective ways I have found to promote safety and stability with a child are: being firm while simultaneously being supportive, and being honest with the child by telling him or her the truth with both good and bad news when you have it. If you are holding back something from a traumatized child, I can almost guarantee that the child knows this, and the actual information you are holding back may not be as scary to the child as what he thinks may be going on.

Jesse Demanded to Be in Charge

Jesse liked to control everything and everyone to the point of angering any child he played with and frustrating most adults who worked with him. We experimented with Jesse's need to control things around him by giving him some appropriate control to see if he would let go of some of his need to constantly be in charge. We gave him choices for the way his room was set up and decorated. We allowed him to "control" which of three choices for an afternoon activity occurred once a week. We even had him pick between two menu items for dinner on occasion. The result was a noticeable reduction (not elimination) of his attempts to control others. We believe part of this reduction was because Jesse sensed that we understood where his need for control was coming from. Once he felt understood, he could relax a little on the control issue.

It is important to avoid asking the child to let down his or her defenses until the child is ready to do so. Traumatized children are hypervigilant about space, so don't physically invade the child's boundaries or space. I recommend that physical touch be an important part of your connection with the child, but be sure to ask permission from the child, and then move forward with touch cautiously. Do not assume if you require the child to be physically close that this translates into interpersonal closeness. I often verbalize to the child that I know he can't be sure he can trust me yet, but we will work together to get to that point. It is common that children need weeks and even months to internalize the safety of a new situation; do not rush the process.

CHECKLIST OF SUGGESTIONS

✓ Ensure the child is not experiencing physical threat.

✓ Don't get in a hurry; the child may pick up a negative agenda.

✓ Provide an extremely predictable environment.

✓ Maximize external structure.

✓ Allow the child appropriate control over some things.

✓ Use rituals for predictability.

✓ Be firm and supportive.

✓ Allow the child to share with you at the child's pace.

✓ Physical touch is important but ask the child first.

✓ Predict to the child that he or she will not easily trust you.

Jesse is a seven-year-old child who will help us through the steps of trauma treatment. I will use Jesse to help illustrate the process and some of the dynamics that may come up in the process.

Jesse will likely be very leery of you for some time. Be aware that he may experience your contact very differently than you do. He will likely be hypervigilant to any attempts to get him to do things and be vulnerable in any way. Jesse was "groomed" by his grandfather over several months before being sexually touched. In the early stages it is not a good idea to ask him to elaborate on abusive sexual experiences, share deep fears, or tell family "secrets" if he is not ready yet. If you want him to know you are safe, give him room and prove you are safe. In fact, tell him he should not trust you until you have proven yourself; abusers don't say that to children. Be patient until he gives you the lead to take the next step. Don't make the beginning therapist's mistake of going too far, too fast with a traumatized child. You may get some information, but you may pay a long term price when the child experiences that you have some agenda and want something from him, like he experienced with his grandfather.

Step 2: Explore How the Trauma Is Perceived, Experienced and Acted Upon

Regardless of the trauma, no two individuals experience the same event in the same way. Knowing what may have happened does not mean you know the child's experience. I usually suggest that whatever information may be available about a trauma, the reality can often be significantly more than what is known, and you should expect this to be the case. It is very difficult to obtain factual information about trauma involving young children, particularly from the child directly. However, factual events are a forensic (legal) concern and much less important in therapy than the internal reality of the individual.

If a child believed her life was in jeopardy, then therapeutically it was. Conversely, there are times that potentially lethal events occur, but a child may be unaware of the threat and therefore not affected by it. The essential element of a trauma is that a child has an experience that overloads the child's resources to feel safe and able to withstand the threat. When this occurs, the limbic system in the brain is significantly impacted, and unless outside help is received, all additional stimuli associated with the event are filtered through the brain's traumatic memory center. Associating new events with traumatic memories is the basis for the potentially lifelong impact of traumatic experiences (Ziegler, 2002).

There is only one way to learn the nature of the trauma to the individual, and that is from the individual himself or herself. The methods for learning from the child will depend on the child's age, ability to communicate in multiple forms, willingness to give you any information, and the degree of safety the child experiences so as to let down his protective guard. There is no substitute for taking the time to do this right. Managed care is not a good model for the treatment of trauma. Some adults can experience success with a brief therapy model (significant trauma is often an exception), but a child will need you to carefully and slowly listen to his story through words, actions, feelings, dreams, play, art, stories, writing, movement and all the other ways that children express themselves.

How the child perceives the trauma is the nature of the trauma. The primary experience of trauma is based on emotions, which is why the emotional center of the brain, the limbic system, is the center of traumatic memories and reactions. Few children are able to sit with an adult and explain feelings in a meaningful way. There are intensities, textures, and colors to emotions that a child does not have the vocabulary to explain. Because children lack verbal skills to share in-depth feelings, expressive therapies such as art are helpful. I believe expressive therapies are critically important as diagnostic tools to ascertain the experience of trauma to a child.

Another important element to identify is how the child is handling the experience of trauma. Some children dissociate (more girls and young children), some children rage with anger (more boys and older children). Some children alternate between going inward, with experiences such as depression, and exploding outward with rage and violence. If the child alternates these behavioral manifestations, it may be very difficult to know how the child may react at any particular time. Observing behaviors is an effective way to help determine the level of the impact the trauma has had on the child. One way to help understand the meaning of behaviors is to translate what the child is saying based on the way he or she is acting. To translate behavior I suggest you first refrain from thinking you immediately know the meaning of a behavior, and take the time to consider at least 3 to 5 possible meanings. I have found that when I have carefully considered a variety of possibilities, I can often narrow down the meaning to the child with more precision.

Lenore Terr has written that essentially all traumatized children could be helped by some period of time in trauma therapy (Terr, 1993). Therapy helps most children because trauma is one of the negative experiences that does not get better with time. The journey of trauma therapy taken by the child and a good therapist gives the child the message she is not alone in her inner pain. Support is one of the mitigating factors in the lasting impact of trauma, and it is one of the essential aspects of healing. The role of the therapist is not to do psychotherapeutic magic on Wednesday afternoons with the child. The therapist must take a journey with the child first to a safe and supportive relationship, and then to the place where the child holds his pain. The general role of the therapist is to journey inside the child's world and learn what things look like from the inside out. Only then can the therapist help the parents, teachers and other supportive adults provide the child the ingredients of a world where healing is not only possible but is promoted. Often, it will not be in the therapist's office where the breakthrough occurs, but on the playground, in the classroom, or on the family vacation. However, the therapeutic compass must often come from the essential deep trauma exploration of the therapist and the child.

Few children with Jesse's experiences will be ready to talk about the fear and pain of abuse/trauma. You will likely first need to show that you can handle the bad things by being matter-of-fact when discussing anything related to trauma. You may think it is supportive to say something like, "Oh, you poor thing" when abuse or trauma is mentioned, but the child may perceive this as your discomfort and believe you can't handle the details. The best place to start therapeutic disclosure (as opposed to forensic disclosure) with young children is through projective methods: art, play, metaphor, puppets, etc. Be supportive, don't pry, ensure that you have fun with the child as well as hear the tears and rage. Take your time on this step — it may take awhile.

CHECKLIST OF SUGGESTIONS

✓ Don't assume you understand the child's experience from the facts, trauma is an internal, not external, experience.

✓ Assume the facts are worse than what is known.

✓ Determine the level of a support system the child had at the time of the trauma.

✓ Pay particular attention to the child's feelings.

✓ Learn how this particular child can best tell her story.

✓ Translate the meaning of the child's behaviors.

✓ Share what you learn from the child with the important adults in her life.

Step 3: Exploration of Trauma Memories

Trauma memories are powerful whether the events have happened recently or many years in the past. Trauma is embedded in the traumatic memory area of the brain's limbic area. After trauma of any significant magnitude, associated experiences will be filtered through this memory section of the brain. This process is by definition not a deliberate process, since it is the cortex of the brain, and not the limbic area of the brain, that is mediated by deliberation of the individual. In other words, a traumatized individual does not give trauma critical consideration. It works on them, not the other way around. Responding to trauma is close to an instinctual process — the individual acts in particular ways without thinking about it, or knowing why.

Time is not a significant concept regarding trauma. If the trauma has been recent, the brain directs the individual to be wary, anxious, and ready to fight or to flee from the worst case scenario. When the trauma has occurred some time in the past, perhaps years earlier, the brain again directs the individual to be wary, anxious and the fight or flight response is engaged. The actions of the brain provide some understanding as to why children who have been abused or traumatized in a significant way will quickly get to a place where they act like the trauma is actually happening in the present. This dynamic is driven by the traumatic memories in the limbic area of the brain (Ziegler, 2002), because as far as the child is concerned, the trauma is happening in the present.

There is little uniformity or even consistency in the emotional or behavioral responses to trauma and events that trigger trauma memories. The only sure thing is that traumatized children can quickly change their demeanor. They will often be hypervigilant, anxious, reactive, and overly focused on their own distress. To help understand this somewhat universal response, consider that you have taken a once-in-a-lifetime safari to Tanzania, Africa. One morning while walking you are either extremely lucky or extremely unlucky (depends on your point-of-view) when you come upon a 4,000 pound black rhino, and you surprise each other. It is not hard to imagine that you would immediately become hypervigilant (what is the rhino going to do next?), that you are anxious (this will be great to tell my friends, if I survive), you are poised to react (if he heads this way, feet don't fail me now!), and everything around you becomes irrelevant and you become totally focused on what is happening exactly at that moment. Years later the sight of a rhino in a zoo or in a magazine may bring up old memories. Traumatized children run into rhinos from their past quite often.

At the same time the child's general reaction is predictable, the specific behavior can be very inconsistent and unpredictable. He or she may become passive and docile, or the opposite, violent and raging. The child may respond one way in the morning, and the opposite in the afternoon. When the fight or flight response is activated, either extreme may be initiated depending on signals from the environment, or perhaps based on random chance. "Jesse, why are you so upset about going to school today, you liked school yesterday?" It is likely that Jesse has no idea why he is reacting, but his brain is picking up distress signals, which are translated in emotional reactivity.

The third step in the process of trauma treatment is to explore the unknown regions of traumatic memories and reactions. This is not an easy or necessarily an enjoyable process. It is not easy for the child or the therapist to have the child go to dark and frightening places in the past and within the child's painful memories. Don't assume that you know all the traumatic events the child has experienced. It is not important that all the recollections of the child be objective truth. There is little difference to the child when six sexual assaults become, "He did it to me hundreds of times." The reality is that he did do it to the child at least a hundred times, in the child's mind, and therefore in the child's experience. Facts are not critical in this process, leave facts to a court of law. The child may communicate more or less of a response than you may expect. Either way, take the lead from the child. If there is more in there, the best strategy is to be attentive and supportive, the rest will come forward when the child is ready.

I ask therapists to be good detectives in this phase of trauma treatment. A good detective is focused and observant. Small details can mean something or nothing, you just don't know yet. The therapist's job is to facilitate the exploration and provide a setting where the child feels safe enough to open the doors to the inner vault of trauma memories. Although the brain processes events through these trauma memories, the last thing the child wants to do is to voluntarily open these doors. Many children will express feelings and recollections through symbolic forms. A good trauma therapist is one who understands the many languages children speak. These languages include play, movement, color, images, and symbolic reenactment. The language you work with is best left to the child's personal choice. If the child senses you are pushing her in a certain direction, you may end up with a fight or flight response, rather than the information you had hoped for. Be ready to receive the information regardless of the metaphor or method, the texture or the volume.

> *Trauma Groups Can Be Powerful Interventions*
>
> To aid in the process of disclosing traumatic memories, groups can be very useful. Most of the children I have worked with were treated in one or more trauma groups with others, both children and adults. Until the individual discloses internal recollections of trauma, the therapist does not have the full picture. One of the most powerful techniques I have found in the process of disclosure is to use videotaping. Use this intervention only with children who do not have an active forensic (legal) case. After six weeks of the weekly trauma group to establish the safety necessary, the children are videotaped as they briefly share something about their abuse while getting support from the group. The next week the children are met with individually, shown the tape of the previous week and are asked to tell the rest of their story. Using this method, nearly every child provided more details than anyone was aware of. It appeared to me that watching the tape let the child know that the secret was out, and this seemed to give the permission to tell the rest of the story.

There are a few hazards to avoid in this step of the process. It should go without saying that no traumatized child should be forced to re-experience trauma in a manner he or she is not prepared to safely handle. However, this obvious statement is lost on some therapists around the country who use physically intrusive methods to "heal" children. Physically intrusive therapies are now appearing on the harmful list of evidence-based practices (Hyde, Falls, Morris & Schoenwald, 2003). Under euphemisms such as holding therapy, psychodrama, holding time, rebirthing or the many related physically coercive interventions, children are theoretically forced into overcoming years of traumatic abuse and neglect. This is of course absurd to anyone who understands the neurological effects of trauma. Children cannot be forced into healing any more than a parent can force a child to love.

Most of the time physically intrusive interventions are promoted by those solely focused on the healing of attachment, not trauma. This statement explains the reason physically intrusive interventions are ineffective for repairing attachment. In these cases, the therapist is focusing on one primary issue — attachment — while not recognizing the trauma is a definitional aspect of serious attachment disorders. Attachment must have a component of trauma therapy to be effective. Never attempt to use physically intrusive interventions, the result will be the child adding another trauma to his or her life experience with the therapist becoming the traumatizer. This is not to say that physical interventions are never a part of the therapy process. Physical interventions were addressed in Chapter 4.

Another hazard to avoid is any type of intervention that pushes the child beyond his or her emotional experience of safety. It is usually clear when this has happened, the fight or flight response will be initiated. It is very difficult to reach a the child in a state of red alert. Timing is critical in trauma therapy, and it is important not to want too much from the child too quickly. Hypervigilant children can sense that someone has a particular agenda, and the child will assume the agenda will be hurtful. Also avoid being judgmental of facts or details related to how the information comes from the child. It may be difficult on the therapist to have the child draw pictures of cutting off the head of his grandfather and feeding his body to wolves, but this is not the time to ask the child to draw a picture without violence or blood. This could be a signal to the child that you can't handle what the child has to communicate.

The most important point of the exploration period of trauma therapy is that the child takes the lead — with the therapist closely tracking the child's experience. This process must be done the way a child communicates, not in the way adults communicate. The therapist must learn the language of children and specifically the language of this one child. The exploration step can be the most challenging and at times the most taxing for both the child and therapist.

CHECKLIST OF SUGGESTIONS

✓ Trauma is re-experienced as if it is still happening.

✓ Fight or flight reactions indicate you need to slow down.

✓ It is typical to observe hypervigilance, anxiety, reactivity, and being overly focused on the child's own distress.

✓ Don't expect consistent emotions or behaviors.

✓ Give the child a chance to tell her story in her own way.

✓ Learn the expressive languages of children.

✓ Don't force the child; he may be traumatized by you.

✓ Don't be in a hurry, you may miss the information along the way.

✓ Don't correct or judge the child's expression.

✓ Be a good detective: listen, learn, and record the child's message.

✓ The "resistant" child may simply be using a language you don't yet understand.

Don't assume that Jesse felt what you would have felt in the same situation. For therapists, sexual abuse is often the most difficult experience to listen to, but repeated studies indicate that other types of abuse are more difficult for most children and leave more lasting scars. Give Jesse permission to tell you what he wants to, or to hold back what he doesn't want to tell you. Give him a chance to "tell" you in nonverbal ways. Your office may not always be the best setting to discover the impact of the trauma on him. Observe or get information from other settings such as home and school. Carefully consider each of the symptoms of Post Traumatic Stress Disorder (PTSD). He may not tell adults all the things he fears, or that he wakes up at night and shakes. Do your detective work and you will learn plenty.

Step 4: Deconditioning Harmful Affective Responses

This fourth step of trauma treatment is an important prerequisite to re-exposing the child to the traumatic experiences. It is much easier to describe this step than it is to actually do it. Just how do you re-expose a child to a traumatizing experience that is not available to the reasoning centers of the child's brain, while preventing the automatic physiological response? This is an important question because if this step is not accomplished, there is a chance that the next steps in the therapy process could be further traumatizing for the child — an unintended consequence of much of the trauma therapy currently taking place. The answer begins with the context outlined in the first three steps of this process. If these steps have been effectively accomplished (establishing safety/trust/exploration, exploring how the trauma is perceived and experienced, and exploring trauma memories) the stage has been properly set.

The task at hand is to show the child how self-regulation works, and then to repetitively teach skills to have the child experience the allostatic process, which is autonomic arousal followed by a return to a relaxed state. The goal of a healthy individual is not homeostasis, where the individual has a constant state of regulation, but an allostasis where the individual goes up and comes down with regularity and proficiency. Only with practice do we learn that when we are in a state of heightened arousal, such as excitement, fear, and anticipation, we will be able to return to a relaxed state if we wish. Without this skill and the internal confidence that it brings, the child is at the whim of events, peers, stress, and the weather. Children who are unable to self-calm react to any and all stimuli as if they live in the firehouse and the alarm keeps sounding.

The concept of self-regulation is very foreign to traumatized children. It was not the child's decision to go through the initial trauma. They are not thrill seekers looking for an adrenaline rush. The child is following the lead of his or her brain to survive threatening situations. Survival is aided by constant vigilance, being ready to act, and at times attacking before being attacked. These primitive laws of the jungle are not useful to the child in the classroom, or in the youth group at church. The lessons learned from trauma are reactivity to events beyond one's initiation or control. The drive to survive does not place self-regulation or relaxation as priorities. Who wants to be a sitting duck when the next assault comes along? Of course the problem with these primitive cognitions is that they have not advanced much beyond what the animal kingdom uses to avoid being another animal's next meal.

The process of teaching self-regulation will be impossible without an established environment of safety. The child's brain will not allow reduced vigilance if there is any possibility of an encounter with something threatening. In a setting that provides the child with assurances of safety, I suggest you take the child on small excursions to relaxation land. You may well find that relaxing at first is one of the child's most uncomfortable feelings. This makes sense to a system familiar with constant hyper-arousal. Explain to the child that he doesn't have to stay long, it is just a visit to an inner world of relaxation.

Brief visits to relaxation land can gradually be extended. Biofeedback has been shown to be a helpful tool to teach children self-regulation. There are even biofeedback "games" where the more the child relaxes, the more he moves the remote control car across the room. If he becomes tense, the car stops. It will take repeated calming experiences that are positive before the child has any interest in relaxing or self-regulating arousal that he believes might be needed at any time. In a sense, you must make it fun and even a little cool to self-regulate for these children to be interested.

Good martial arts, where the emphasis is not on "kicking butt" but on self-discipline, can be a cool way to learn self-regulation.

To combat internal and almost instantaneous autonomic arousal, the child must be taught skills to have some internal control of physiological responses. This control can be achieved by teaching a variety of self-mastery skills such as: relaxation, guided imagery, concentration, or other techniques that put the child in touch with internal states. While some people think these techniques are too sophisticated for children, my experience is they are effective if used in developmentally appropriate ways.

Internal self-regulation will need to be well-understood and frequently practiced in order to move onto Step #5 where the child will be re-exposed to traumatic memories.

CHECKLIST OF SUGGESTIONS

✓ Safety is a prerequisite to this and each step of trauma treatment.

✓ Teach the child to increase and decrease arousal.

✓ The child must learn what it means to turn off tension.

✓ Have the child experience that it can be fun to be calm.

✓ Make the process of learning self-regulation skills fun and cool.

✓ Do a little at a time. Repetition is key.

✓ See if you can get the child to ask on his own to do more practice.

✓ Of the many forms of self-mastery, find one that interests the child.

✓ Don't underestimate the ability of the child to learn self mastery skills.

Jesse will need some tools to relax and calm himself. He will need to learn to control his thoughts by purposely deciding what he chooses to think about. He can be shown how to select his own movie in his mind, kids like to do this. Point out that he can control what he thinks about and what he feels in your office. Make it interesting for him by telling him that when he's bored at school, he can close his eyes and go to Skateworld or to the water park, it's like magic. Teach Jesse how to turn on and turn off his ability to internally self-regulate. You are not teaching him to dissociate, you are teaching him self-mastery; the difference is he is the one consciously deciding his own experience.

Step 5: Re-exposure to the Trauma

Re-exposure to the traumatic experience, a universally accepted step in the process of trauma therapy, does nothing but harm if not done at the right time and in the right way. Every time the brain processes stressful events using the neural pathways established by trauma, the neurons in these pathways are reinforced to continue processing new stimuli as a new traumatic event. The research on effective trauma recovery indicates that re-exposure must take place, but the organism must find a new way to process the experience of being re-exposed to associated traumatic events — or harmful and destructive trauma responses will get worse. This step of re-exposing the individual to the traumatizing events is the most important and also the most sensitive and complex step of trauma therapy — proceed with caution.

One of the most important mitigating factors that helps many soldiers return from war without post traumatic stress disorder, and keeps crime victims from losing more than their valuables, is support. Having an effective support system helps an individual move from being victim to the survivor better than any other prescription for trauma relief. Re-exposing the individual to the trauma must be done with at least the therapist as a major part of a support system. The importance of a supportive therapist points out one of many reasons why it is not therapeutic to have the therapist pushing, coercing, and adding to the trauma in any way. To have a therapist using something like physically coercive interventions puts the child in a state of inner panic, producing fight or flight responses and in the long run adding to, rather than eliminating, the harmful effects of trauma.

The therapist is a support to the child when a safe and trusting relationship has been established. The child must experience that the therapist cares what is going on with him or her. The therapist can verbalize and then practice taking only the therapy steps the child is prepared and ready to take. Giving the child a choice over some of the steps and the timing of moving forward gives the child a message that he matters to you. While I do not suggest strong emotional responses from the therapist toward the child, particularly in the initial stages of therapy, I do suggest giving the child frequent messages that you are right there with him, and the two of you are taking the journey together. As with any therapeutic alliance with a child, it takes time to develop trust, but it takes very little to damage the trust.

It is also helpful to have other components of a support system for the child. Generally the child has a family that is concerned. It is important that the parents look at their own trauma associated with what has happened to the child. The non-abusing parent may feel guilt. The neglectful parent may have a need to minimize the damage to lessen the magnitude of the responsibility he or she feels. Many caring parents project their own pain from the experience onto the child, and most of the time the child dutifully absorbs the extra burden. For these and other reasons, the parents must take care of their own trauma without adding it to the weight the child already feels in order to be an effective part of the support system.

A support system for the child can include grandparents, teachers, coaches, youth leaders, rabbis and family friends. Caring adults do not always instinctively know how to handle a situation in which a child has been harmed through trauma. The best way to handle such a difficult situation for all concerned is to normalize the environment around the child, and encourage the child to have fun and enjoy activities with supportive adults.

Begin the process of re-exposure with a foundation of support. Do not begin this step until steps 1 through 4 have been firmly established. Now the complex work begins.

The effects of trauma that do not receive outside intervention seldom resolve on their own. The trauma recollections in the brain are indelibly embedded in the neural pathways of the midbrain. Re-exposure to trauma is the opposite of the technique used with adults called "flooding." The goal of re-exposing the child to traumatic recollections is not to desensitize the individual simply by having the traumatic stress become more familiar, because this approach may actually make the situation worse for the child. The purpose of re-exposure is to enhance the allostatic process of arousal and then relaxation. There is no effective way to have the brain completely turn off traumatic memories. These memories are automatic and not controlled by conscious thought. Someone who has been a part of domestic violence will be agitated by yelling and arguing. A wartime PTSD survivor will likely have a visceral and automatic reaction to a loud sound like a car backfiring. However, the internal emotional response that is automatic with a traumatized individual can with practice quickly have a cognitive response that assists the individual to return to a relaxed state. Every time the allostatic process is successful, it becomes more routine and successful.

The methods to re-expose the child to the trauma can vary greatly based on age, the nature of the trauma, and the individual characteristics of the child. Younger children in general may need more symbolic re-exposure, while older and more sophisticated children can have more direct re-exposure. To re-expose the child to the trauma is to lead the child, who is feeling safe and trusting with you, to the inner state of reactivity to associations of trauma. It does not necessarily mean that you read the child the police report or have her close her eyes and remember the smell of the attacker, although these approaches could be possibilities in some situations.

The principle problem with trauma is that it is not in the past but in the present for the child. You do not necessarily need to go back, you just need to find the triggers that cause the reactivity that hinders the child in the present.

A role play or videotape of two adults having a heated argument may trigger a child who has been physically abused. The sight or smell of alcohol could be a trigger to the child abused by an alcoholic parent. Re-exposure may involve showing a picture book of the child's past. It may be a trip to a gas station like the one where the child was assaulted in the rest room. The best way to re-expose the child will depend on many factors. It might also take some trial and error. However, one thing is essential, monitor the response of the child and ensure that the child maintains a sense of safety regardless of how directly or indirectly you proceed.

Re-exposure to trauma must be done very carefully while the child has significant support, and is provided sufficient power over the process to impact the internal arousal of trauma memories. For example, although physically intrusive or "holding therapy" re-exposes the child to trauma, it lacks all of the safeguards to prevent the internal perception of trauma, and the arousal system is activated to defend against, rather than work with the experience. The child must be given some power over the process to say when and for how long she will recall the memories. Re-exposure should occur with thoughts and feelings, and generally not be physically experienced, at least initially.

Once you find the best way to re-expose the child to the internal reactions caused by trauma, the work turns to de-conditioning the harmful internal reactions. It is not always harmful to avoid large angry dogs after you have been attacked by one, this could be called learning from experience. It is harmful if the same person becomes agitated by the presence of a miniature poodle at a friend's home. The important work of re-exposure is to have the child learn ways to prevent the typical maximal arousal to minimal stressors. Beginning steps involve brief re-exposure in a process similar to systematic desensitization. With each progressive step that increases agitation, the therapist has the child practice the self-regulation and self-mastery skills learned in step 4. This process is repeated until the child can go from reactivity and back to a state of calm. The repetition of the allostatic process strengthens critically important neural learning.

Gary Learns to Relax

We started with several practice sessions teaching Gary methods of meditation, or focusing on an inner state of calm attention. At our next session we moved to relaxing his body, and then inviting the mind to visualize a calm setting. I had Gary visualize sitting on a beautiful beach by himself in the warm sun and listening to the waves lap up on the beach. Since Gary had his eyes closed, I asked him if he could feel the warm sun. To my delight he said, "Yes." I asked him to just relax and sit in this comfortable relaxed place for a few minutes. Two minutes later, without opening his eyes, Gary said, "Dave, can I move over under the palm trees? It's getting pretty warm in the sun." Being one of the most reactive children I have ever worked with, this one experience with Gary taught me that even very troubled children can learn self-regulation.

This second half of the process of re-exposure is to bring the techniques from step four, such as calming and relaxation, to de-condition the internal response to trauma memories. De-conditioning of the body's arousal responses can be assisted by approximation to stressful thoughts or situations, while at the same time promoting relaxation. The child must be allowed to have control over how far to go and how long to work on these steps. The child can verbally say when to slow down, back up, or to stop. The child may be given a signal to share when he has gone far enough. Giving the child some power and control over the process in itself changes the nature of the trauma memories due to having personal control over them.

CHECKLIST OF SUGGESTIONS

✓ Effective trauma treatment requires re-exposure to traumatic experiences.

✓ Firmly establish yourself as a support for the child.

✓ Facilitate reactivity and then use of self-regulation to a state of calm.

✓ Give the child choices in the methods of re-exposure.

✓ Give the child power over how far and how fast to go, this level of control will make the experience fundamentally different than the trauma.

✓ Have the child practice tensing and relaxing while you compliment the strength you see.

✓ Repeat the process until the child can go up and come down effectively.

You should now have been working with Jesse for some time to take this next important step. You should have already discussed the trauma in specific detail a number of times. Now you let Jesse know that you think he is strong enough to imagine events like the ones he lived through, but this time he is in charge, not the abuser. Give Jesse a sign, head nod or lift his hand, to signal when he needs to calm himself or put on the brakes. Let him know that he decides how far and how fast. He needs your support, and he needs to hear how strong he is, regardless of what happens. He is strong to take this step with you, and to go back to where he never wanted to go again. Remind him to use his special powers that he has learned to calm his thoughts, his feelings, and his ability to stop and go when he decides to go. If he can do so, give him some ways to tell his abuser what he thinks of him, or to call the police and hand him over.

Step 6: Cognitively Restructure the Meaning of the Trauma

At this point in the process, the therapist and the child have done a considerable amount of work. Safety has been established, the internal experience of the child has been identified, self-regulation skills have been taught and practiced, harmful affective responses have been reduced, and the child has been carefully re-exposed to the internal trauma experience. The next goal is to alter the past by altering the present.

The saying that the only thing you can't change about your life is the past is not entirely true when it come to trauma. Following trauma, the past remains very much alive in the child's brain, to the degree that, given specific circumstances, the child continues to experience past trauma. To help prevent this from happening to the same degree in the future, it will be useful to put the past in a new and different perspective. One method to do this is to cognitively restructure the memory of trauma, or said another way, when we change the meaning of the experience, the details of the trauma can be relegated to a state of reduced impact on the individual.

Cognitive restructuring sounds more complex than it needs to be when working with children. One of the best ways to help the child change the impact of the past is to change the trauma story — specifically the ending of the story. We are not asking the child to be internally dishonest or to ignore the fact that something terrible has happened. However, we are asking the child to bring to the traumatic experience the one thing the child lacked up until now — control. This step is most effective after the step of re-exposure, because at this point the child has faced her inner fears and learned to reduce the emotional impact of memories of the experience. Now the child can add the final chapter to the trauma story because the final chapter has yet to be written and is up to the child to decide.

In step 5 it was stressed that the child must hold some of the power if he or she is encouraged to re-experience aspects of traumatic experience. How, when, and where this happens should be details of the process over which the child has some choice. My experience is that children do not always avoid looking at their traumatic past. Rather, they avoid being re-traumatized. If the child has some power, and he or she feels safe and has some level of trust in the therapist, he usually will go willingly into the past. We can help the child add to the power he experiences by now deciding how this trauma story is going to end.

It is important that the child understands the last chapter in the trauma has not been written — no matter how bad it was, or how far in the past the events occurred. The child must be given the power to write his or her own ending to the trauma story. This ending is not creating some make-believe fantasy; instead it is adding the real ending. Typical ending themes include: the perpetrator was the one who was bad and therefore did not win, the child grew up to understand who was responsible for the abuse and it was the abuser, the child told other adults and the perpetrator was not able to keep his bad secret, the child was able to move on and not let the abuser continue to have power, etc. Each of these endings disrupts the secret acts of abuse, identifies right from wrong, affixes responsibility, and has the child escaping the control of the perpetrator. The abusive adult tried hard to win, but lost because of the strength of the child — who goes on to come out the winner.

There are many methods that can be used to change the ending of the trauma story. It can be reenacted with puppets or other expressive medium, or it can be done with the therapist helping the child write and/or draw the story. The methods to accomplish this step are as varied as the approaches used in Step 2 (of going inside the world of the child to learn the child's experience of the trauma).

Although the majority of traumatic experiences that bring a child to mental health treatment are related to child abuse and domestic violence, there are other traumatic experiences that affect children. At times serious and invasive medical procedures can be traumatic for children. Accidents such as a serious car collision can create lasting traumatic memories. Children can also be profoundly affected by witnessing serious events such as a parent being assaulted, a violent crime, or witnessing the death of a person or animal either by natural or accidental means. All of these experiences have the potential to be impactful on a child in ways similar to child abuse. Therefore these forms of trauma can be helped by the steps in the trauma recovery process.

Although victims of a traumatic experience seldom have power or control during the traumatic event, they often feel a level of responsibility for the event. Children can feel responsible for the trauma even when someone does something to them against their will. For a child the fact that she was involved brings with the involvement responsibility for what happened. The responsibility aspect must be a part of changing the ending of the trauma story. Since the traumatic effects did not end with the event itself, the story has not ended until the child decides it is time. Help the child place responsibility where it belongs, and to have the upper hand with the traumatic events, and prevail by successfully going on with life and not being willing to be further traumatized by the past. Anytime we change the meaning of an event, we change the event.

The brain has several types of distinct memory. Most memories are not encrypted factual events, such as sights, sounds, and behaviors. These memories are very personal recollections based on emotions connected to experiences and factual events. The memory of an argument with a friend will have a very different place in our long-term memory if it ended the relationship, or if there was a reconciliation. The final chapter of the story provides much of the meaning of the event. Changing the final chapter can be a very powerful tool in the long-term emotional inner disposition to the event itself. We can change how we remember events by the context we give the event. When children have power over part of the story, such as the ending, the big picture changes, and the child's emotional responses change as well.

Help Jesse decide what he wants to do with his story, or with the abuser. He can decide this part of his story. He can even make the abuser disappear from his world. He lived through the trauma, he prevailed, and that is the most important point. This is his story, so there are no inappropriate ways to end the story. Encourage him to decide what should be done to the abuser. If the abuser is a loved one, give him the chance to decide whatever he wants including forgiving the person. Point out that he is in charge of the end of his story, and he can have it any way he wishes.

CHECKLIST OF SUGGESTIONS

✓ Use cognitive restructuring to change the meaning of events.

✓ Change the past by changing the meaning of the past in the present.

✓ Have the child change the ending of the trauma story.

✓ Help the child feel powerful by controlling the ending.

✓ Have the child understand he can win in the end.

✓ You can use art or puppets, make a storybook, or act out the ending of the trauma story.

✓ Make sure the responsibility for the trauma is a part of the story ending.

Step 7: Replacing Problematic Behaviors with Adaptive Behaviors

Some professionals believe that behavioral therapy is the only effective way to promote change in clients. I disagree with this position because behaviors are manifestations of the thoughts and feelings of the individual, which need attention in any effective therapy. However, I do agree that a behavioral component is important. Since behaviors are the result of inner states, we have first addressed these inner states and can now address behaviors. In trauma therapy, the outward manifestation of traumatic memories and feelings will often be behaviors that negatively affect the child and/or the people around the child.

To replace problematic behaviors with adaptive behaviors is another step that is easier said than done. With many clients, increased awareness can assist in gaining some control over problematic behaviors. However, traumatized children are not like most clients. Behavior is principally affected by perceptions, and when trauma has occurred, perceptions often come from regions of the brain that are not mediated by reasoning — mainly the limbic system which holds traumatic memories.

So how can you replace maladaptive behaviors with adaptive ones? The solution is in the question. The goal of the brain is to ensure survival through adaptability. Even though an individual has been traumatized, causing a variety of problems, the goal of the brain is still to adapt to whatever the situation happens to be. The therapeutic challenge is to create an environment that promotes further adaptation. While it is true that negative adaptation seems to develop more quickly than positive adaptation (one very bad experience can have more impact than dozens of good experiences), the process remains the same. The brain takes in information that signals whether the situation is safe, and whether there is something of value to be gained, and what it will take to obtain it.

Whenever possible, adults should promote opportunities for the child to make choices related to the child's desires and the consequences of getting or not getting what the child wants. Making good decisions and understanding consequences are not routine and will need adult encouragement. Adults literally must help the child to think about the situation and his or her responses. Adults must also set up conditions where positive adaptations will bring the child more success than maladaptive behavior.

Children with traumatic histories often missed developmental periods since they were focused on survival concerns rather than learning effective and pro-social behaviors. If a child perceives threat, he will be less interested in making a friend than getting out of the situation unharmed. Missing developmental period of social knowledge leaves major gaps in the child's understanding and ability to correctly perceive social situations. The result is the dynamic where adults indicate that the child "Just doesn't get it!" When the cognitive building blocks are absent, it is unlikely that repeated opportunities to progress will end up any more successful than past opportunities have been. In other words, if the child has misperceived and behaved poorly the last 10 times, the odds are that a new opportunity to do better will end in similar failure. The answer to the problem is not to become frustrated with the child, the answer is to provide the missing insight you have to help the child positively adapt and change negative behavior.

It is frequently the role of parents, teachers and other adults to provide missing insights to children. We teach skills when we intervene with two toddlers fighting over the same toy. We point out to the angry child the consequences of throwing his new radio onto the floor. The primary ways for children to learn moral values and behaviors are to observe the modeling of adults, and to have adults help the child think about the situation from a broader perspective than, "How do I get what I want?"

Whatever the adult wants the child to think about should be the input from the adult to the child. This process is essentially to help the child think through the situation. You can still give the child choices as to how they want to behave; but you will need to help bring more accurate perceptions and reasoning to the gaps in the child's thinking process.

Allowing the child choices as to how to behave in various situations may require that the adult help the child identify the options. This process of reasoning for the child will provide other opportunities that would not likely come from the child's thought process without such help. The process of helping the child reason aids in the ability of the child to adapt more successfully. Once the brain experiences successful adaptation, when the child feels safer and receives more supportive attention, the adaptation process of the brain kicks in. When the child practices pro-social behaviors and the results are good, the child experiences success. The brain of the child acknowledges this process by saying, "Let's do that again." Successful repetition of the process of thinking and then acting helps to establish neural networks that were not established during earlier developmental periods.

Learning adaptive behaviors may take a long time with significant repetition required. Assisting the adaptation process requires the adult to be actively involved (and not stand back and lament the repeated failure of the child to figure things out), and then act in a way that promotes improvement. There is a reason that children repeat behaviors that do not improve their situation. Like the path of water, stimuli are processed by the brain in the path of least resistance. Repetitive processing establishes a neuro pathway that has more likelihood to be involved at the next opportunity. This can also be said of positive and successful behaviors. If the child experiences responding in a way that the results are desirable, the child is more likely to repeat this behavior. Keep in mind that the complexities of becoming a functioning and successful human being are the most demanding set of skills in the animal kingdom. It appears that the complexity of social success is the reason why humans mature much more slowly than other animals. All children need many years of helpful instruction to get it right. Traumatized children can take even longer, so remain patient.

As Jesse goes through this therapeutic process, help him to consider what is happening. Jesse's ultimate power is in his ability to think and to use his reasoning ability to adapt to his situation. He will want to spontaneously feel and act without considering the consequences. He will need help to learn to effectively think, feel, and act. Don't assume that because of his young age or troubled past he is limited in his ability to think about himself or the situation. Give him your ideas and guidance at every stage. It will help to reinforce any signs that he is thinking about himself, his past, his future, his preferences, and any other sign of using the reasoning centers of his brain.

CHECKLIST OF SUGGESTIONS

✓ The child must receive outside help to correctly perceive and understand social situations.

✓ Use the brain's ability to adapt by helping the child experience social and behavioral success.

✓ Help the child think through situations.

✓ Stay patient — the child likely missed important developmental learning due to trauma.

✓ Give the child choices but help her with the alternatives.

✓ Take one step at a time, then repeat.

Step 8: Building a New Internal Self-Perception

Thus far in the journey of trauma therapy we have started within the child to understand the child's needs and perception of trauma; we then moved to manifestations of the trauma both internally (perceptions and emotions) and externally (behaviors). It is now important to come full circle and return to the child's inner experience and substitute a new efficacious self-perception in the place of being a powerless victim of abuse or trauma.

Understanding the meaning of past trauma to the individual, which is Step 2, will help the therapist understand what the post trauma self-image is. This self-view is not likely to be positive nor comfortable for the child. The presence of a negative self-view must change if the child is to emerge from the fog of inner trauma.

One of the insidious aspects of child abuse is that the child will re-experience the abuse again and again, even after the perpetrator is not in the picture. Because of how the brain records trauma, the experience is relived repeatedly, often resulting in one of the symptoms of post traumatic stress disorder. The child is not sure the abuse has really ended, since perhaps it has just paused momentarily. After all, what is to prevent an abusive adult from coming back into the picture? A frequent question of badly damaged children is, "Can he find me and hurt me again?" The perpetrator does not need to find the child, because the child's brain has recorded the voice, the smell, and the image of the perpetrator. These sensory experiences are some of the brain's most vivid recollections from the past.

Some memories the brain must work hard to recall, for example, the name of our second grade teacher, the tune of a song from our childhood, but this is not so for specific recollections of trauma. If the whole nation recalls where they were when President Kennedy was shot, when the Challenger exploded, or when the World Trade Center collapsed, even more so does the traumatized individual retain the indelible memories from the horrible events the person directly lived through. The child needs help to remove the intrusive recollections that force her to remember — rather than the child deciding when and if she wants to think about an experience in the past. It is therefore essential that a new sense of personal power becomes a part of a new self-perception.

One of the steps of developing a new inner self-view is to reframe the experience of the child abuse or trauma. Child abuse must be made to seem like any bad physical injury. For example, I broke my arm ten years ago. It was painful and I clearly remember the situation and the pain, but I seldom think of it, and it does not negatively affect my life today. In fact the opposite is true — the experience helps me empathize with the pain of others in similar situations. My broken arm was a very minor trauma compared to child abuse, but this event points out the important process of being able to recall the memory but not be haunted by it, or constantly reactive because of the experience.

The child will need help not to define herself permanently as the one who was hurt. The hurt was temporary and must now take its place in the memory banks of the conscious brain. The reasoning mind must consider the facts and events, and not be controlled by the reactive limbic system. The way to accomplish putting the past in the past is to build a new sense of self.

Self-perception is made up of many factors. It involves an awareness of the body, and how it is similar or different from others. Our view of our self involves our demographics such as gender, age, grade in school and hometown. Self-perception includes our connections with others, such as being a part of a family, a school, a church, a team or a neighborhood. Our inner view is affected by the messages we hear from others. Some children learn to see themselves as valued, loved and competent. In contrast, maltreated children develop an inner view of being in the way, and being a burden to already overburdened adults. The negative self-view of maltreated children makes them much more likely to fail than to succeed. Such a negative self-view can have a significant impact on the child's experiences in creating a self-fulfilling prophesy.

To counter an already negative inner self-view, the child must hear new perceptions and begin to see a very different picture when looking in the mirror. The child's experience has often been to hear much more about personal weaknesses than strengths. Here is a good place to start. What are the child's strengths? What are the things she loves to do? What are her goals and dreams? The process of discovery of self is one of the most enjoyable aspects of psychotherapy. Traumatized children need this opportunity more than anyone else.

However, self-discovery is not a journey individuals with a negative self-view want to take. Why find out more negative things about yourself? Do you choose friends who primarily give you criticism? Self-discovery is a journey the child will only take with a supportive therapist or adult, and even then the child will be reluctant at first. It is your job to turn this process from painful to enjoyable from the very start. Children who have heard only criticism (or only pay attention to the negative) at times can quickly learn to enjoy hearing good things. However, you may need to be persistent until they begin to believe you mean what you say.

After many years of drought, these children may also begin to absorb quite a bit of positive feedback to the point of believing they deserve to be on the next cover of *Sports Illustrated* or *Time*. I do not get concerned with this dynamic of overestimating the child's abilities and their importance. I see this as a swing of the image pendulum that will soon swing back in the negative direction and eventually to a point in the middle.

There are many ways to have a child begin to experience a positive self-view. If you think back to your own childhood, most of us gravitated to the skills and tasks we excelled in, and avoided the things that we did poorly. I have for some time found this fascinating that our proficiency often dictates our preferences. It is as if our ability is more important than if we enjoy something. It also seems that we learn to enjoy the things we do well, even if they did not start out important to us. I can offer an example of this dynamic from my life. While growing up I was keenly interested in athletics. I learned to play as many games and sports as I could. I found that the more games I played, the more well-rounded I became. I therefore focused on being good at many games rather than being very good at any one. This experience has been a metaphor for my life to date. I continue to enjoy multiple activities and areas of interest, and I do not dwell on any particular one. I look back with gratitude that I was not a standout in one area, because I think it would have enticed me to stick with what I was very good at and miss many other opportunities. I actually feel sorry for the child who is a prodigy at anything, not for the presence of a unique skill, but for the way it may hinder the child's choices about the future.

I mention the impact on our lives of our strengths to highlight several points. If a traumatized child does not see herself as good at anything, she is likely to not see herself as a good person. Since external feedback is very strong with children, it is important to consider what reflection has been provided to a traumatized child. If the mirror adults have held up to the child has been very distorted, it will take considerable effort to rectify this internal image. The positive point to mention here is that experiencing strengths, and all children have them, can have a strong impact on the child's self-perception. In my work done with children individually and in groups, I have spent week after week just talking about and exploring the strengths the child has.

Sharing the Good News

George was at the point of trauma therapy where we were working on his being proud of himself and everything about his mind, body and spirit. George was enjoying his new experience of pride in his abilities and in his body. He was not shy about sharing his thoughts. Our program had a minister on the Board who visited one day. George was quick to share his new appreciation for his strong and able body. He innocently was talking to the minister about this when he stopped and said, "Are you proud of your penis?" Having never before been asked this particular question, the minister uncomfortably did his best to reply and then took me aside to find out what that was about. I could then tell him that George was learning to be proud of all aspects of himself and just wanted to share his version of the good news.

It is time for Jesse to build upon his sense of self. There are many techniques that can be used here. You could ask him to say which storybook characters he most admires, and then point out traits that he shares with the character. Help him to see his unique traits and skills. Work on his view of his body and personality. Have him write as many positive things as he can about himself and reinforce his ideas (perhaps give him a coin for every positive thing he can come up with about himself). Spend some time in each session talking about his strengths. The new image he needs to develop must come initially from the outside, from you and others. Be real, but lay it on until he can hear you in his sleep saying how capable and talented he is.

CHECKLIST OF SUGGESTIONS

✓ How we act says a great deal about our inner self-perception.

✓ Use the information learned in Step 2 to know what needs to change.

✓ A sense of personal power is essential to stand up to perceived threats.

✓ Reframe the past as being in the past and over for good.

✓ Help the child look at all aspects of who she is.

✓ Spend considerable time on newly-discovered strengths the child has.

✓ Don't be concerned if the child starts believing he or she is Superman or Wonder Woman. This will level off over time, and you are on the right track.

Step 9: Learning Coping Strategies

The previous step outlined increasing adaptive skills and decreasing maladaptive behaviors. The child's day-to-day life will require him to be able to work with others in one form or another throughout his life. Learning to adapt to the each situation is an essential step for social success. While learning adaptive skills is important, it is also important to recognize that the world is a difficult and demanding place. The best of us struggle on the worst of days. As Woody Allen has said, when things go from miserable to horrible, it is not so much succeeding at the challenge at hand, but to simply cope and get through the day. Being able to cope with events we are confronted with may be a form of adapting, but adapting is more concerned with adjustments that are ongoing, and coping is more concerned with the here and now.

If you watch a young child who is frustrated, she may become angry, sad, tearful or all of the above. In that moment, the child not only intensely feels not getting what she wants, but she may also believe she is alone in her pain because others get everything they want. To make matters worse, in her mind she is convinced she will never again get anything she wants. This type of catastrophizing is common in young children and all too common in adults traumatized as children. While some of us are better off in life than others in one way or another, the human condition does not include getting everything we want. We must all learn to cope with disappointment, loss, and unfair treatment.

I have observed that traumatized children are generally much more transparent than other children with their words and energy. This is helpful in knowing what the child is internally experiencing, and gives a hint as to what the child needs from others. Traumatized children often learn survival adaptations during traumatic abuse (dissociation — distance from self, and attachment disorders — distance from others). However, these adaptations do not serve the child well after the abuse has ended. While survival requires adaptation, it does not require successfully coping with disappointment. For this reason, traumatized children are often devoid of the ability to cope with even small matters.

Whether moving from being the pawn of an abuser, or overcoming the disappointments in life, coping skills must be specifically taught. At this stage in the process, the child must have a new sense of self, and feel more confident about her internal abilities to be able to win the battles in the present, by first keeping the past from continuing to interfere indefinitely. To help the child, you must have some ability to teach, to model, and to reinforce coping skills. The methods to teach coping skills are as varied as many of the previous steps. Illustrated story books can be useful, and play therapy can role play ways to cope with disappointment. However, there is no substitute for helping a child learn to handle disappointment in real time.

I have found it helpful to have the child practice handling disappointments. I let the child know that I plan to have a small disappointment for him, and we will handle it together. For example, I might say that in a few minutes I have a small toy car as a gift. When the time comes I reach into the bag and realize I have left the car at home. This may be disappointing or not, but let's pretend like it is. The child is helped with choices of what to think: I was tricked, I will never get the car, adults can never be trusted, or I can ask if I can get the car tomorrow. The child can also be given choices of how to act: I can cry, I can get angry, I can say hurtful things, or I can be calm and say, "Thank you, and maybe you could bring it for me tomorrow." I believe it is helpful to have the child anticipate the disappointment you are practicing, so he is involving his cognitive process due to the anticipation of what is coming. In life, the child may do better to remind himself that there will be disappointments, and his job is to cope with them.

For some children it is helpful to have visual teaching tools. This can be done by drawing figures of a person getting disappointed and handling it badly and of others handling disappointment well. It can help at times to give the child a laminated card with coping steps to take. This could include a variety of strategies such as taking a deep breath, closing your eyes and thinking of a happy time, counting to 10, telling yourself things will get better, etc. It is better to have the child come up with ideas that may be helpful to him, but this must be done when he is in a relatively good mood.

You will know when you are getting through to the child with learning coping skills. The child will begin to take an interest in the process, and at times cannot wait to learn more in order to feel the power of self-mastery and come out ahead for the first time. This step often releases energy like a volcano that has been building up pressure for years. Be prepared, at times the only thing worse than Jesse in a bad mood is Jesse in a good mood! But when this step begins, it makes this difficult trauma journey worthwhile for therapists as well as the child and family.

Everyone Must Learn to Cope

The story goes that a rich, powerful, and brutal king battled with depression because even rich and powerful people have bad days. He sent for the three wisest sages in his kingdom. He put them in his dungeon with the royal command that they had until dawn to give the king the solution to his depression. As motivation, the wise men were to be executed if the king did not like their solution. After some discussion, the wise men had the answer that they would stake their lives on. The next morning the king called them to his chamber and demanded their solution to whenever he was disappointed. One of the wise men stepped forward and handed the king a gold ring. The king became angry and said, "I have many gold rings, how will this help me feel better when things go badly?" The wise man said, "Read the inscription on the ring, Sire." The king then noticed the inscription, "And This Too Shall Pass," and spared their lives.

As one of the last steps in the process, you will need to assist Jesse with new coping skills, and life will provide plenty of opportunities for him to practice. He might be rejected by a classmate, and you can help him demonstrate his power to decide how he wants to think, feel, and act about this situation. He will need reminders of how powerful he is to influence every situation he is in. If he is now able to move beyond his trauma even a little, it will be new territory and he will need your help learning how to manage this new world. Don't just give advice, show him: role play, read stories, use puppets to demonstrate, and be sure to make all this as fun and enjoyable as possible.

CHECKLIST OF SUGGESTIONS

✓ Help the child understand that everyone gets disappointed.

✓ He has the right to be disappointed and upset when things go badly.

✓ Help the child with choices of what to think.

✓ Offer some choices of how to act when disappointed.

✓ Read stories or use play therapy to teach the child.

✓ Practice handling small and anticipated disappointments.

✓ Visual cues may be helpful showing steps to take to cope.

✓ Have the child come up with coping strategies she likes the best.

✓ Look for signs the child is feeling more personal power with practice of coping skills.

Step 10: Practicing Self-Mastery

The term self-mastery describes the many ways an individual can have an influence on his or her experience. To be able to have an impact on what goes on within or around you is not a typical experience of a traumatized child. To successfully overturn the long-term detrimental impact of trauma the child will need to be able to learn some level of self-mastery.

Self-mastery can turn trauma and other stressful situations into experiences producing resilience. The final step is similar to rewriting the ending of the trauma story; the individual can be stronger because she has survived the abuse or the trauma. Overcoming trauma can make someone stronger, more resilient, smarter, more empathetic of others, and more prepared for the many challenges of living. The essential aspect of this step is to be in control of internal processes, or what can be called self-mastery.

I recommend that self-mastery be taught and experienced by the child in incremental steps. Self-mastery is something that must start in small ways and build to larger and more important things. If we cannot be in charge of our feelings, our memories, our perceptions and our behavior, we will not be successful adults. But this is demanding a great deal from the traumatized child. However, practicing having control over the child's actions and thoughts in small matters can make the learning more accessible to the child. Internal control is a major goal of trauma recovery. If we can achieve these steps with something as challenging as a traumatic past, we can handle most of the pressures in life by comparison. Abraham Maslow and Victor Frankl emerged from the Holocaust somehow more than men. Christopher Reeves became a real Superman only after his spinal cord was snapped and he lost most of his physical abilities; and our entire nation was shocked into a new appreciation of life, our country, and hope following the events of September 11, 2001. It is not always the best of life that brings out the best in ourselves.

Teaching self-mastery techniques involves developing self-awareness. Learning these skills involves listening to and cooperating with the teacher. Self-mastery gives the child a glimpse of what is possible and how he or she can have a very different life than the one relegated to the child by the abuser. These children crave control, it is a fundamental drive. Being able to experience self-control, sometimes for the first time, can be magical. The gains can be great, and the potential interest of the child can be substantial if this process is done in an enjoyable way for the child.

Several of the techniques described throughout this trauma therapy process can fit under the general heading of self-mastery skills. In Step 4 the child learned to increase and decrease internal arousal. In Step 5 the child was helped to face fears from past events while using skills to stay calm. In Step 6 the child practiced changing the meaning of the trauma, and in Step 7 the child experienced changing how she responded to situations. All of the techniques used for these steps are some form of self-mastery. This theme of teaching the child internal and external control of thoughts, feelings and behaviors, is part and parcel of trauma therapy by helping the child move on from a history of trauma.

This final step in the process of trauma therapy also moves beyond simply recovering from the trauma to slow ourselves down when we are feeling or acting at excessive levels. A socially successful person will be able to do a quick internal check to see how another person or event has affected him and then consider what would be the best way to handle the situation. We all are invited to accept the negative scenarios provided to us by others who have little interest in seeing us succeed. The ability of an individual to promote her own thoughts, feelings and behaviors will put her in a very strong position throughout life.

Certainly each aspect of self-mastery is difficult to do and will take years for the child. It is the role of trauma therapy not only to remove the impediments to success, but also to teach the tools that will help the child reach his or her goals in life. Self-mastery can be the difference between being governed by trauma, or the individual having control over a traumatic past. Self-mastery also can allow the child over time to turn the negative experience of abuse into positive resilience for the future.

Jesse will need outside help frequently throughout new developmental periods, and throughout his life. Making or not making the team, not being invited to a party, or being rejected by a love interest — all of these situations will invite him to relive his trauma all over again. He will need his therapist initially, and then trusted family and friends, to form an all-important support system throughout his life. Self-mastery includes the wisdom to surround yourself with supportive people who can help you. Give Jesse the keys to unlock his past, and then give him the keys to the city, while you encourage others in his life to continue the work you have started.

CHECKLIST OF SUGGESTIONS

✓ Self-mastery skills are the skills we use to live our lives as we choose.

✓ The best trauma treatment turns a bad experience into a helpful one in the long run.

✓ Start with small steps and build upon successes.

✓ Teach the child the internal control she can have.

✓ Teaching self-mastery is more about the future than about the past.

✓ This step teaches resilience, something that will come in handy at every stage of life.

We have now taken the conceptual journey of trauma therapy. This is a journey that I have been privileged to take countless times with both adults and children. As I was writing this chapter, I was contacted by a young lady who was seriously abused when she was young. I had the chance to take this journey described above with her over a two year period of time. I have to say that before this recent phone call I was not at all sure that the end result of the treatment in her case was what I was hoping. This young lady was a handful, and she was cold and controlling. She was very smart and could quickly see what the adult wanted from her, and she used her skills to prevent it from happening, whether positive or negative in her mind. Control was her goal. I hear back from most of the children I have worked with over the years, but I guessed this young lady would be an exception and never contact me. I just figured I was right since there had been no contact for over eleven years following the trauma work. Sometimes I love to be wrong, and it appears I was wrong in this case. In a long telephone call and subsequent e-mails, I not only heard about a success story of going from a victim to a survivor, but I was also treated to a barrage of appreciation for taking the journey with her more than a decade ago. She also offered perhaps the greatest compliment I have ever received when she said, "I can only repay you by trying to do for my infant daughter what you did for me." It doesn't get any better than that!

The seven-year-old was tired of taking his daily medication so he said, "I am done with pills, I am going to do the mind over the med." [We could only wish.]

Chapter

9

Residential Treatment — Still an Important Solution

This is the most difficult chapter of this book for me to write. It is difficult not because I am unsure what to say, it is difficult because I must condense so much content and so many points into one chapter. I am placing this subject into Part II of this book because I believe residential treatment has been and will continue to be a cornerstone of intensive treatment services for the most troubled children. This is a message I want to send to parents of very challenging children. I also want to support the many hard-working professionals who make a difference in the lives of children every day, often with little recognition for their efforts.

I state in the chapter title my position on the role of residential treatment. The implication of the chapter title is that I am surprised that some would question whether residential treatment is indeed a solution, and you will find those who do question "congregate care." Despite criticism, I am surprised that residential treatment would be the target of continual criticism, despite what I believe are the obvious logical reasons for its importance in the overall system of care for children.

I frequently criticize authors who attempt to change people's opinions without letting the reader know this is the author's objective. I am most critical of authors of research who misuse science to manipulate opinions and market a particular agenda. It works both ways, and I need to abide by my own rule, so I will begin and end this chapter by stressing that my intention is to explain my belief that there is no reasonable argument against residential services being an important component of our system of care for difficult children. I quickly point out that my opinions are based on the premise that only children who are a safety risk and who cannot be safely and appropriately managed and their needs met in a family and community setting, should be considered for an ongoing residential setting. For children who cannot be effectively treated in families, it is my position that residential treatment is the placement of choice, has the best chance of success, and is in the long run the most cost-effective option of the alternatives available. As far as trying to change the reader's mind on the importance of residential services, I believe the facts will do that for me.

I will do my best to state my points clearly with very little attempt to be politically correct or careful. I understand why other providers of residential services tend to be more careful, but I believe the points I am making should be clearly stated. My personal experience on this issue has developed over the last 32 years of referring challenging children for residential services, visiting multiple residential programs, consulting with many others and operating outpatient and inpatient services. I would offer that no one knows the true weaknesses of residential treatment quite like someone who operates such a service. With my background, I know the issues from both the outside and the inside, which I believe has given me a unique vantage point to review both the strengths and weakness of this level of care.

The History of Children's Residential Services

The initial role of services in a residential setting, going back well over 100 years ago, was to provide a place for children who had no families to provide for them. The lack of a family could have been caused by a variety of reasons: orphaned by accidents, illness, war, abandoned due to physical or mental disability, incarceration of parents, or simply being abandoned by parents who did not want the responsibility. The orphanages of the 1850s until the 1960s have been much maligned; however, there have always been exceptions to the "David Copperfield" or "Little Orphan Annie" type of institution. Those exceptional programs were places where children actually received the care and learned the skills they needed to be successful in life. The current governor of my state is a product of a caring orphanage, and he is quick to speak fondly of his upbringing and the care he received. Boys Town, Nebraska has been another example of a caring and respected orphanage where good things happened to thousands of children without families. It is also true that abuses have occurred, and there have always been marginal or poor homes for children, just like there are poor schools, abusive families and impersonal and uncaring welfare departments.

In the middle of the last century the conditions that produced orphanages did not immediately change, but society's response to children without parents moved away from congregate care to family-based services such as foster families. In part this came from a realization that children who could live in a family should be allowed to do so. At the point our society began to wake up to what C. Henry Kemp was saying about the presence of child abuse within families, in the 1960s and 1970s, the sheer numbers of children removed from abusive families made group care unfeasible as the primary resource. At the turn of our new century, so many children now grow up in substitute care that it is hard to imagine our society without foster care.

Although at times connected to maltreatment or abandonment, another purpose for group care came about with the struggles of teens growing up and the delinquency, substance abuse, and pregnancy issues that resulted. Teens who once would be incarcerated with adults were first provided safer and more age-appropriate correctional settings such as detention homes, training centers and other terms that essentially describe youth jails. However, it is ironic that after 30 years of separating children from adults in correctional facilities, we are now heading in the opposite direction with charging and sentencing more children as adults than ever before.

Since the 1970s our system of care has developed three separate aspects of residential services: 1. Delinquency and Corrections, 2. Child Welfare due to dependency, and 3. Mental Health programs. Critics of group care often combine these different settings, but they are all quite different. A frequent error made by critics of group care is to criticize all congregate care for problems found in any of these three separate types. Another error is to generalize research from one type of group care to the others without the validity to do so. For example, most of the cited research on group care comes from juvenile corrections. Similarly, most of the evidence-based programs are designed for adolescent delinquent populations. Research from youth correctional facilities is seldom applicable to mental health programs; and what has been found effective with delinquent populations cannot be generalized to young mental health populations.

For the most part, we have eliminated the reasons most children were in residential care 100 years ago through the use of foster and kinship care. As the response of society changed, so did those who have always worked to help children. The orphanages of the past became at first group care homes, and some developed the clinical expertise to become residential treatment programs. You can still find programs helping children today that have been in operation for over 200 years.

Although there has been extensive attention to the abuses that have occurred in residential settings, there have also been many positive and even mythical portrayals of places such as Boys (and now Girls) Town in Hollywood movies. It is not hard to imagine why most orphanages were viewed more positively by the public than they may have deserved. First, no one wanted an orphanage with "those type of children" in their neighborhood. Taxpayers grumbled about the financial responsibility of the biological parents, and stories of child abuse or at least harsh treatment in children's institutions were too frequent. The stigma of orphanages appears to have developed with each of the transitions of group care over the years; and even today there are many people who don't want a children's home in their backyard.

That "Weird" Place That Houses "Those Children"

Two years after we started our residential program we began to get attention, the wrong kind of attention. Restless teens in the area were enjoying "drive-by baseball," where they would drive along destroying mailboxes with baseball bats without stopping the car. My wife was in the post office picking up mail one day when a customer said to the postal clerk, "We had our mailbox destroyed last week." The clerk said, "I'm not surprised, I understand the retarded children at that Jasper home have been doing this." Normally an easy-going person, my wife found herself in tears and snapped back, "That place is my home, the children are not retarded, and they are never left unsupervised, so blame someone else!" and she left without getting the mail. Over the next four years, the local public school district continually attempted to have our permit to operate revoked because they didn't want "those kids" in their district. We prevailed in all ten legal challenges that were finally decided in our favor in the State Supreme Court. There have always been many more supporters than critics of our program, but the list is long of those with judgmental and unfair attitudes toward helping abused children have a better life.

At each change in the orientation and services of residential care over the many decades, there have been opponents who argue against such services and programs. The recent detractors are mainly in the camp of questioning the value of residential treatment at least in comparison to other more recently developed types of services. In the first 10 years of my career, I was a referral source to residential programs. I was a counselor and then director of the largest youth agency at the time in a large state. I made it my business to visit and get to know all the residential programs.

What was true in the 1970s is true today, there were all levels of quality in the available services — good, bad and ugly. Opponents of residential services tend to get stuck on the bad and the ugly. The energy of opponents of residential services often surprises me in its intensity. However, Dr. James Whittaker has said that negative beliefs and attitudes in the past and the present have hampered an objective review of the appropriate place residential services have in the system of care (Whittaker, 2000). It is time to get over the emotion and look at the reality of what children need and how best to provide it to them.

In my own case, it was only after my first 10 years in the field that I could clearly see that our outpatient services did a very good job with 85% of the children and families but 10% to 15% of the cases did not improve. When I learned that 80% of society's energy and resources for corrections and mental health were going into 10-15% of the most troubled populations, it was clear that helping 80% of the population was not good enough. I decided to go into the residential treatment business to learn to work effectively with the most difficult children. Perhaps I was not paying attention, but in the early 1980s most people wanted to help rather than criticize our work with residential care (other than our local school district). We received then and continue to receive today a continual outpouring of goodwill and financial help from all areas of the community. However, as our program became more defined and successful, the criticism from a few grew as we grew.

Five years after starting our residential program, I was attending meetings where I heard for the first time professionals saying things like, "No child should ever be in a residential program." I noticed that a few service providers would spread untrue rumors in a direct attempt to harm the reputation of what we were doing. I remember the moment I realized what the primary issue was with the covert attacks. It was all about "my model is better than yours" and about funding.

In the professional community, there has always been an element of criticism of residential services. On a global level it was about the high cost as well as the questions of whether children actually improved in any residential treatment environment. Over the last 20 years there have been new models of working with children and families. The good models tend to become incorporated into community programs and the "flash in the pan" approaches go out like clothing fads. In the last ten years new approaches have sought to gain attention through evidence-based research. And like treatment programs, research runs the gamut from the good, the bad and the ugly.

As the research has been mounting concerning new alternative services, and as the proponents of these new services have become more aggressive in comparing the latest approach with the current system of care, there has been a distinct silence coming from providers of residential services. In part this silence has been due to the everyday demands of keeping their primary focus on the challenges of daily operations. With all their beds full and a waiting list of children and families to be served, why get concerned with random critics of residential services? Another reason for the silence is that many of the new approaches have ties to academia and have the time, expertise and financial resources to conduct empirical academic research, which residential treatment advocates do not have.

Unlike many new behavioral approaches that lend themselves more easily to research, an ecological multilevel treatment program has never been easy to research — even if programs had the time, expertise and money to conduct the studies. Perhaps the best way to research the multilevel treatment "village" is with ethnographic or qualitative research. However, causal research has been more fashionable, which is all about finding the outcome and determining why this result occurred. Most residential treatment programs have hundreds of variables that are not easy to isolate and control, and the outcome (improvement with the child and family) is much more important to them than who or what caused the improvement.

I believe the argument for and against residential services is as meaningless today as it has been over the years. This is not a criticism of attempts to improve services. However, most of the current detractors of residential services have a new and improved alternative approach to offer the system, complete with their own research studies. Other detractors are consumers and advocates who want to make the decisions on where the system's funding is spent. I cannot speak for all residential treatment programs, but I believe the closer anyone looks at my agency's programs, the more an objective person will see the value it has for the most difficult children and their families.

The fact is that throwing stones is not the best way to build an effective system of care. It is time for the adults to start getting along with each other for the sake of the children, and to set an example of collaboration. I will own my opinion that the arguments against having any type of residential services are, at best, unhelpful and at worst, divisive and self-serving. I have some company in this opinion. James Whittaker of the University of Washington and an expert in the field of child and family services has said, "...the greatest tragedy would be to extend into the next century the polarizing debate that has engulfed group child care throughout much of the last 100 years" (Whittaker, 2000). With a similar message E.C. Teather has written, "How on earth did we ever let ourselves get led into this argument... I believe this argument to be the ultimate in nonsense" (Teather, 2001). Although I agree with both of these statements, it may be helpful to look closer at the criticism of residential services.

Arguments against Residential Treatment and a Response

The criticism of services based in a residential setting has a long history, which is more true today than ever. There have been many blatant abuses that have occurred in residential settings. To institutionalize a child has become synonymous with warehousing in a cold and insensitive environment where more negative than positive outcomes are likely. At times this has been true of institutions. But even in the past, the black orphan asylums of large cities, the foundling houses of religious organizations, the poor houses of England, and the Eastern bloc orphanages of today all were established for an important reason — the alternative was generally much worse for the child. However, the abuses that have occurred in the past in residential settings do not provide a good reason to categorically condemn residential treatment programs of today. Good residential treatment programs are well-designed and are nationally accredited by meeting standards of excellence, and they ensure that they prevent the problems associated with institutionalization — while safely and effectively meeting the needs of children and families.

The arguments of today against services provided in a residential setting are most likely to be based on research findings, and the implication is who can disagree with the evidence against housing children as a group. However, it is essential to critically review the cited research to see if these studies stand the test of rigorous science that is generalizable: objective, completed in a real-world setting, recognizes its limitations, and does not claim to be applicable to settings not a part of the research. I find the majority of the frequently-cited research used to criticize residential treatment does not stand up to the test of good, generalizable, scientific evidence.

Before giving my opinion as to why there is so much criticism of residential settings, I will outline some of the most frequently cited reasons why some would like to see residential treatment either marginalized or eliminated altogether. I will briefly give my response to each point.

As a rule children do better in family settings than in institutions (Barth, 2001). This statement has been supported by numerous studies and appears to be accurate. However, there is at least one major reason why this statement is not a valid argument against residential services. The reason this is not a valid criticism of residential treatment is that only children who do not do well in their own and other families, or in less restrictive community based interventions, should be admitted to a residential setting in the first place. There has recently been expanding discussion in the field to consider residential services as something other than the last recourse for young people, but finding what the residential settings do best. While I appreciate the reasoning behind this discussion, I still believe that if a child can grow and develop in a family setting, and there is a safe and healthy family available, this should be the first resource of choice. Even if all children who could live with families are placed there, there are still many children in our communities who are not safe, cannot be maintained in the community, and will not thrive in a family setting and need a residential setting. The word institution often has a negative connotation. Most anyone, particularly children, will do better in a non-institutional setting. Good residential treatment has few similarities to institutions, and in fact seeks to prevent institutionalization of children needing treatment.

Residential treatment is used too frequently when other community and family based services have not been tried (Barth, 2001). If a child is placed in residential treatment when the child could have had mental health needs addressed in a family or community setting, then I agree that community services should be tried first. However, most parents, caseworkers and referring professionals would say the opposite of this statement. They would like to have the funding available to more frequently place an appropriate child in a good residential treatment program, because in most cases the parents, schools and community have tried everything available to help the child with little or no progress.

Children develop delays in interpersonal and social development while in residential settings (Barth, 2001). This statement has been repeatedly shown to be the case in institutions such as the orphanages of Romania and Russia. However, good residential settings allow children much more opportunity than in families to interact with peers and multiple adults throughout the day. Standardized data from a residential treatment center I operate, has shown in the area of social and interpersonal skills, that very difficult children progress during treatment at a more accelerated rate than normal children in families. The argument could be made that group settings provide children much more practice than families for learning many interpersonal skills. The determining factor is the quality of the program, not whether it is group care or not.

Outcomes are better in families than in residential settings (Berrick, Barth, Needell, & Jonson-Reid, 1997; Chamberlain & Reid, 1998; Barth, 2001). This statement has also been supported by repeated research. But once again, this statement cannot be used as a valid comparison since children appropriately in residential settings are placed there because they have already had very poor outcomes in community services and cannot continue to be placed with families. Therefore comparing outcomes of children in families and children appropriately in residential settings is not comparing the same population.

Children in residential care lag in educational progress due to a lack of individualized attention and few extra curricular activities (Barth, 2001). If a residential setting does not have a rich environment of educational and extracurricular activities, it is a poor program. Most residential treatment programs have a distinct advantage over family and other community-based programs by integrating academics, treatment and a wide variety of activities into one setting. The potential exists for there to be many more child-oriented activities in a residential treatment program than in most families. Children leaving residential treatment often struggle much more in public school than in residential schools, and they miss the amount of child-focused activity available in all good treatment centers. One of the frequent concerns of parents of children graduating from good residential treatment programs is how they can possibly provide the rich array of educational and extracurricular activities the child is used to in the treatment center.

The cost of a residential placement is more than most other types of interventions (Barth, 2001; Chamberlain & Reid, 1998). The comparisons of cost depend on what comparisons are being made. It is true that residential treatment is generally more expensive than family or community-based interventions. However, in many cases the better comparison is to juxtapose residential treatment with the most likely alternative — inpatient psychiatric hospitalization. In this comparison, residential treatment is substantially less costly (generally 50% to 75% less). If cost includes the damage to property, and the human cost to families, residential treatment can also prevent very costly outcomes in less intensive settings. A comparison of dollars may not always be the best measure.

Institutions are particularly bad for young children (Berrick et. al., 1997). This is another position that has been shown to have strong validity in research. However, it could also be said that young children heal better in their own homes than in institutional hospitals. The challenge for both physical and mental health care is to not have the young child out of a family setting for any longer than is required. With the priority of reintegrating the child into an appropriate family setting, neither treatment programs nor hospitals can be said to be bad for young children if this is the level of care they need for a limited period of time.

Putting troubled children in proximity to other troubled children creates more problems than it solves (Chamberlain & Reid, 1998). This statement is also based on research, but the research has been generalized beyond the sample population — delinquent teenagers. Young children are in a more normalized setting with other young children. It is not a good idea to put delinquent teens together (although this is consistently done in correctional programs), but the data is not available to say combining young children generally has poor outcomes. Having difficult young children living together has shown a number of advantageous outcomes. For example, troubled children tend to be marginalized by normal peers, but can compete socially, academically and athletically with more success with peers who have had similar histories or problems. Children may learn poor behaviors by peer example, but the opposite is also true that they can see what not to do when peers act poorly with poor results. Young children can learn prosocial behavior by peer example facilitated through close supervision by trained adults.

Who Criticizes Residential Treatment Most Often and Why?

Actually the most frequent critics of residential services are the residential providers themselves, but they don't write about it, they work to improve upon all the weak areas many programs have. The typical residential treatment program of today has little in common with services of 50, 25 or even 10 years ago. Good programs have made the majority of internal advancement through the means of extensive quality improvement programs. The field of residential services has been quietly evolving based upon past experience, internal questioning, and evidence from new research on effective services. The best organizations that provide residential services also provide a host of step-up and step-down services to form a continuum of care. Today it is more the norm than the exception to find that organizations with residential services also have treatment foster care, home-based services, emergency respite for families, and care teams that include all the adults in a child's life designing an individual plan to fit each child. The majority of changes over the last 30 years have taken place because service providers have chosen to look critically at their own failings and want to be at the forefront of developing new and effective interventions for difficult children.

There are also many detractors of residential settings who are not providers of residential care. The authors and researchers I reference above are just a few of many that I could list. I used these individuals because they represent the often-cited criticisms, and are some of the most frequent detractors of residential programs. All of the mentioned authors have at least one thing in common, they all have a model they wish to see promoted. This by itself does not make their arguments invalid, but when research is not done by an independent party with no vested interest in the outcome, the responsibility falls on the author to ensure against marketing research — attempting to use science to sell a product by arriving at a predetermined outcome.

The frequent criticism of the financial cost of residential treatment is another hint as to the agenda of continual critics of residential services. Many critics do not have direct experience with residential interventions, but they do have alternative approaches for which they are seeking funding for. In my opinion, many of the new alternative approaches to helping difficult children make the error of believing their new approach is the answer to all situations and all children — rather than identifying where the new approach is likely to be most effective. I also believe that some decision makers misuse research and erroneously believe, because there is a study that produced positive outcomes with one population, it must be good for other populations.

The new approaches, often aligning themselves with evidence-based practices, generally have a significant research base (not always independent or replicated research), and prefer to make comparisons of cost and outcomes with residential care. However, this research is often generalized from one setting or population (correctional settings or delinquent adolescents) to all settings and populations in the system. Unless a child is inappropriately placed in residential treatment, nearly all comparisons of residential care and outpatient care are not valid, because only children who cannot be safely placed in community settings should be in residential care. Therefore the outcomes and the costs are comparing apples and kumquats. Recently it has also been acknowledged that comparing a specific intervention (the latest new approach) with a level of care (a residential setting) is not an appropriate comparison, yet it is frequently found in the literature of new systems of interventions.

The argument about costs has receded somewhat in the last few years since a milestone project led to the growing opinion that community-based intensive services may have a number of advantages, but lower cost is not one of them. The study I am referring to is the Ft. Bragg comprehensive demonstration of community-based care. To the dismay of many proponents of alternative community-based systems of care, this massive six-year research project involving 42,000 children was funded by the Defense Department to the tune of $80,000,000 and did not support either improved outcomes or cost reductions. The results of the most comprehensive implementation and evaluation of switching to a community continuum of care were that client satisfaction went up and access to services improved, but the goals of the project were not met because outcomes did not improve and the actual costs of the community continuum of care nearly doubled (Bickman, 1996). There are several likely reasons why this project did not produce the desired result, but one thing appears true — the fact that an intervention is well-funded and community-based does not ensure better outcomes or lower cost.

I believe the frequent goal of research (and thus researchers) with alternatives to residential care is to divert some of the funding from one established, well-regarded level of care to the newest approach *du jour*. I call this the "Avis Syndrome" in mental health, where the new intervention has to try harder. From my vantage point, it seems somewhat ironic that established mental health agencies with well-deserved reputations for effective interventions, including residential services, are generally the first to incorporate the newest ideas in the field of working with difficult children. The irony is that the supporters of alternative treatments are often criticizing the very organizations that are the first to embrace their new approaches.

It is the norm rather than the exception to find organizations with residential services incorporating the core principles of evidence-based practices of newer interventions such as Multisystemic Therapy, Functional Family Therapy, Treatment Foster Care and other interventions that have shown promise in research studies with delinquent teens. There is as yet little or no evidence to support the long-term effectiveness of these approaches with young mental health populations — much less to be able to say they produce better outcomes than residential treatment.

Mental health providers know that they must proceed cautiously with the newest approach to come along. Over the last four decades a great many new approaches have come and gone without demonstrating effective long-term outcomes. The most recent group of evidence-based programs that are getting considerable attention have not originated in mental health settings but rather with delinquent teen programs. Although there are some similarities between delinquent teens and children with serious mental health issues, there are also very real differences.

Recent research is actually questioning the long-term effectiveness of the latest evidence-based programs with young children with mental health needs (Hoagwood, 2003).

I will again state that, for the best interests of children and families, all aspects of the system of care should work together to build new and creative ways to deliver what children need, and what will help families do the difficult job of preparing children for a demanding world.

Why Residential Services Are an Essential Part of the System of Care

In the present and in the years ahead, residential services will play an important role for the same reasons they have played an important role in the past. In child welfare, corrections and in mental health, residential services have been the recourse when all else has failed. If for no other reason than this, residential services will probably always be with us. However, this argument indicates that residential programs are important by default. The indication is not so much that these programs are innovative or effective, they simply need to be there as a last ditch effort. Some residential providers are sensitive to this and object to being a service of last recourse. Actually this description suits my residential programs just fine. By design we work with the children with whom no one has had success, and we provide the ingredients to be successful for the first time. However, in the larger picture I can understand some providers not wanting to be best known for being the last stop on the treatment highway. There are other reasons that residential services are a critical part of the system of care.

- Psychopharmacological Assessment and Interventions — Medications have developed into an important aspect of working with very difficult populations. It is important that medications to improve behavior and/or emotional health are not misused as a type of chemical control. When used effectively, medications have been shown to be a critical element in working with conduct disorders, depression, mood disorders, violence, hyperactivity, and other common themes among troubled children. The understanding and use of psychotropic medications has improved over the years, but there are still many mysteries as to when, why, and how they impact the person. Miracle drugs of the past have fallen out of favor, and there is little doubt that, in the years to come, some medications in use today with children will turn out to be considerably less appropriate than was believed. Medications are one area where research on adults is often used to guide use in children, which provides serious built-in deficiencies. The role residential services can play may be vital in many cases. The roller-coaster ride of medication trials is at times extremely difficult to do in a community setting. In a residential setting with professional staff, including medical staff, medications can be prescribed, altered, or removed, all while the results are measured in a safe and secure setting.

- Stabilization/Respite — Residential settings can greatly assist in the management of serious behavioral and emotional outbursts where safety becomes a major concern. Good residential settings have all the ingredients of an excellent place to stabilize a child. Such a setting is staffed around the clock by trained employees who have the skills to meet the needs of either internally or externally violent children. Residential settings can also provide the families with seriously needed respite. This is more than giving families a few days off, it is allowing parents to regroup, rest, develop a new plan, and connect with consultants who can help the family reunify with the child and implement the plan to make the family setting work for everyone.

- Trauma Treatment in a Safe Setting — With the majority of troubled children suffering from the effects of one or more traumatic events, trauma treatment is a necessary part of addressing serious behavioral and/or emotional problems. Although there are many therapists in the community who understand and practice good trauma therapy, there is no question that this process will at times destabilize the child.

Bringing a child to a therapist who may further escalate the child's serious behavioral problems puts a very difficult strain on the parents and family members. However, in a residential setting, the important trauma treatment can move ahead without the concern of the destabilization of the child going beyond the ability of the care providers to handle the results. A residential setting also allows for multiple therapeutic interventions in a single day, rather than waiting until next week at the same time.

- Strengths Identification — It can be very difficult to celebrate the strengths of a child who is being suspended from school once a month or causing your neighbors to circulate a petition to have your family move to another town. However, in a residential setting, there are multiple adults who play many roles in the child's life. This sharing of responsibility helps the adults avoid focusing only on the problems, by having some staff focus primarily on the child's strengths. The typical parent of a difficult child feels like a combination of police officer, prosecuting attorney, judge, jury, and prison guard along with being mom and dad. When the demanding roles are shared, there is more opportunity to notice what is going right with the child, as well as what is going wrong.

- Skills Training — Life skills can be learned in many settings. However, there are unique possibilities for learning skills in a residential setting. To use my own program as an example, there are multiple peers not only at school but throughout the day; and there are multiple adults every child must interact with all day long. We believe the variety of people and the variety of situations is one reason that the troubled children in our program improve in life skills much faster than their normal peers in the community. Every minute in a residential setting is an opportunity to learn from doing, from modeling, from instruction, and from discovery.

- Family Coaching/Consultation to School and Community — Residential programs historically have developed some of the most knowledgeable professionals in working with difficult children. Ask any parent who goes to a therapist, within minutes the parent can tell how experienced the professional is with very challenging children. Parents can usually tell if the therapist "has been there." Residential settings are magnets for difficult children, and professionals who are successful in this setting have earned their stripes. The best parenting coaches are those who have been in the trenches many times. There is no joy for a parent quite like finding a coach who can help them better manage a difficult child. Residential programs also typically have staff with community development experience along with a practical understanding of the needs of difficult to manage children. These staff can be very valuable consultants to school staff, youth groups, sports programs, churches, and other community settings where difficult children are found.

- Crisis Backup — The most efficient path to success with difficult children is to have a team of adults working together with a well-developed plan that involves every aspect of the child's life. As good as the team and the plan may be, I have noticed that the cases that succeed are often those where there is a backup, or a Plan B, when things get chaotic or safety concerns grow to a critical point. In many situations the backup may not even be needed, but it is there and available. Residential services can be an excellent crisis backup, when the parents, teachers, and other members of the team need a place for the child to stabilize while the team gets ready for the next step. Residential settings provide crisis backup more effectively and to more serious situations than any community-based alternative.

- Continuum of Care — Few agencies have the ability to provide a full continuum of care to rival an organization that has the capacity for residential services. Children who need intensive services can best take advantage of step-up and step-down care. Agencies that offer a full continuum of services are less likely to fall into the trap of fitting the child into a program rather than having a program that fits the child. The best organizations that serve difficult children are those that have a variety of levels of care that child can: access, move through as their needs change, and potentially return to at a later date to receive a "booster shot." Agencies that have a continuum of care with no residential component will not be able to provide all that is needed for the most difficult children.

The Future

Just as in the past, the future of mental health and other systems of care will include services in residential settings. However, in the future I predict there will be less tolerance of the "my model is better than yours" arguments of the past. A theoretical model is important, but not the deciding factor of a successful program. "At present, there is no empirical evidence, and it is unlikely that there ever will be, to suggest that one model of residential treatment is superior to another... advocates for "innovative models" typically claim superiority over traditional models, their claims are never substantiated" (Mordock, 2002). Greater reliance on evidence-based services will continue to aid in the identification of core components of effective treatment. As adults committed to helping children, there will likely be less adult squabbling and more collaboration from components of a broad system of care.

I believe, like others knowledgeable in the field of service delivery, that the future will promote more multi-service organizations that provide a variety of levels of care with an array of approaches. Different types of services, innovative approaches and differing models will be encouraged because, in the end, the system will have more choice, more diversity, and opportunities to learn more about effective interventions. The multi-service organizations of the future will not necessarily be the large Wal-Mart style social services of today where size is the most distinctive feature. Part of the reason we have mega-agencies today is the economics of survival. As funding becomes scarce, programs merge to stay alive, although there are often losses in service quality that come with financial gains. In the future I believe smaller programs, with multiple components within a coherent philosophical orientation, will be able to ensure quality care one client at a time and have the financial stability of today's very large multi-service organizations.

In the future, the separation of professionals and parents will be a thing of the past. Already good treatment programs are open to and partnering with families. At the same time, the pendulum will likely not stop swinging where it is today. Because families have been kept too far from the treatment decisions in the past, the attitude today that the family always knows best will also not prevail. There is no question that the parents must be at the decision-making table when discussing intensive treatment services for difficult children, but so must all the other knowledgeable voices on the team. In the same way parents don't take their child to the cardiologist and pretend to know the answers and tell the physician what the child needs, the care teams of the future will listen to special skills areas of the team members around the table without the tension of the family (white hats) vs. the professionals (black hats). All members of the team are experts at something related to the child, and outcomes will improve if everyone is respected and heard.

Effective interventions of the future will have well-developed theoretical models. Including the increased amount of research being done over the last few years related to mental health treatment, a consistent finding over the last fifty years in research has been that positive outcomes are linked most often to a well-developed theoretical model. From a common sense perspective, this makes sense. When practitioners in a program know what they want to do, why they want to do it, and when they believe it will have the greatest impact, the outcome is likely to be more positive than the unsure practitioner "playing it by ear." However, this finding, which has been shown repeatedly in research on the effectiveness of therapy, has not been well received by those who have a model that is "better" than everyone else's model. After the initial claims and the early research that is usually conducted by the pioneer of the "better" approach, the repeated finding is that one well-conceptualized and implemented theoretical approach has been shown to essentially be as good as any other. Lambert and Bergin (1994) identified six treatment factors that appear to make the real difference in outcomes, and these factors need to be a part of any good theoretical model — catharsis, positive relationship with the therapist, gaining a new perspective, learning behavioral regulation, cognitive learning and mastery. Although in the literature on outcomes of therapy, effect sizes (improved outcomes) have been influenced by: type of problem, age, education, skill of therapist, race, IQ, social class, level of participation, client expectations, gender, and even physical attractiveness and likability of the client. However, the most important ingredients of positive treatment outcomes come back to having a model the therapist and client believe in, along with the six ingredients of effective therapy mentioned above. The theoretical model is the road map that guides the program to stay on course, and to avoid "drift" away from what the program and the staff believe will make a positive difference.

An issue of growing importance in programs of today and the future is the ability of the program model to incorporate interventions for trauma recovery. As we have become more aware of the amount of child abuse in our culture (currently America's most common and serious medical problem), and as we learn more about the short and long-term impact of abuse, it is clear our treatment programs must be prepared to assist in the healing of trauma. The numbers are ominous: 5,000,000 children traumatized each year in our country, approximately 25% of our children sexually abused while growing up, threat of harm and exposure to violence in the home have become one of the most frequent types of abuse, and neglect still holds first place in both the frequency and the level of long-term negative consequences. The effects of trauma have been directly linked with most mental health issues.

The frequency of trauma, particularly in populations of people in mental health programs, indicates that a majority of clients will be traumatized in some form at some time in their lives. A concerning finding related to trauma is that, due to the way trauma is processed by the brain, the negative effects tend not to improve on their own over time. Stated in another way, some form of outside intervention will be important, particularly with children and adolescents, in order to prevent lifelong debilitating symptoms of being traumatized. Faced with this level of need, we must have all treatment programs staffed by knowledgeable and competent trauma counselors.

Final Thoughts on Residential Services

In an ideal world there would be no need for services that essentially take the place of the family. However, with the pressures on parents, the level of violence that can accompany some mental health problems, the presence of child abuse and neglect, and a host of other all too common realities particularly for children, our world is a long way from the ideal. In the helping professions we have improved in our ability to assist some families to provide for the needs of many children in the home — who previously would have been treated in a residential setting. We have developed treatment resources that are community and family-based, rather than removing the child from the community. However, as good as we get at assisting families and developing new service approaches, there has been and will continue to be a need for: comprehensive, responsive, effective residential services that partner with families and other community services, have a well-developed theoretical model, and only keep children out of a family setting for the time it takes to optimize treatment gains.

As I began this chapter, so will I end it: there is no reasonable position for residential treatment not being an important component of a system of care now and into the future.

STRENGTHS OF RESIDENTIAL TREATMENT

✓ Residential programs have nearly always been better than the alternative: children in dangerous homes, on the streets, or in community settings unable to meet the child's demanding needs.

✓ Residential settings have some distinct advantages in promoting living skills.

✓ Residential settings can effectively work with the most extreme problems.

✓ Combining treatment with academic learning in one setting can have advantages.

✓ The costs of residential treatment are far less than the alternative placements for children with serious medical and mental health problems.

✓ Evaluating medications can more effectively be done.

✓ Stabilization and respite are effectively provided in a setting designed for these purposes.

✓ Trauma treatment in residential care can handle the child's temporary deterioration in symptoms.

✓ With more adults, more attention can go to the child's strengths rather than problems.

✓ Professionals that work with very difficult children have more credibility with families.

✓ Residential settings have built-in crisis back up.

Part III

Adoptions, Attachment & Academics

What to Do When Things Go Badly

The angry six-year-old girl who was tired of following adult directions proclaimed, "I know you want me to do cartwheels down three flights of stairs for you, but I am not going to do it!" [You're right, that's unreasonable — how about two flights of stairs?]

Chapter

10

Post-Traumatic Adoption

If you work with troubled children very often, you will end up working with families who have adopted. The conditions that create a child available for adoption are often very difficult on the child. Whether the child is abused, abandoned, or put up for adoption at birth or afterward, each of these situations can result in psychological problems for the child and challenges for the adoptive family.

In my career I have worked with many adoptions — before, during, and after the adoption has occurred. Because of the nature of my work, most of the adoptions have been of the difficult variety. I have not worked frequently with the typical adoptive situation in which there are children who need a home and a family fully prepared to provide one. The overall statistics provided by adoption agencies indicate the vast majority of adoptions succeed, at least by the definition that the adoption does not disrupt. In the State of Oregon, for example, which prides itself on its success with adoptions, figures are thrown out that over nine out of every ten adoptions are successful. What a successful adoption is may be a matter of contention, but let's accept that most adoptions do not disrupt.

I work with the hard-to-place, and the exceedingly hard-to-place children. Many of these adoptions are the ones in the one out of ten group that does disrupt. In fact, in the first five years of my adoption work with children, who were adopted coming out of our residential treatment program, a full 64% of the adoptions of our children disrupted when placed by the state adoption program. In response to this serious problem, we developed a new way to approach adoptions that we called the Adoption Courtship Model. This model was initially printed in the book *Handbook for Treatment of Attachment-Trauma Problems in Children* (James, 1994). It will be included in the second section of this chapter.

I want to stress that good programs are similar to good interventions – they must be designed around the particular needs or issues in the situation. The model that will be described is a program designed for very difficult children. There are components that would not work as well, or perhaps work at all, in the average adoption. As adoption agencies face the task of finding homes for the challenging children in the system of care, I believe that our experience may be of use in many of these situations.

As we implemented this model, we began to have successful adoptions for the first time. This was back in the 1980s. It would be years later before I was to face another major problem for both the child and the family related to the aftermath of disrupted adoptions. After developing the adoption courtship model, over the next ten years were spent working to place children coming out of our program into homes that were fully informed, prepared and ready to take on the challenges that came along with each child.

After initial resistance to handing over some of the control of the process, the state adoption agency allowed us to follow our process due to the severity of the past problems with our children. With this new approach, we experienced immediate success and had no disruptions for the first five years. We continue to this day to find success with a model that was based on the family and the child mutually progressing through three levels of commitment: from a commitment to spending time together, to a commitment to developing a relationship, and, finally, to a commitment to a relationship for life. We found that when children felt a real choice in the matter, as well as taking the process one step at a time, our success rates with the most difficult children went from 36% to 84% long-term success with the same population of children.

In the early 1990s, I began to see a different type of problem with adopted children and their families. By this time, our program had developed some specialization in treating attachment problems in children. Over the next decade we began to have children come to us who had divergent pasts, but who also had a recognizable dynamic occurring between themselves and their families. These children came from pasts that included: drug-affected children who were adopted very young, only to present problematic symptoms years later, foreign-born adoptions, and all varieties of serious abuse and neglect resulting in the child pushing the families away with all their might.

We were able to develop some methods to deal with the attachment problems the children displayed. These methods can be found in my book *Raising Children Who Refuse To Be Raised* (Ziegler, 2000). However, as we became more skilled at working with attachment disorders, another problem began to arise when it came to children coming into our program from adoptive families. Put briefly, the better the child became, the more stress we observed in the families. At first this surprised us, but over the next five years, the names changed but the dynamic was frequently the same.

The overarching fact we observed was that, regardless of the progress of the child with the attachment disorder, who came into the program from a previous adoption, the child invariably did not return to the adoptive family. At times the family called a halt to the relationship and disrupted the adoption; and at other times the family remained fiercely loyal to the adoption, but not to the child who returned to their home. As I mentioned earlier, some of these children improved considerably in treatment, and yet it seemed that the more they improved, the more stress was observed among the family members. Along with this dynamic came considerable tension and sometimes conflict between the family and treatment staff within and outside of our agency. I watched this dynamic occur over and over until the pattern began to make some sense to me.

I now believe this dynamic to be what I call *Post-Traumatic Adoption*. This PTA is a very different than the PTA most parents belong to, and it is not fun for anyone — the family, the child, or people trying to help both. Basically, what Post-Traumatic Adoption entails is that the family members have exhausted their resources while the child was in the home and the results were seldom what they wanted, and often times were damaging to family members. The combination of giving their all and continual failure became the traumatic experience for family members in relation to both the child and the adoption itself. The subsequent steps usually were: continual fruitless efforts searching for help, convincing the adoptive agency such as the state to assist with the cost of treatment, and a very exhausted family coming to our program for help with their child.

Our program does considerable work with post-traumatic stress disorder. This problem initially was associated with soldiers in combat and adults who were the unlucky victims of life-changing traumas such as rape, car accidents, and other terrible events. However, it was later recognized that children who had been through serious child abuse and neglect had the same symptoms as adults following serious trauma. In the mid-1980s Dr. Michael Reaves, a psychiatrist, and I identified that not only were abused children every bit as seriously affected as soldiers with combat PTSD, the children appeared even more deeply affected by the trauma they had lived through.

Although I had experience with both adults and children with PTSD, this problem was something individuals experienced and I never connected it to a common experience with a group of people, such as a family. I did not make this connection, that is, until the last few years when I began to see the same dynamic in the traumatized adoptive family as in the traumatized individual.

I need to explain that the term Post-Traumatic Adoption may sound like a mental health diagnosis, but it is not. It is more of a description of the dynamic following an exceedingly difficult adoption where the family members individually and even collectively exhibit symptoms that are remarkably similar to post traumatic stress disorder. I am using a similar term because I believe it is a useful association and has some similar implications for treatment.

The Diagnostic and Statistical Manual – Fourth Edition (APA, 1994) is useful in this discussion as a reference for the types of symptoms associated with PTSD. Before discussing the similarities, it is important to say that Post-Traumatic Adoption is not about fault nor blame. The victim of trauma is not held responsible for the negative impact on his or her thoughts and emotions. In the same way, the symptoms of trauma exhibited by family members in a Post-Traumatic Adoption are not the responsibility of the family, instead the problem lies in the trauma they have experienced. If this was a question of blame, we would need to look at whether the placement was appropriate in the first place, whether sufficient information about the child and the child's past were available to ensure a reasoned decision about the adoption, or we would need to look at the perpetrators of the violence, abuse and neglect in the child's past that led to being adopted in the first place. But the discussion of Post-Traumatic Adoption is not concerned with fault or blame. Much like any other symptoms stemming from trauma, it is not the victim's (in this case the family's) fault, despite internal guilt or responsibility the victim may feel.

Similarities Between PTA and PTSD

The DSM-IV defines a variety of clinical criteria that are helpful in considering this paradigm of symptoms associated with trauma within an adoption. PTSD has six general criteria and 19 sub-criteria within the six areas. Each of the criteria will be briefly addressed to see if they relate to difficulties experienced by the family in an adoption.

221

The diagnosis of post traumatic stress disorder is always experienced by an individual. PTSD is an intensely internal experience. To consider PTA we need to view the trauma as experienced by a family unit, although it is possible that just one member of the family would be affected. This is not to say that everyone in the family has a qualitatively similar experience of the difficult events in the adoption. All family members have their own internal experience of the adoption, with some family members being more traumatized than others. I will mention that from my experience the family member who typically pays the greatest price from an adoption that has gone bad is the mother. This makes perfect sense in that mothers are, more often than not, the glue that holds family units together. Accordingly, when the family begins to come apart, the mother often feels the most pain, responsibility, guilt, and other forms of distress. To complicate matters, the adopted child often targets the mother.

The first DSM-IV criteria is that the traumatized party (in this case the family) experiences or is confronted with events that are serious, a threat to the integrity and well-being of others, and experiences fear and helplessness. There is little doubt that this criteria roughly describes the comments I have heard from family members in an adoption where nothing is going quite right.

The second criteria requires at least one of five events: recurrent and intrusive distressing thoughts and images of the trauma, distressing dreams, feeling as though the trauma has not ended, intense psychological distress related to cues of the trauma, and physiological reactivity when exposed to events that resemble aspects of the trauma. Again, these descriptions are quite close to how families often respond following months or years of effort to make an adoption work; and they feel like the harder they work, the farther from their goal they find themselves.

The third criteria includes an avoidance and numbing of general responsiveness involving three or more of the following symptoms: efforts to avoid thoughts and feelings of the trauma, avoidance of activities or people that arouse traumatic feelings, inability to remember aspects of the events associated with the trauma, feelings of detachment or estrangement from others, restriction of affect such as the ability to keep loving others, and a sense of a foreshortened future of the marriage or the family unit. The serious PTA cases include all or most of these factors. Parents, particularly the mother, associate helpless feelings with having the child in the home, and often have little interest in repeating past problems by allowing the adopted child to return to the family's environment.

Parents almost always remain strongly committed to the adopted child after the child leaves the home, yet they cannot bring themselves to expose members of the family to continuing difficulties associated with the adoption. This leaves the parents in a quandary: how to fulfill their commitment to the adopted child, while also fulfilling their commitment to every other member of the family? I find that one of the only ways parents can resolve this dilemma is by fiercely advocating for the child, while they attempt to ensure the child is not returned any time soon to the family, if at all.

The fourth criteria involves increased arousal of two or more of the following: difficulty sleeping, irritability or anger, difficulty concentrating, hypervigilance, and they startle easily. One of the battlegrounds of difficult adoptions is during the evening and nighttime hours. It seems that when the adoptive child often has difficulty is when the family can least afford the consequences. In this case the consequences, of behavioral problems late into the night and even nighttime mischief by the child, are an increase in hypervigilance leading to sleep difficulties, and general exhaustion occurs when quality sleep is absent for extended periods. The result of this dynamic is usually irritability, trouble concentrating on other aspects of life (such as work), and other heightened stress responses.

Chuck and His Family Were Both in a No-Win Situation

Chuck was referred to our program at age eight due to years of attachment issues and acting-out behavior. Chuck was adopted at age three by his well-educated, middle-class family. The parents were told little of Chuck's early history, apparently because the details were not known. After a few months in their home, Chuck did not settle into the family, but instead, gradually escalated his problem behaviors. After coming to us, Chuck responded well to the structure of our residential program, and over the initial nine months of treatment, he was not showing his former serious problems with enuresis, violent rages, destructiveness, sexual behaviors and stealing. However, our treatment staff noticed that the more Chuck's behavior improved, the more reactivity and tension were being expressed by his parents. They began to question treatment reports and our assessment of Chuck's progress.

"How do you know he is really improving?" This was the continual question from his family. The more we observed Chuck's progress, the more his parent's questioned our staff and confronted Chuck on every minor issue. Chuck believed they no longer wanted him. In fact, his parents ended up deciding that Chuck was not safe to return to their home, although he was demonstrating no unsafe behavior. Eventually the family decided Chuck would never live with the family again, but they were committed to maintaining the adoption. Since they did not trust "the system" to meet his needs, Chuck needed them to advocate for him as he grew up in substitute care. We saw a no-win situation emerge for Chuck and his family. The family wanted to let go, but couldn't "for his benefit." Chuck grew up in group homes while having an adoptive family that he was not allowed to either live with or even to visit in their home. As legal guardians, the ultimate choice was the parents' decision to make. I could not help but believe their decision was one in which no one could succeed.

The last two criteria are essentially givens: the duration of the difficulties has lasted more than one month, and the problems associated with the adoption difficulties are causing significant distress in the functioning of the family and/or the parents and other family members. In a PTA, both of these will be true.

The above criteria from the *Diagnostic and Statistical Manual* is used as a means to show that significant trauma and resulting symptoms can follow from an adoption that is very difficult on a family. These criteria are not appropriately used to say the family has PTSD, because this is an individual diagnosis and not a disorder experienced collectively by a group of individuals. In this discussion, I am borrowing these criteria to outline a different way to look at the stress and the struggle that the family is going through — and to help explain how the resulting dynamic may affect social service professionals who are trying to help the family.

Over the last year, in my experience, I believe the conceptualization of Post-Traumatic Adoption has shown some validity. Families with PTA often present to my program when the adopted child has been removed from the family to a psychiatric hospital, foster home, or residential program of some kind. Sometimes the change is agreeable to the child and fewer serious behaviors occur, which can further stress the adoptive family. In cases of serious attachment disorders, such as child adopted from Russian or Romanian orphanages, the reduced requirement of intimacy can calm some of the child's serious behaviors, or may change the way the behaviors are exhibited. Care providers outside the family who are unaware of the dynamics of these children may incorrectly believe either that the child is fine and the family is the problem, or they may believe they have given the child what he has needed all along and now the child is much improved. Both of these conclusions are probably erroneous. These families are not child abusers, and in fact, they will often put up with abuse from the child until they have no other recourse but to have the child removed, often for the safety of other family members or pets. Just because a child is not exhibiting serious behaviors in one setting, especially where there may be little required intimacy such as that associated with a permanent family placement, does not mean the behaviors will not come roaring back when the environment signals that closeness is once again required of the child.

We must take one further step in considering the plight of the family. Families open their lives to a child who they are often less familiar with than they need to be. Too often, families are not told about all the important details of the child's past — including abuse or serious neglect. The family gives and gives for years, spends all their emotional and financial resources trying to make the adoption work, only to feel the internal guilt when they have the child temporarily leave their home for professional help. At this point, the child often initially improves and the family must try to explain that this may very well be temporary, while the family agonizes with what to do next.

In the above paragraphs, I have tried to show the most important step of effectively working with a family experiencing PTA. If you, as a helping professional, cannot show the family that you truly understand their experience and their dilemma, they cannot trust or effectively work with you. When the family does not have the assurance that you understand their situation, the results are various degrees of anguish for the family, sometimes the child, and often the professionals trying to be of help.

PTA families that have not received the assurances they need, to trust the understanding and expertise of the therapist or other helping professionals, can appear resistant, controlling, hostile, unworkable, negative, demanding, manipulative and lacking in concern for the child. However, each of these impressions held by the helping professional is a misunderstanding of the experience of the family. As I was formulating this paradigm of the Post-Traumatic Adoption, I described the general premise to several families in this situation, and every family said something similar to, "Yes, that is exactly what we are going through." There is no better feeling for a client than to hear that your therapist understands the deepest aspects of what you are going through. In the case of families dealing with PTA, it is not a matter of making them feel better, it is a matter of make it or break it regarding the recovery of the family and any remaining hope for the adoption. If this level of trust from the family is not obtained, the result is a state of limbo for everyone. The child will likely not be going home, the parents find themselves in the terrible place of wanting help for their child while they must stress that the child is not really getting better, adoption agencies often are paying the cost of expensive out-of-home care, and the helping professional attempting to work with the family is so perplexed she goes home and wonders what can be done about the situation.

Navigating the Fire Swamp of Healing

A number of years ago, a Rob Reiner movie came out called *The Princess Bride.* In this fairy tale, the hero had to take the heroine on a treacherous journey through the darkest and most foreboding place one would ever want to find themselves — the dreaded fire swamp. I like to use this analogy for any very difficult journey that is necessary for the healing process, and it fits nicely with the healing of Post-Traumatic Adoption. An essential point of this discussion is the PTA family will need to go through the healing process, it is not just about the adopted child getting professional help. The starting place in helping the family is to have them understand the family must go through a healing — whether they have the child returned to the family or not. In fact, it is not unusual to find that the family has been more damaged than the adopted child by the problems in the adoption. The child often has the self-protection of an attachment problem; the same wall that prevents emotionally bonding with the family also tends to protect the child from further trauma. As is true with PTSD, the trauma of PTA that is untreated does not often improve over time. I have observed marriages break up, other children in the family step into the problem child role when the adopted child leaves the family, and many families find the adoption has taken the wind out of their sails in all aspects of family functioning.

The trip through the fire swamp involves both knowing the route and also what hazards to avoid. Although I am not a believer that typical human beings need a professional therapist to get by in the world, trauma is a different sort of beast. As I said before, research has shown that untreated trauma usually does not go away, and can actually intensify over time. The traumatized individual cannot always trust personal instincts and an internal compass for the journey of healing. It is wise to get a trauma guide, at least to acquire a road map, if not for support throughout the journey.

The hazards to avoid on the journey of healing from Post-Traumatic Adoption are potentially many. The blame game is the first roadblock. It is not helpful to look for who is at fault for the problems the adoption has brought the family. Finding fault does not make a situation better. The fault finder often becomes more upset when blame is placed because, once determined, there was no reason to have gone through the blame game in the first place. Blaming the child frequently occurs, but few adults within themselves will allow blame to go to a child who was abused, neglected and/or abandoned. Parents who put the most energy into blaming the child are likely the parents who are trying unsuccessfully to convince themselves that fault belongs not with themselves, but with the child. Parents who blame themselves take on an internal psychological weight that they will carry a very long time. Extra weight is not helpful on any journey. For those who must find blame, it can often be shared by all family members, the biological parents who initially did not provide the child what they needed in the early years, and potentially the adoption agency and the adoption process itself. However, blame never solved a problem, but it does take a great deal of energy away from the journey toward finding solutions.

Another hazard to avoid involves the lasting effects of grief and loss. It is often the case that a family must grieve the loss of the dream they had of successfully adopting a child, who would accept the love of the parents and learn to reciprocate. In a PTA, this has not happened and the fact is that it will likely not happen in the way the parents initially hoped it would. Therefore, they must say good-bye to the image they had of a successful adoption if there is any chance for the adoption to succeed. It is very difficult to let go of our dreams, but this step is not unlike what most successful marriages must go through — the difference between what we dreamed our partner would be like and/or the marriage would become, compared to what actually happened. Adults who hold onto an image of an ideal relationship will most likely go from one partner to another looking for "Mr. or Ms. Right," rather than creating the right relationship with the person to whom you commit. After we let go of an image of what we want, we have a better chance of developing a working situation with what we have.

We are not yet done with hazards along the healing journey. One of the most typical effects of Post-Traumatic Adoption is the inability of the adoptive parent to trust professionals trying to help. This often comes out as a lack of trust that the professional really knows the problem and how serious it is. This often results in the tragic dance of on the surface the parent asking for help, but appearing not to accept it. Another way this comes out is an apparent resistance to believing either the child can improve, or in the face of data indicating improvement, not being willing to accept it. Although frustrating for the helping professional, it is even more stressful for the adoptive parent who desperately wants to see the child improve, but, due to the trauma of the adoption, cannot come to believe it is real improvement. The end result of this dynamic is that the child continues to reside away from the family in some form of substitute care, while the professionals try to reunify the family, and the family resists reunification. This is a roadblock that will stop any further progress on the journey to healing for the family.

What Can Be Done with PTA

Can this complex dynamic be avoided or worked through? I believe it can, and here is how. Preventing a problem is always preferable to trying to get out of a pit after you fall into it. If adoptive families know that the dynamic described above will lead to a dead-end, they are much more likely to avoid going very far down this road. The best prevention is to get as much information on the child as possible to make an informed decision on adoption. The second step is to be prepared for the worst and hope for the best. The third step is to have the resources on your team to face the difficult times that nearly all adoptions, and for that matter all families, will have. And when all other attempts to prevent an adoption trauma are tried and have failed, get the child out-of-home intensive treatment the child needs *before* the family has exhausted all personal resilience and family resources and is exhibiting signs of serious burnout.

Once the Post-Traumatic Adoption has happened, the first step of the healing journey is to want to heal. This is generally not a problem for families who have struggled unsuccessfully with a difficult adoption. These families want things to improve. However, what will bring improvement is often unclear to the adoptive parents, although their instincts say that keeping the adopted child away from the family is an important element. In the short run this may be true, but if the adoption has any chance of success, keeping the child away is part of the problem and not part of the solution.

The second step after the adoptive child leaves the family for some intensive treatment is for the parents to take a step back and see the landscape of where they have been and where they wish to go. This may seem obvious, but it is often true that traumatized individuals focus on going from day-to-day rather than looking with a long-range perspective. This long-range view not only requires reexamination of the adoption decision and what has actually happened to date, but it also requires the parents to consider where they want their family to be a year, two, or more down the road. Without this perspective of having long-range goals, the family will be unlikely to reach them. Trauma produces a very short-term focus, which is one of the insidious aspects of trauma. The individual, or in this case the family, thinks about surviving right now, not a year from now. But without a plan, the family cannot develop a road map to reach the destination they desire.

The next step to healing is to get the right type of help. The right help is not a function of a professional degree or completion of a special certification program to work with adoptive families (something that has been put together in my state). Perhaps the most important ingredient of the right person is someone who comes highly recommended, someone you can trust, and the most important credential — experience with helping traumatized individuals and families. Once this person is found, it will be important for everyone to move forward together with the realization that there are many hazards along the way. Every family will be unique, every family will need to have their own individual long-term goals. Sometimes the family will want to invest much more effort into making the adoption work, while other families will need help to verbalize that they cannot go any further with the adoption. However, although the specifics of the healing journey must be individualized, this chapter can be a general road map, and one that both the helping professional and the family can discuss and use to help plot a direction.

A Message to Helping Professionals

There is no substitute for supportive, knowledgeable help for the family that has experienced a PTA. Similar to other trauma survivors, the adoptive parents will not always be the easiest of clients to work with. Traumatized children often have considerable stored-up anger that may only come out once they feel safe with you. You are rewarded for your efforts with being the target of the rage that rightfully belongs to the child's abuser(s). This dynamic is true for adults with PTSD from wartime experience, serious accidents, assaults, and other causes of trauma. Just when trust is beginning to develop, the adult lashes out at the person helping them. Unless you are ready for this, it can be very disconcerting when it happens. Traumatized adoptive parents can take the helping professional by surprise even more than other trauma survivors. They often appear not only normal, but very successful, conscientious, and loving parents. Most adoptive families have a great deal to give, and have made the altruistic decision to share their lives with an adoptive child, oftentimes a child with a problematic past. These are good people, very good people. You may find yourself believing these very good parents sitting in front of you are on board with the plan and trusting your help, only to run into what appears to be "resistance," as less and less progress toward reunification begins to occur.

I recommend that the question of reunification be raised at the first meeting you have with the family, and this topic be a frequent discussion point along the way. I also recommend that some of the hazards and pitfalls described earlier in the chapter be on the table and discussed before, during, and after they appear in the process. Your ability to let the adoptive parents know that you have an understanding of their family's and their own internal experience with the adopted child can go a long way to establishing trust. But even after you have established respect and trust, the hard work of healing is still ahead.

I will not go into great detail in this chapter on the specific steps of trauma treatment, as this can be found in chapter 8, but I will briefly mention some important steps. For trauma to heal, some level of "re-exposure" to the trauma must occur as the stressful reaction is altered. With PTA the reexposure includes contact between the parents and the adopted child, and then the more important reexposure — the child being in the home with the parents and any siblings. As with other traumas, this step must be taken carefully because, if the ground work has not been laid, the results could reinforce the trauma rather than counteract it, and the trauma is magnified. The parents must have new skills to work with some of the child's old behaviors. Regardless of the success of treatment for the adopted child out of the home, the child must do some testing when returned to see if the parents will be able to handle the difficult issues. As you can imagine, unless the parents are prepared to face some of the old behaviors, the PTA symptom of reexperiencing the earlier trauma will kick in. When this occurs, the parent will believe nothing is different and can quickly feel hopeless. However, if the parents have learned the skills that have worked with the child in the out-of-home setting, and implement these approaches when the child tests, the child is reassured and the parents have begun the process of feeling successful with the child. This positive dynamic will need to be repeated over and over to overcome the legacy of past traumatic failure of the adoption.

At any point in this process that the adoptive parents begin to hedge on having the child returning to the family home, even for visits, the issue of eventual return of the child should be discussed. If the parents indicate they have considered disrupting the adoption, the odds are they have done more than just considered it. If they indicate they are 50/50 regarding disruption, the odds are they are closer to disruption than they are saying just to see how this possibility will be received. If they say they are fairly sure they want to end the adoption, take this at face value and look closely at the consequences for everyone of a disruption. It is important not to try to talk a family out of disrupting an adoption. To give the adoption a chance, it is actually more helpful to spell out the details of a disruption, and families that are not sure will more likely want to put more effort into the reunification process.

The dynamic that is most troublesome is when parents indicate that they have lost none of their commitment to the adoption, but they do not see that it is feasible for the child to return to their home anytime soon, if at all. The parents want to advocate for the child and not leave the child "adrift" in the world, but do not plan on parenting the child in their home. This is nearly always a losing proposition for the child, for the funding source paying for out-of-home care, for the helping professional, and for the adoptive parents as well. This is one of the scenarios in which no one can win. There are many reasons why this roadblock must be avoided. The child will not have the chance to grow up in his or her family regardless of the improvement they make, the funding source must fight with the parents to avoid paying out-of-home costs indefinitely, the helping professional working toward reunification is thwarted by the parents at each stage in the process, and the adoptive parents have all their internal guilt enhanced by pushing away the child and even by the help that is being offered to them. The way to avoid this trap is to work toward the goal of either giving the adoption another chance with the child in the home or disrupting the adoption. To not go in either direction is to not go in a healing direction. There is nothing easy about making this decision or helping adoptive parents make such a wrenching decision — but taking the non-decision direction (status quo) will not be the easy way or the best way in the long-run.

A final note to the helping professional. Remember that there are no bad guys in adoptions. The child is confused and is in no position to determine what she needs, although she usually has a lot of demands. The family wouldn't have adopted the child unless they felt they had a lot to give a deserving child, and the adoption agency likely did the best they could with the information they had. You certainly are not the bad guy because your only agenda is to be of help. At times, the adoptive child is pathologized based on the testing that all children must do to ensure they are safe — so they can turn their attention to being a child learning about the world. At other times the adoptive parents are pathologized because they are "resistant" to reunification, or want the child to be considered dangerous or mentally ill. This happens when parents are not sure they can trust that progress has been made, and that the initial trauma, that tore apart the family the first time can be prevented from happening again.

Remember to avoid labels and avoid blame. Remember, as in all trauma therapy, if you do a good job there will be times you will be rewarded with the wrath of your client, who desperately needs to express her rage at the trauma she has gone through. The fact that it is directed at you means that she trusts that you care enough and are capable of accepting her most intimate feelings — her pain. Just as with a serious medical diagnosis, trauma may require some painful interventions that may be as painful as surgery before the road to true healing can begin to give the patient hope for eventual success.

Tatiana Made a New Start

Her story was familiar — Romanian orphanage, adopted at age 18 months, and over the years did not really bond with her two American adoptive parents. Tatiana had "soft signs" of being prenatally affected by drugs or alcohol. She was either withdrawn or would rage violently. Either way, she did not look at her parents, which they said was one of the most painful things for them. When she raged, she clamped shut both eyes until she was done screaming in a way the family just couldn't continue to live with. Tatiana underwent an intensive focus on attachment and bonding in our program. After 14 months, Tatiana was clearly improving. However, her family was remaining very much the same. After three difficult months, the family decided that she was different but they were not, and they would end the adoption. Initially very sad about the decision, Tatiana was placed with a family and maintained contact with her former adoptive parents. She continued to improve and did very well in her new family. Although painful, the results was that she was allowed to move on while maintaining a connection with her former adoptive family.

PTSD Symptoms Associated with Post-traumatic Adoption

✓ A family is confronted with events in the adoption that are serious, a threat to the integrity and well-being of the family, and there are feelings of fear and helplessness.

✓ Recurrent and intrusive distressing thoughts and images of the problems, distressing dreams, feeling as though the problems have not ended and may never end, intense psychological distress related to cues of the adoption issues, and physiological reactivity when exposed to events that resemble aspects of problems that happened in the home.

✓ Avoidance and numbing of general responsiveness involving three or more of the following symptoms: efforts to avoid thoughts and feelings of the adoption, avoidance of activities involving the child or situations such as contact of the whole family with the child, feelings of estrangement from others, restriction of affection such as the ability to keep loving others, and a sense of a foreshortened future of the marriage or the family unit.

✓ The duration of the difficulties has lasted more than one month, and the problems associated with the adoption are causing significant distress in the functioning of the family and/or the parents and other family members.

Adoption and Attachment — The Adoption Courtship Model

In our program, we have had some success preventing

adoption disruptions and the potential resulting post-traumatic aftermath. We have used a model over the last 14 years that takes into consideration these points: the children are very difficult, the family will need full information, the parents will need considerable coaching, and everyone will need support to overcome the hurdles involved. The model does not fit every situation. It has been used primarily with children over age six. Obviously the model would need to be modified for either very young children or for children with significant developmental delays. However, after many years of successfully placing very difficult children in adoptive homes, I would still recommend consideration of the components of this model.

Out of necessity, Jasper Mountain Center (JMC) staff have attempted to isolate why, during the first five years of our program, some adoptions worked and why most did not. The result of two years of considering this question has been the development and implementation of an adoption model for children who:

- Are emotionally disturbed,

- Are difficult to place, and/or

- Have had single or multiple adoptive failures.

The operating principles for our Adoption Courtship Model are the following:

- Standard adoptive procedures are insufficient for special-needs children and their prospective families.

- The odds are often against a successful adoption with these children without preparation, training, and professional support.

- The child and the family must be prepared for the *reality of this adoptive relationship.*

- The adoption commitment must be made by **both** the child and the family, and can only be made based on the actual experience of a relationship, not on information or interest.

The model has three phases:

- *Phase I.* The child is prepared for the adoption by understanding his or her role in making it work or not work. The child's considerable power in the situation is made clear. The family goes through the regular certification steps and is selected by the adoption committee. The family meets with the caseworker and our staff to learn what to expect from the initial meeting with the child. The child also undergoes preparation for this meeting. The two sides meet with the caseworker and family therapist. The child begins to build trust by getting to know the family as a unit, then the family members as individuals, and finally in the home environment of the family.

- *Phase II.* This is where the reality must begin to come in. Both sides have an image of what they are doing and who they are doing it with, but it must become very clear and very real. This phase is characterized by extended visits and family counseling. The process starts with a focus on the strengths and positive attributes of both sides, moves to the faults and flaws of both sides, and finally underscores the realities of the combination of strengths and weaknesses of the adoption.

- *Phase III.* There are three necessary commitments for the adoption to work. The initial commitment on the part of both child and family is a commitment of interest, time and effort in regard to the potential adoption. The second is a commitment to relationships — the family with the child, and the child with the family. The final commitment is to family for life. The last commitment is the final step in a successful adoption of special-needs children, not the first step as is normally practiced. The commitment for life must be made to a person, not as a concept. The commitment to the reality of how difficult the adoption is with this disturbed child must clearly be stronger than the commitment to the adoption as a concept.

Suggestions and Techniques

PHASE I.

Preparation. Phase I starts long before the family and the child meet. One of the keys here is preparation. There is an important question to ask before the specific adoption work begins: "Has everyone received some preparation for the adoption?" Too often the family receives more preparation than the child. Preparing the child for an adoptive placement should ideally begin a year prior to meeting a family, and should include specific counseling on the issues that will surface. Along with adoption classes, it is valuable to have the prospective parents meet with the adoption worker or counselor who will work through the transition process to prepare the family for the probable struggles that are ahead.

Initial meeting. After the adoption committee gives its blessing to a match, and the Adoption Courtship Model is decided upon, it is then important for the family to meet with the adoption worker(s) and the counselor who will provide the transition counseling and discuss the model, the process, and the goals. Keep in mind that most adoptive families are in a mild to huge rush to have the child. A rushed courtship is almost always problematic. Gain the family's agreement and commitment to the process or don't use this model (in general, the bigger the rush the family members are in, the more concerns there are about their readiness).

The initial meeting of child and family. The suggestion here is for the worker(s) and counselor to be actively involved. Often meeting the parents alone before children are included is less complex and overwhelming for the adoptive child. There should be informal time between the child and the parents, as well as the worker and counselor outlining what will be happening over the next few months and why. Keep the meeting from being stuffy or too formal. Make it clear that the goal is to see if in the long run this is a good match for everyone concerned. All sides will have a voice (empower the child to influence his or her future and you will have a much better response).

Process. Start with meetings in a counseling environment to get to know each other. Have the whole family come the second time.

Use techniques to rapidly point out the different personalities in the family (who is the clown, who is grumpy in the morning, etc.) One technique is to have the members of the family write on a sheet of paper the things they like and dislike about the family member to their left and right. The counselor reads the items and has the family guess whom it was written about. Start with afternoon visits away from the family home. Go to day-long visits, and then an overnight visit, again away from the family home. The individuals get to know each other in a neutral setting to equalize the playing field. In the family home, only the adoptive child is unfamiliar with the environment. In a park, restaurant, or motel at the beach, the focus is on the relationships, not on getting familiar with the family's turf. The adoptive child should have a chance to get to know all family members at least a little, both individually and together, before going to the family home.

Counseling. The initial meetings and discussions should take place in the counselor's office. After each visit there should be a counseling session. The counselor plays the role of bringing the family and child together and facilitating the process so both sides know that the situation is organized and under control.

PHASE II.

Counseling. Counseling continues to be frequent but not necessarily occurring each time. Involve foster care providers to help make the child's strengths and weaknesses clear.

Process. GET REAL! Arrange extended visits, primarily in the home environment. Get away from special events like getting ice cream or going to the zoo, and get down to everyday life. The goal of this phase is to make it clear what this adoptive combination will really be like.

Techniques. Stress the strengths and weaknesses of the match, the family, and the child. It may be difficult or embarrassing, but it is time to air everyone's strong points as well as dirty laundry. Use techniques like having everyone answer such questions as "When I get really angry, I...," "I show sadness by...," "When I am grumpy, the best way to deal with me is...," etc. Role-play some of this. Have children act like Mom in the morning before coffee.

How do the parents fight with each other? Have the adoptive child act out some of his less impressive qualities, such as being rude, disrespectful or hurtful. If the child is unwilling, the counselor can be the child. Whatever behavior family members will see later should be talked about, even acted out, now.

Can You Really Give the Child a Choice Regarding Adoption?

I am a believer that on most important issues in a child's life, the adults need to be the decision-makers. Adoptions with troubled children are one exception. The reality is that children do have a voice, they speak with their actions. Any child can eventually disrupt any adoption in any family. We have had good success with giving the child the opportunity to have his or her voice heard. Most adoptions proceed too rapidly mainly because the parents are usually more ready than the child. This can spell trouble. Slow down, give the child a chance to let you know, through words or actions, if the process is going too fast. Few children end up saying no to the family, but some do. If the child is not interested, I would prefer to know this now rather than a year or two down the road when everyone has paid a high price for a match that won't work. Children feel empowered when they are asked, when they are consulted, and when they get to decide how far and how fast. If the decision to be a part of a new family is not a place to give the child a voice, then I'm not sure what would be. At the same time, it is critical to correctly translate what the child is telling you about the adoption. As with other communication with troubled children, don't rely solely on words.

PHASE III.

Process. Now that everyone has met and should know a lot about one another, the emphasis shifts to commitments. There are three levels of commitment: (1) time and effort, (2) relationship, and (3) lifelong commitment. Commitment 1 should have long since been made and operationalized. It will be important to review and evaluate how everyone has handled this commitment because it will be an indicator of the next two. How interested is everyone in a commitment to relationship? In the case of children with serious attachment problems, the relationships must be reviewed carefully to result in realistic expectations. It is clearly time to begin putting out on the table the issue of lifelong commitment. Again, the commitment must be to people, not just to the concept of adoption.

Counseling. Here is where the skill of the counselor is most needed. There is much complexity in commitments. There may be resistance on everyone's part to addressing this. Everyone may be thinking, "If things are going smoothly, why upset the apple cart?" No one really wants the final analysis to be halting the adoption because it is not overall a good match, but this may be the case. The counselor must be firm and willing to be the bad guy. The capacity of the child to commit himself may be problematic, and the parents may have better intentions than abilities.

Ritual. If the adoption gets a green light, then some have found a formal recognition of the adoptive commitment an important step. Consider having a ceremony. Invite friends and throw a party. Our culture does this for most important events.

A Final Thought

Adoptions can work with special-needs children, but the work is never fully completed (yet when is any parent's job done?). Despite an excellent placement for both the child and the family, the work has only begun. The transition into the home will set an all-important tone, but don't fool yourself that the job will get easier. Our experience is that new struggles come up with each physical and developmental stage of the child. But that just makes adoption like life—a new challenge around every corner!

THE COMPONENTS OF THE
ADOPTION COURTSHIP MODEL

✓ *Phase 1*, Preparation for both the child and the family. The stakes are too high for both sides to just be thrown together and see what happens. Visits in neutral settings focus on relationship building with family members.

✓ *Phase 2*, Time for reality, longer visits are combined with family counseling to help make the issues real. Strengths and weakness of everyone are put out for all to see.

✓ *Phase 3*, Time for commitment, #1 commitment to time and getting to know each other, #2 commitment to relationship, and #3 commitment to a life together. Both sides have a voice in how far they wish to go.

The staff member was trying to gain some rapport by showing a four-year-old that he had a skin scrape just like the one the child got on the playground. The four-year-old, who apparently was part lizard said, "Oh no, I'm not hurt, I am growing out of my skin."

Chapter

11

Attachment Disorders And Success In Life

The attachment process has been a particular interest of mine for over fifteen years. Based on my assessment and treatment work in the field of attachment, I was asked by Beverly James to contribute to her 1994 volume *Handbook for Treatment of Attachment-Trauma Problems in Children* (James, 1994). Fourteen years ago, I developed a scale to determine the severity of attachment problems in children. This scale was printed in *Raising Children Who Refuse To Be Raised* (Ziegler, 2000) and is a tool our program uses today. Also found in Chapter 3 of this book is a comprehensive section on attachment, both theory and treatment. While appreciated by professionals, many readers found this discussion of attachment too technical and complex.

It is my intention in this chapter to approach attachment somewhat differently. I will outline the many areas that affect the bonding process and hopefully provide an easy-to-understand look at the problems of and the solutions for one of the most serious precursors to interpersonal, social and mental health problems in our society. If we can prevent the disruption of attachment and skillfully restore attachment that has been

245

damaged, this will do more for the mental health of our nation than any single endeavor.

The Biological Role of Attachment

The role attachment plays for humans can be summed up in one short statement — attachment enhances survival. Humans are poorly prepared on a physical level for their environment at birth. Most of the elements that other members of the animal kingdom possess to physically manage their environment are missing in newborn humans. For example, humans cannot withstand temperature variations due to the absence of fur to keep us warm. Our vision is poorly developed at birth. We have very limited ability to move and are completely unable to physically fight off or flee from danger. Our strongest weapon to enhance survival in the long run is a liability early in life, and that is this large head that is so out of proportion with our body size that we can't even support its weight without outside help.

Because humans are so slow to mature when compared to other animals, nature builds in elements that promote survival through instinct. It is clear that among the endangered species on the planet, humans are not one of them. In fact, from a Darwinian perspective, it could be said that humans are such a dominate species and have eliminated predators so successfully (other than other humans) that the planet is suffering from over-population and the resulting consequences of so many members of one species on the larger ecosystem. Despite the fact that humans are not independently ready to face the world at birth, what provides their excellent success at survival is their instinctual drives.

For an infant to survive, many factors must come together. Nourishment must be obtained quickly and frequently. Threats must be avoided. A proper temperature range must be maintained. All these and a long list of other basic needs must be met. The infant must be able to enlist the help of a care provider to take care of all the survival issues for the child. To accomplish this critical task, nature builds in very specific instinctual methods to gain the attention and elicit help from the care provider, which is usually the mother. Survival requires instinctual attachment. Taking a closer look, we can see that the vulnerability of the child enlists the instinct of the care provider to step forward and provide help. The child's poor eyesight first develops close range vision, just in time to imprint the face of the mother and to remember this face. The child may have a limited ability to move, but instinct will drive the child to move toward the mother. It is critical for the child to communicate to the mother the many basic needs that will come up. The child has a well-developed ability to cry and scream at a decibel level rivaled only by rock bands and ambulance sirens. The sounds of distress are met with the mother's instinctual response to reach out and help. When successful, the child communicates pleasure through cooing sounds, smiles, and cuddling. Very few mothers can resist the call to action set off by the communication of young children. This instinctual response is so strong that women, in particular, generally find all babies very cute and generalize to all little creatures. For example, my wife finds most any small living thing cute except for roaches and garden slugs (this nuance may have reincarnation ramifications that I dare not pursue).

The overwhelming percentage of time that the instinctual process successfully plays out its role within both the child and the mother to ensure survival is a testament to the wonder and mystery of attachment itself. However as we will see, this process does not always play out so successfully.

Why a Secure Attachment Is Critical for Success in Life

While attachment is an instinctual process in humans and as natural as breathing and self-preservation, it is also a very complex process that is greatly influenced by multiple factors. Among these factors are genetics, environmental influences, instinctual imprinting, and brain development. Through genetics, the normal, healthy human has been provided the ability to recognize and to accept the protection and nurturing the individual needs. This same individual will be prepared to have all his or her basic physical and emotional needs met early in life by a supportive family. The instinctual process will flow both ways, from mother to child and back to the mother. The healthy attachment process will promote within the brain a positive disposition toward connection with others, along with the neural pathways that promote attachment.

Attachment is a complex process that is vulnerable to disruption if any of these factors becomes an obstacle for the individual. People do not decide to develop attachment problems. The foundations of attachment are some of the earliest neurological developments taking place within humans. We don't have conscious memories of the early bonds we develop (or don't develop), but our brains retain strong associations from these early events. Well before a child is two years of age, the fundamental disposition of the individual toward others is established at a personality level, unavailable to choices or decisions by the individual. If this process, either positive or negative, is not changed, it will usually continue throughout the life course of the individual, and will be one of the most prominent influences on the individual's social personality.

It is easy to imagine that individuals who distrust other people and attempt to avoid them have a profound barrier to finding fulfillment and happiness in life, which is usually based on interconnectedness to others. The disposition to mistrust and avoid connections with family and friends is usually caused by factors occurring early in life and related to attachment. What we can logically expect to find in negative attachment experiences is, in fact, what the research has found. Insecurely attached preschoolers do not do as well as securely attached peers (Belsky, 1988). Socially withdrawn children are more likely to have future social problems (Rubin, 1988). Insecure attachment has been linked with later behavioral problems (Erickson, 1985): negative disposition, poor empathy, and poor peer skills (Lewis, 1984). Less securely attached infants are less enthusiastic, persistent and cooperative than securely attached infants (Matos, Arend & Sroufe, 1978). Antisocial behavior stemming from poor early attachment has been correlated to: disproportionately high rates of alcoholism, accidents, chronic unemployment, divorce, physical and psychiatric illnesses, and welfare involvement (Caspi, 1987). Attachment is one of the more frequently researched issues in child development starting with the work of John Bowlby and Mary Ainworth and continuing today. Clearly, successful attachment is one of the most significant foundations for a successful person.

Because humans are inherently social creatures, we do not have the option to skip the part where we get along, trust and become interdependent on others. Our society has many adults who do not get along with others. They can even periodically appear successful either through becoming wealthy or gaining political power. But these adults are not among the happy nor fulfilled, and they make up a disproportionate number of our prison population, substance abusers and wandering street people. The goal of every major religion is to become one with self and/or a higher power. The foundation of love is to become one with the beloved. The inability to connect with others dooms the individual to roam the planet much as did Jacob Marley, epitomized in Dickens' *A Christmas Carol*. Either we are successful in human connections or we fail, but the result of this fundamental test is perhaps the most influential psychological predictor of success or failure throughout life.

Trauma and Attachment

It takes many factors to produce the ability to successfully connect with others, but it may only take one major deficiency to disrupt this ability. One of the most influential factors that affects successful attachment is significant trauma in the early years of life. Infants not only want to connect with a primary care provider (almost always a mother), their survival depends on it. Since we have a very strong drive to survive, the instinct to attach is every bit as strong. It takes a significant influence to dissuade the infant from attaching, and trauma is often that significant influence.

By the term trauma, I mean a substantially negative experience in which the child's life is either threatened or the child experiences enough pain and threat to believe survival is at risk, and the child's ability to cope is seriously compromised. While childhood trauma is most typically some form of child abuse, it can also be a serious medical problem or living through a natural disaster or wartime experience. A traumatic experience is exactly what humans do their very best to avoid at every point in their lives. The problem is that children seldom have any ability to influence their environment enough to avoid trauma on their own. The child's vulnerability adds to the fear and the threat of traumatic events. Vulnerability can also result in the child reliving the trauma repeatedly, because of the inability to guard against a repeat of the trauma.

In the very early days and months of life, the newborn does not have much room to make mistakes. If anything goes wrong, survival may be the price the child pays. The child is unable to consider this predicament in a rational way (the ability to reason will come later), but the child's survival mechanisms are tuned-in to good and bad messages coming from the environment. When the child runs into threats to basic needs, there may be little room to adapt and avoid the threat. In the past, we were wrong to assume that events that happened to children before they are able to have voluntary or explicit memory recall, could not affect the child in the long run. In fact, it is the early precognitive experiences that are the most profound for the child. In the normal attachment process, the infant seeks the warmth, nourishment, and touch from a primary care provider. When these basic needs are met by proximity to the care provider, the drive to attach is strengthened. However, the reverse is also true. When the basic needs of the child are not met, anxiety is created along with a variety of emotions that signal distress in the child's nervous system. When the child's basic needs are not met, as in child neglect, the child's internal alarm signals all go off. Because neglect produces such strong internal anxiety, it has been shown to have the most profound long-term negative ramifications. Either trauma or threat of trauma can cause distress related to vigilance, regulation of affect, attention and sleep patterns, and may result in a persistent stress response state. These biological responses can be compared to the anticipation of a soldier the night before going into battle. In such a state, little is important other than issues related to survival.

The Brain and Attachment

The human brain has one primary task — to ensure survival. Any threat to survival receives maximum attention from the child's mental processes. The brain develops from the more primitive to the more complex regions of the brain. This makes sense when you consider that the child will first need to have internal processes take care of body temperature and blood pressure, long before the child will need the discriminative ability to choose between orange or apple juice. The first area of the brain to develop is the brain stem that controls the involuntary body functions such as heart rate, breathing, digestion, some reflexes, blood pressure, and body temperature. The next region of the brain to develop is the diencephalon which controls motor regulation, balance, sensation, arousal, and sleep patterns. The next stage of brain development occurs within the limbic system, which controls emotions, hormones, appetite, the immune system, sexual appetites and attachment. Early trauma will have a direct impact on all three of these brain regions. Since the limbic system is more complex than the lower brain regions, it is in the developmental during the first year of life. Trauma during this time will substantially impact the developing limbic system, which not only controls attachment but also is associated with emotions and trauma memories.

To facilitate adaptation to whatever it finds in the environment (in order to ensure survival) the child's brain is 75% undeveloped at birth. The autonomic nervous system is developing its ability to respond to threat early in life by relying on the sympathetic (arousal or the on switch) and parasympathetic (off switch) nervous systems. These systems will allow the child to begin developing the fight or flight response to threat. Before the child has the ability to either fight or run, the only response he has is to signal interest to attachment figures or signal disinterest to threatening figures. When trauma impacts the early developing limbic system, a pattern develops of signaling disinterest to either certain adults or potentially all adults. All of the above brain functions are conducted without the influence of the higher brain functions in the neocortex, where thoughtful consideration will be the last stage of the brain to fully develop.

For the child traumatized early in life, the lower regions of the brain in essence do the thinking for the neocortex. By this I mean that, long before the child takes the time to consider if the adult in the room is the same or similar to the adult who caused the trauma (a higher reasoning function of the brain), the limbic system has already connected the adult to past trauma and signaled emotions as well as hypervigilance and heightened physiological arousal. The child will signal disinterest, fear, or rage before the higher regions of the brain have the time to consider the situation. Reactivity to associations of past stress is not restricted to infants or young children. Because trauma memories are associated with the limbic system and unavailable to the thoughtful regions of the brain, the child may develop a standard cycle of reactivity not only in early childhood but continuing into preadolescent and even teen years.

When trauma negatively affects the developing brain, particularly in the limbic area, the result is often the inability to regulate emotions. Most troubled children have this trait. When life goes differently than they wish it did, either in large or small ways, the result is an emotional meltdown. The inability to regulate affect is not only an issue with negative emotions, such as anger and frustration, but positive emotions are affected as well. Many adults love Christmas morning to see children opening presents with anticipation and excitement. Not me! My last 21 Christmas mornings have been spent watching troubled children face the positive stress of Christmas presents, and usually handling it badly. Children who have problems with self-regulation scream when they tear open the present, and yell what the present is as soon as they can tell, then they toss it aside, often in a rough manner, grab another present and start the cycle over again. I think Christmas morning is a challenge for most children, but it is an over-the-top experience when you have a room full of children who are unable to regulate all the feelings that are flying around. Teaching affect regulation will generally be a part of working with traumatized children.

When children are unable to modulate or manage their feelings, they lack the ability to understand or to care about the feelings of others. The result is a partial or complete lack of empathy. Empathy is both a simple concept and it can also be quite complex. We learn as young children not to hit our friends because it hurts when someone hits us back. Primitive forms of empathy can be taught to preschool children. More advanced forms of empathy are lost on many teens and even adults. Advanced levels of empathy involve the ability to put yourself in another's place and consider the implications of your actions or the actions of others on someone else. Antisocial personalities find such a process irrelevant. Criminals have little interest in the impact of their crimes on others. Developing the ability to empathize with others is a key factor in preventing criminal behavior.

Empathy must be taught to all children; it is not an inherent trait of humans. When the cavemen went hunting and only returned with one small animal for dinner, some ate and some did not. Survival might depend not on considering who else is hungry but on making sure some of the meal comes to you. It is not a surprise that the Old Testament transitioned into the New Testament with the message of Jesus to think of others, not just of yourself (the first shall be last, no greater love has a man than to give his life for a friend, the son of man did not come to be served but to serve, and treat others as you want to be treated). The 2,000 year-old message of Christianity is fundamentally about empathy. At times, standing in the parking lots after a Sunday service shows the message has not yet taken root with some Christians.

Teaching a troubled child empathy is a conceptual challenge. Even if you can encourage the child to consider the well-being and the feelings of someone else, what sense does it make to miss out on something just so someone else can have it? But if we are unable to help children learn empathy, the child will be caught in a world that cannot include real love, which requires consideration of the beloved, in other words empathy. Difficult children don't mind you thinking about them, they just don't see the point of thinking about you. However, as Francis of Assisi said nearly 1,000 years ago, the goal is not to be loved but to love. A life without love cannot meet the minimum requirements of a rich, successful life. Knowing why empathy is difficult for traumatized children does not always help a parent know how to instill this important element in a child. The interventions that lead to improved attachment will also help with the training of empathy.

Chemical Processes in the Brain Related to Attachment

The brain operates on electrical and chemical transmissions. Electrical impulses are transmitted within the neuron or brain cell. An electrical charge is transmitted from the receptors of the synapse through the axon and out the dendrite to the next neuron in the chain. The chemical transmission is stimulated by the electrical charge in the synapse and neurotransmitters pass over the synaptic cleft to stimulate an electrical charge in the next cell. If the chemical transmission is unsuccessful, the entire neurological process is disrupted, as in disorders such as depression and other mood disorders. Serious problems can also arise when electrical transmissions are disrupted causing disorders such as multiple sclerosis and other disorders in which brain signals are not transmitted effectively.

Trauma affects the chemical transmission of neurotransmitters. The brain has special neurotransmitters in case of emergency. These special chemicals include adrenaline and cortisol. These chemicals are like a smoke detector in a home, they are always ready to signal a serious problem. However, traumatized individuals frequently sense danger and the smoke detector is going off all day long. Each time the alarm is sounded, adrenaline and cortisol are released to aid in the response to serious danger. The problem is that the brain, like someone in a home with a faulty smoke detector, can never really relax since it is just waiting for the next alarm to go off. The other problem is that neurotransmitters like cortisol are harmful to neurons and to the synapses that they cross. If these substances are released only in real emergencies, they do not cause harm. However, when cortisol is released multiple times a day or perhaps many times an hour, the result is neurological damage. The brain must learn how to control how much cortisol is released. The off switch in the brain to cortisol release is directly affected by secure attachments in the individual's life. The allostatic process, which is the cycle of feeling increased stress and returning to relaxation, is enhanced by the individual's attachment with others.

Attachment Problems are Not Always Disorders

Before discussing how to work with children with attachment issues, I want to touch on some common misconceptions related to attachment. Although a major way attachment problems are indicated by children is through a variety of negative behaviors, attachment is not fundamentally about behavior. It is more accurate to say that behavior is the last step in the cycle of perceptions, impacted by past memories and recollections, resulting in feelings, that finally prompt behaviors. It is unhelpful to list all the common behavior problems found with children with attachment issues. The reason this is unhelpful is there are no definitive behaviors that distinguish attachment issues from several other psychological disorders. Books that print the litany of behaviors associated with these children tend to make parents believe that they have one of these attachment disordered children, which may or may not be true.

In *Raising Children Who Refuse To Be Raised* (page 190), I listed 20 of the most frequent characteristics found in difficult children. The big 20 are: inflexibility, oppositionality, irritability, explosive when tantruming, destructive, assaultive, sneaky and covert, rapid mood swings, anxious, erratic sleep patterns, excessive activity, precocious, preoccupied with death, reactive to change, rigid, controlling, over-stimulated, poor at making and keeping friends, manipulative, and intrusive. Reading this list, when it is associated with attachment problems, would lead parents to believe their child had the problem being discussed. The problem is that these 20 behaviors do not differentiate between the most common psychiatric disorders in children. Therefore, looking at behavior is not enough.

Another misconception is that children who show problems attaching with care providers always have an attachment disorder. Again, this may or may not be the case. Just as attention deficit hyperactive disorder has been over-diagnosed during the last fifteen years, attachment disorders have been frequently over-diagnosed in the last five years. While it is true that most children who have spent any time in substitute care (foster care, group homes, treatment centers) have developed issues around attachment, very few have an attachment disorder. Popular books that list problem behaviors and ask if you have an attachment disordered child in your home, inaccurately give parents and therapists the message that we have millions of attachment disordered children across the country. In reality attachment disorders are rare among children, however, attachment problems are frequent. What is the difference? A disorder is the most serious form of attachment issues, and most attachment problems are not serious enough to be a disorder.

If behavior is not enough to determine whether a child has an attachment disorder, how does one identify a disorder? It takes three factors: 1. Early developmental problems with trauma, abuse, separation from mother, serious inadequate care; 2. The quality of the attachment with present care providers measured in physical, interpersonal, emotional and core or spiritual traits; and 3. Behaviors consistent with the inability to bond and attach when it would be in the best interests of the child. All three issues are required. However, whether you have a child in your home with attachment problems or an attachment disorder, you are probably wanting to know what you can do to improve the situation. This is our next step.

What We Need to Know before We Fix the Problem

Children are not born with attachment problems, in fact natural instincts work to ensure the opposite. Attachment problems come from the brain's adaptability function that alters the goals of the individual based on what will best assist survival. When closeness to others results in threats to survival, the brain adapts to avoid closeness. This fact must be kept in mind if attachment problems are to be improved. This is the Hippocratic oath (do no harm) for attachment work — whatever you do, don't make it worse. The way you make attachment problems worse is to continue to reinforce the threats the child has previously experienced related to physical and emotional basic needs. You do not have to intend to reinforce the threats, the deciding factor is whether the child perceives you as a threat to basic survival needs.

A traumatized child does not have accurate perceptions. Early trauma has activated the brain's critical response system (the limbic system) to function most of the time on Code Orange (to borrow the Homeland Security color code) and to move to Code Red at the first sign of trouble. Because the brain has been through one or more threats to survival, new situations will be processed through past traumatic memories. The result is like our national defense system experiencing repeated false positives, or an alarm going off when there is no real threat. The first step with traumatized children with attachment issues, as it is with all children, is to avoid any threats or perceived threats to a child's basic needs. Ensuring safety and security would seem to be self-evident, but in fact, it is remarkable how many "attachment therapists" use interventions that precisely threaten the child. The reasoning provided is to get the attention of the child. Threats to basic needs will get the child's attention all right, as well as the attention of the limbic system's internal alarm producing fight or flight responses, release of stress neurotransmitters, and all input to the brain will be routed through the trauma memories. This systemic response will eliminate any potential of positive steps toward attachment, which require the absence of perceived threats to basic needs and therefore survival.

We need to understand that the child does not take into consideration bad things that have happened in his or her life and decide to keep adults at a distance. Consideration of a situation and developing a response are cognitions that take place in the neocortex or higher regions of the brain. The survival system in the brain steps in long before the child is capable of higher reasoning to understand environmental factors and developed a plan to address them. In a sense, both the parent and the child are dealing with a third party — the child's threat response system in the brain. This threat response system is not accessible to either the parent or to the child. It is much like a thermometer or barometer that responds to environmental sensors that record temperature or air pressure. The barometer is incapable of consideration, it simply is capable of reacting. The brain's threat response system (the limbic system) is similar in that it is set to automatically react under conditions of perceived threat.

Since the problem is in the brain, it is within the brain that real change will need to take place. We cannot scare a child into attaching. We cannot use physical pain as a part of attachment therapy. No amount of threat will make a child override the trauma memories and get the child to use higher regions of his or her brain to figure out that this a good person to attach to and not like others from the child's past. Every aspect of the solution must pass one central litmus test — any improvement must be made in the child's brain. We cannot simply observe the child's behavior and say our intervention was helpful; there are negative reasons why some children "bond" with persons they perceive as threatening. We cannot simply watch the child's emotional expressions. It may be that improvement in the brain has created honest but negative emotions, which is a good sign for children with attachment problems. To know if our interventions have been part of the solution and not a continuing part of the problem, we must understand the way the child's brain works, and the way it has processed our intervention.

It is important that we understand that there are several ways that children experience attachment. I discuss these in detail in

Raising Children Who Refuse To Be Raised, Chapter 3. I will briefly touch on the four ways here. The deepest level of attachment is a core level of the individual that I call spiritual attachment. Spiritual attachment is not the same as a religious experience, although a religious experience could be placed into this category. All humans begin life not only connected but also as biologically one organism with the mother. Our first experiences are of being a part of something greater than ourselves. We have an instinctive drive to remain a part of this larger self throughout infancy and into childhood. I would add that we continue to pursue in our lives the drive to become one with our larger self through intimate relationships, connection with our higher power, or pursuing any of the world's religions that all have a common denominator — to become one with God, our eternal or great spirit, the source of life or other expressions for the source of our deep internal longing. The infant experiences connection with the mother before experiencing separation as an independent self. This level of attachment is the most difficult to repair if damaged.

The second way we experience attachment is interpersonally. At the point we begin to differentiate ourselves from our mothers, we begin the long road to understanding that the social needs of humans requires connection to significant others as a necessity for true contentment.

The third way we experience attachment is in physical ways. Most of our basic needs relate to physical needs — nourishment, temperature regulation, and avoiding pain and discomfort. The midbrain is wired to sense if these physical needs are being met, and attachment is synonymous with meeting our physical needs.

The fourth way we experience attachment is the most fragile and sophisticated, which is emotional attachment. Much of life is measured by our ability to emotionally connect with others, particularly with significant others. It is difficult to call a person a success in life if he or she has been unable to connect with others emotionally. Successful interventions are going to address one or more of these ways we experience attachment. It is a good idea to develop a plan that will touch on each of the four areas.

The final point that we need to know before we develop interventions to improve attachment is that the age of the child is a very important consideration. We expect children to demonstrate a broad range of attachment, and as they age, the expectations grow exponentially (they double, triple and quadruple). This is one of the reasons why troubled children get more lost as they move into ever-widening social networks. Our large middle schools and massive high schools are frightening places for troubled children who do not understand the social requirements and nuances of social connections with peers and adults. We must take the age of the child into consideration as we plan to help the child bond and attach. The chronological age of the child is somewhat useful, but the developmental age of the child is more important. Traumatized children tend to have arrested development at the age the child was first exposed to significant threats. Since any real progress will take place in the brain, we must understand when, how and for how long the trauma affected the child, because this is where the brain's threat response system was first set into motion. With the above thoughts in mind, we can now consider interventions to improve a child's ability to attach to others.

Interventions Promoting Attachment

I received a call some time back from a psychology professor at a university. He had heard of my work in the area of attachment and had some pointed questions. His major question was "What is attachment therapy?" He was polite, but seemed to have made up his mind about the question before calling me. His energy suggested that he didn't believe there was such a thing as attachment therapy. What he had observed that went by the name of attachment therapy had not impressed him. My response to him was a suggestion that people should avoid most of what is called attachment therapy. My experience has been that, with the exception of professionals who devote much of their professional lives to studying, writing and researching a specific psychological problem area, many therapists who call themselves "specialists" can cause more problems than they solve. What children and families need is the wisdom and understanding that comes from seeing the big picture of problem areas such as attachment. A specialist often means no more than a therapist who has seen many cases of a particular problem. If a professional sees too much of one type of problem, he or she runs the risk of getting into a diagnostic and therapeutic rut and seeing children in categories rather than as unique compositions of history, genetics, environment and the individual's response to all of this.

The professor pressed on and said no one had ever defined attachment therapy to his satisfaction. I told him that I believed there was such a thing as attachment therapy, as there are such things as depression therapy or trauma therapy. This does not mean that attachment therapy is a packaged model, in fact a packaged model would be on my list to avoid. He again asked for my definition of attachment therapy. To lay the groundwork I said attachment therapy could include a variety of approaches, settings and styles. However, unless the treatment includes the following components, I would not consider it attachment therapy.

1. Within the context of a safe and secure setting, which the child experiences as safe and secure;

2. The child's basic needs must be unconditionally met, including not only air, food and water, but also the psychological needs outlined in this book;

3. Consistent invitations to connect are extended by people in the child's life; and finally,

4. A reciprocal world must be created where the child only receives what he or she wants (other than basic needs) if the child gives something in return.

The professor seemed surprised and said that my definition of attachment therapy made good sense, and he proclaimed that I had passed his test. He told me that what had been presented to him as "attachment therapy" would not have met my definition; however, he could support a therapy based on my four principles. Before he hung up the phone, I cautioned him that much like the simplicity of Jesus' statement that forms the basic foundation of Christianity: love God and love your neighbor as yourself, the four principals of attachment therapy are easier to list than to live.

Principal #1 should be easy to understand as the first requirement. Attachment problems are created early in life when any threat to basic needs develops a reaction that can lead to long-term problems. I would hope that meeting a child's basic physical needs would not be questioned, but I have found otherwise. Some interventions done under the banner of expensive attachment therapy actually withhold basic needs on purpose. I have consulted on "attachment therapy" cases in which children are deprived of contact with their mother, deprived of food or made to eat food tainted with a foul taste, deprived of water or forced to drink excessive amounts of water, deprived of sleep, threatened with physical harm, held in painful ways while the "therapist" yells in the child's face, or an adult prods or physically irritates the child until she screams, etc. These approaches would meet a general definition of tactics used to brainwash prisoners of war; but by definition, the use of these threats to basic needs would eliminate the intervention from my conditions or for that matter from acceptable and ethical psychotherapy. Without this first step, treatment and improved attachments cannot be successfully achieved.

Principal #2 builds upon #1 but adds that basic needs cannot be conditional. Most of us have had a parent get so flustered they have said something like, "Pick up your room now or you will go to bed without any dinner." In a home where food is plentiful, an occasional less than impressive parenting intervention of this type will not cause real harm. This cannot be said of children with serious attachment issues. If the child's basic needs become conditional upon anything, this means the environment has signaled the ability to and interest in withholding survival needs. The child's brain processes this information in relationship to past trauma, and the child goes into hypervigilance and survival reactivity. No treatment can be successful when a child is in flight or fight mode.

Principal #3 may be the most difficult step in working with a child with a serious attachment disorder. The difficulty is that children say and behave in ways to push you away. The child is often very skilled at increasing the pressure on you to walk away and leave him or her alone. It takes a very special adult, in the face of unpleasant and distasteful behaviors and attitudes from the child, not to give the child what she says she wants — to be left alone. The wise adult knows that, at a deeper level, the child does not want to be left alone, but these children can be very convincing and effective in having you look elsewhere and give your love to someone who wants it. In the face of abuse, foul language, constant disrespect, name calling, and disgusting habits, principal #3 requires that invitations to connect are still extended. I used the analogy of Christianity earlier, and it may be easier to love your enemies than to constantly extend invitations to connection with this unpleasant little terrorist in training, posing as an adoptive or foster child in your home.

Principle #4 is the long, hard road to improvement. Steps 1 through 3 are prerequisites, but without #4 they may not create more damage, but they will not move the child in a positive direction. Reciprocity is fundamental to successful social relationships. Children learn very early that hitting a friend with a stick may cost you the friendship. Reciprocity is basic to the golden rule, treating others as you would like to be treated. Reciprocity is the foundation of friendships, partnerships, lovers, business associates, politics, and all social relations. It is precisely the principle of reciprocity that causes concern for significant political contributions, as in what does the contributor expect in return? By definition we call relationships in which one person gets what they want and the other person pays the price an unhealthy arrangement. Children with serious attachment issues missed this important lesson along the way while they were preoccupied with surviving. If the child is to have any future social success in life, a precondition for being a successful human being, the child will need to learn reciprocity.

No young child comes to adults asking for lessons in reciprocity. They want ideas in how they can get more of what they want from others, not how to give more to others. Children with attachment problems are much less interested in whether other people get something out of an interaction with them. The only way I know to interest these children in learning reciprocity is to require the child to learn this principle regardless of his interest or willingness to do so. For years I have run into criticism of my use of the term emotional coercion. I have been asked to find another term because of the harsh associations with being physical or violent coercion. This term does have some very strong meanings in the dictionary, but I use emotional coercion in the same context as compelling the child to do something she would not do on her own, and there is quite a list of these lessons — sharing, listening, bathing, and many others.

One meaning of both to coerce and to compel is that the individual simply must to do it. My method of accomplishing this is to set up the condition that for the child to get the many things he wants (and children with attachment problems want a great many material things), the child must give something in return. Give and take begins as a primitive lesson in giving something to receive something in return, but it must become habitual and eventually natural for the child. The only way I have found to have this happen is to ensure that the child is successful in getting much of what he wants, and along the way he learns more and more not to object to the other person getting something as well. I am not saying that the child for the near future actually cares about the other person, but over time the child learns that these two factors go hand-in-hand: I give something, I get something. Even monkeys can be trained to perform a task for a treat. Your little monkey may be more challenging because he knows what you are trying to do. You can still have success in teaching reciprocity even when they know what you are after, if the return is worth the child's investment.

Repetition is an essential ingredient in the brain forming new neural pathways to assist in changing feelings and behaviors. The fact that, the child does not care if the other person gets something as long as the child gets what he wants should not be of initial concern. Just as parents should not refrain from teaching a child to say polite words, such as please and thank you, even when the child does not care about the concept of being polite. We often use the expression, "fake it until you make it." What approximation of behavior means on a brain level is that the brain will need to repeat a certain process multiple times until it becomes habitual, and then the higher regions of the brain can understand the significance of the process that is now ingrained.

In this discussion of attachment therapy you have noticed that I have not talked about using any particular system of interventions, I have not even mentioned professional help. This comes from my belief that children with attachment problems heal (or do not heal) in real life and not primarily in a therapist's office. It is often helpful to have a therapist on your team working with you, but there will be no magic insight that happens on the psychiatrist's couch. However, other than ensuring that 1) safety is not threatened or 2) made conditional, 3) a relationship is desired by the adults, and 4) reciprocity is built into the skill training, how you want to achieve all this is really open to your preference, skill level and your creativity. The good attachment work being done will meet these four principals, and the attachment therapy that does not meet them should, in my opinion, be not only avoided but banned to protect children from harm.

What about the situations in which children who go through systems of "attachment therapy," where the parents pay large amounts of money for two-week intensives, physically intrusive interventions, and other interventions that do not meet the four principals, and yet parents report improvement? This is a common question I receive. I attended a show by a magician recently and I came away with the lesson "do not believe everything you think you see." There are many ways to explain a short-term change in the behavior of a child with attachment problems. Here are some principles traumatized children live by: *If you are threatened, go along with the person to stay safe. Pay special attention to anyone in the environment who can prevent you from getting what you need or want. Align yourself with the one who has the power in the situation. The quickest way to get rid of professionals is to tell them what they want to hear.*

It is not a mystery that a child's short-term emotions and behavior often change when subjected to a holding therapy intensive including harsh behavior, deprivations and physically intrusive interventions. Even the most self-assured among us if abducted, held for ransom, and during a two-week ordeal were subjected to deprivations and threats, would radically change our emotions, and behavior as well. However, this change would last in full force only during the abduction, and then gradually return to what was normal before the event. This is one aspect of the Patty Hearst or Stockholm Syndrome, in which the abducted person aligns with the captive holding the power in thought and behavior but only for the short-term. In relation to brain development, the change can only be short-term because there is the need for continual repetition over a long period of time — not days or weeks, but months and years.

The national network and industry built around "holding therapy/physically intrusive therapy/attachment intensives" is not the only professional help to avoid. There are other types of ineffective treatments that accomplish nothing except reducing excess money in your bank account. Among these I place long-term non-directive therapy with few goals and little involvement by the parents. I also do not recommend hoping one approach in isolation will have any major impact (it will not), such as only using play therapy for young children. Any treatment that promises quick progress should be avoided. As we have discussed, the only quick change that can happen to a traumatized child is a quick negative change. I also would suggest that any treatment not showing some progress in meeting goals after six months should be reconsidered. Finally, if a treatment defies common sense, stay away from it.

Interventions That Work

For over fifty years a great deal of energy and interest has gone into the question of the effectiveness of psychological interventions. New therapies and approaches have come and gone, each saying they were the newest idea and more effective than the rest. However, over and over again the result of independent scientific research has been that the newest approach not only fails to be better, but for the most part, the approach or technique is not what actually produces success. There are core elements that have been shown to be the determining factors to an approach being effective regardless of the techniques used. These core elements are: facilitating catharsis, developing a positive relationship between the therapist and client, providing a new perspective and ideas to see the problems in a new way, teaching behavioral regulation, and enhancing cognitive learning and mastery by practicing making life changes (Lambert & Bergin, 1994). I believe attachment interventions are like all psychological interventions. It is not the techniques that make the difference, it is whether the approach addresses the core elements of effective therapy as well as the four additional principles I have outlined for traumatized children.

To do effective attachment interventions, you do not need an institute or attachment center, you do not need a specialist with an M.D. or Ph.D., you do not need an expensive battery of interventions. What you need to have effective interventions is an environment where the adults work together and create the conditions that will train the child's brain to adapt to a new and more positively social world.

In the long run it is unlikely to accomplish effective attachment work without a family which is committed to and knowledgeable of the child's wants and needs. At times attachment therapy may need to begin in a residential setting due to the seriousness of the child's behavior. However, the proof of the pudding is when the child is faced with the expectations of bonding with a family; this step cannot take place without the involvement of an interested family.

The most effective attachment work happens in a family setting. It is possible that a family can do excellent attachment therapy without the involvement of any professionals. However, because of the complexity of understanding what the child really needs, regardless of what he says and how he acts, and the pressure these children place on parents, I suggest it is a good idea to have a team of people working together. Such a team may include a professional who acts as a coach, respite resource, school staff, relative, youth activity leader, youth pastor, or whoever is involved in the child's life.

Recent research in the effectiveness of interventions with difficult children has shown that the more involved the "village" is with the child, the better the chance for success. Community teams are simply the best way to go. This is despite the potential need to have the child spend some time in a residential placement to extinguish behavior that is dangerous to self or others. The team needs to form early in the treatment process, meet often initially, and ensure that everyone understands the treatment direction. The team's feedback is an important way to assess if progress toward goals is being achieved. It may be that problems at school increase while improvement at home is starting, or perhaps the reverse. It takes multiple views of the child to determine if the overall approach is working. The goals I suggest are to follow the four points outlined earlier. Problems with attachment are long-term issues. It takes years for such problems to develop, and it will take years of focus to prepare the child to learn the skills of being a social success.

Residential Treatment Can Help with the Most Serious Attachment Problems

A decade ago I was asked how we develop an environment to work with children with serious attachment problems. My answer was the following, which was first printed in *Handbook for Treating Attachment-Trauma Problems in Children* (James, 1994).

An attachment disorder is much like many other issues in our society wherein we coin a new term for a very old problem, and then scare ourselves with details of how bad it is. Don't misunderstand, an attachment disorder is a serious problem, but it is not what it has been presented to be by sensational stories and made-for-TV books. Children with attachment disorders are just that — children. They are difficult, yes; they can be hurtful, yes again; but they are not lost causes, much less developing serial killers, as some would have you believe. Our program works with these difficult children every day, and we see clear progress in nearly all of them.

But Does It Work?

This is my favorite question to be asked. We have a comprehensive pre- and post-testing analysis of every child in our program. We collect seven measures on each child including: skills, treatment issues, health, behavior, attitudes, overall functional assessment and level of attachment. These measures include over 200 factors. We also formally track all program graduates for 5 years after discharge. The results? 94% of serious behaviors were eliminated or no longer serious. There was an 89% improvement in daily living skills, 87% improvement in communication, and 86% improvement in socialization measured on a standardized instrument. There was a 62% average improvement on specific clinical objectives, and 94% of the children with an attachment disorder improved relationship skills. In our follow-up after 194 interviews over six years tracking 21 measures of success with very seriously disturbed children, the data indicates they are functioning much better in nearly all areas than they did before treatment. The children actually show more progress six months after treatment than at graduation and show no deterioration in skills at the five-year follow-up. Five years after treatment, the children as a group are demonstrating strengths in 75% of the success criteria, and demonstrating problems in only 5% of the areas we believe reflect personal success. Does our treatment work with the most difficult children? The data leave little doubt.

In our program's assessment and tracking over a five-year period with 67 children having a Reactive Attachment Disorder diagnosis, nearly all are living with a family and 94% have improved relationship skills.

There are tens of thousands of children in our systems of "care," which means we have far too many children who have not been cared for where it counts — in their families. These children often have defenses and a tough shell that few people can penetrate. Without a knowledgeable and understanding care provider, the child's defenses often lead to problems in reaching out and bonding.

Most children in our substitute care system have attachment issues rather than attachment disorders. Without someone reaching them while they are still more connected to family than to peer groups (usually under the age of twelve), these children may well become the delinquents and criminals of tomorrow. The cell blocks of our prisons today are filled with the youngsters whose needs were not met by our system of care in the past. For these children it is either pay now — with additional resources for social workers, therapists, and trained foster parents — or pay later with free room and board in our correctional institutions. These children may well be the criminals of tomorrow, but they should not be confused with children with a true attachment disorder.

Children with a severe attachment disorder have never had a successful attachment to anyone. Children with a mild to moderate disorder have had only partial bonds and have never truly attached to care providers in their short lives. These children start life in the first twelve to eighteen months with failure in the most basic of instincts in human beings: bonding immediately. Bonding skills are essential first of all to survive and then to find a successful place in the interdependent world of other human beings. When things go badly to begin with, the instinct to bond (promoting physical survival) is overridden by avoiding the pain and neglect of attaching (emotional survival). The seeds of attachment are often sown long before the results are observed. Without a disruption in the cycle of an attachment disorder, it may grow into a lifelong and unsuccessful search for a place in the social network of our society.

I believe we are still in a phase where as a society we are not sure how to help these children. In our confusion and to some extent desperation, we have developed what appear to be desperate therapies, and some parents, professionals, and programs believe these intrusive approaches are all that can work [this is as true in 2004 as in 1994 when I first wrote these words]. I suggest that we take our desperation and first work to clearly understand the problem and its causes; and then commit the necessary resolve and patience to test our solutions. I would like to share with you one such patient testing ground, which is a small residential treatment program call Jasper Mountain Center.

How Jasper Mountain Started

The center was founded by three baby boomers who were raised by their own families with varying levels of health as well as dysfunction. Armed with college degrees, professional experience and seemingly unlimited energy, the three of us set out to make a difference in the world, following the advice of Mother Teresa — one person at a time. The goal was to create a seamless integration of our home life and our professional work. This goal has been quite effectively reached, and we are not clear to this day whether this has been as good for us as it has been for the program's children. The practical steps are easy enough to recount: endless meetings to determine the criteria to find the healthiest place in the United States to live, moving to the promised land in southern Oregon, and purchasing a rural ranch.

After six months of acclimating and very long days fixing-up the old ranch, we informed the state child protection agency that we were ready for their most challenging young children. The reaction from the state's workers was one of equal parts elation and suspicion. Elation that people interested in accepting very disturbed children into their home would also be experienced professionals with counseling backgrounds. There was also suspicion as to why people who had a choice would want very disturbed children in their home. Eleven years later [*this has now grown to 21 years at this point*], there are those who still have suspicions. When you commit your life to helping children, over time you learn to ignore the suspicious people.

Jasper Mountain Center was founded in 1982 on an eighty-acre ranch in the foothills of the Cascade mountains southeast of Eugene, Oregon. The scenery was beautiful enough, with two major rivers, heavily wooded forest, waterfalls, an artesian spring, miles of hiking trails, and sheer cliffs rising to a thousand-foot mountain, all of which were on the property. The ranch even had quite a history as part of the second homestead in this region of Oregon and the end of the Oregon Trail for the pioneering parents of Jasper Hills. To this beauty and history we worked to bring hope to some very confused and abused children.

From the beginning the children came to Jasper Mountain telling their stories of abuse and pain. The program quickly turned its focus to healing the scars of sexual abuse, which was present in almost all the children. We soon learned that some children healed very differently from others, and that some didn't seem to heal at all. Of all the children, there were those who didn't look at you, would push away any affection, and were quick to use and abuse you as they had been used and abused themselves. In the early 1980s, we began identifying children who had bonding problems, and invariably they were the most difficult of our difficult children.

How the Program Works

Jasper Mountain is based on principles of health in body, mind and spirit. The program ensures clear air, clean water, plenty of exercise, and treatment components in a context of a family where the parents are professionals. This family focus has turned out to be the most important ingredient in the therapeutic stew. Not that being in a family makes much difference to attachment-disordered children; but in the final analysis, it is the ability of the family and its staying power that will make the difference in the bonding process. In the early years, the three of us did everything without outside help. At this point the program has the state's highest classification for supervision and treatment, which requires one staff for every three children [*ten years after originally writing this the State of Oregon has now closed its State Hospital for young children and the funding and children are sent to us*].

The program uses four basic categories of intervention: environmental, behavioral, psychotherapeutic, and self-esteem.

- Environmental intervention creates a therapeutic Disneyland, but rather than the happiest place on earth, we strive for the healthiest place on earth. There is close scrutiny to every environmental aspect of the program, from the architecture of the buildings to the diet the children eat; from the amount of natural light to the control of violent themes that reach the children from the outside world (e.g., we have no commercial TV).

- Behavioral interventions include the mundane but important behavior management systems wherein the children earn points that determine privileges and earned money. At Jasper Mountain the children have a behavioral system for the residence and another for the on-site school [*ten years later we base points on progress in specific treatment issues*]. Although the point system is the most traditional part of the program, the children get up each morning and go straight for the chart to find out what level they are on for the day. Modifying behavior is an important step, but is only a beginning step in treatment. Behavioral ways to require a give-and-take framework are essential with children with an attachment disorder.

- Psychotherapeutic interventions include all the individual, group and family therapy interventions, as well as art and play therapy and much more. Interventions also include occasional medications and sessions with the program's psychiatrist. Each child has a therapist and an assigned staff person serving as a type of big brother/big sister to promote skills at developing relationships with multiple adults.

- Self-esteem intervention is where some of the unique aspects of the program can be found. These include a variety of routes to the self-worth of the child, including concentration and meditation training, therapeutic recreation, an equestrian program, hiking and rock climbing, jogging, gardening, visual and performing arts, computer competency, positive video feedback to enhance the self-image of the children, and many others.

But even with magical interventions like the above (and on the full list there is something that every child will find magical), there is no guarantee that an attachment-disordered child will use any of these interventions to improve his or her disposition toward others. With this background, the focus turns to specific approaches used for these challenging children.

What Makes the Difference?

At Jasper Mountain we are often asked why children with attachment disorders who can strike fear into the hearts of parents, caseworkers, and therapists are not feared in our program. And here is step #1 in making a difference with these children: they must not be feared or their controlling nature takes over. Relationships with these children are often initially no less than warfare. In this struggle for dominance, if the child wins, everyone loses; and if the adult wins, everyone wins. I see it as just that simple. Of course, how to win the struggle with these masters of control is not simple at all.

The fact that we do not fear these children in our program may come from the fact that no matter how skilled they are, so far none has been able to win the control war at Jasper Mountain although they all try [*ten years later we can still say this*]. In most cases the children, who are usually very bright, realize within weeks that they may be able to control an individual staff person momentarily, but not for very long and certainly not the whole program.

Let The Battle Begin!

Allen arrived at our program with the confidence he would soon rule the roost, much like in each of the four families he had lived with. He was well-practiced in ignoring, arguing, refusing, glaring, threatening and if needed, striking out physically. He had a swagger that said, "Back off or pay the price." The first couple days he was sizing me up as he tried his tricks on other staff. Finally he let it fly with me, he tried ignoring, arguing, etc., but to no avail. He would have to go the distance with me, the director of the program, but the victory would be well worth the extra effort. One morning he demanded to go to his room and I told him to wait. He went anyway and I entered his room and asked him if my instruction was unclear, he ignored me. I matter-of-factly told him he could leave the room of his own power or he would receive my help. He glared at me and I brought him out of the room. He called me a jerk and said he was going to "kick my butt." Later in the day he told another staff person, "I think I threatened the wrong jerk." The next morning when he saw me, he not only followed my directions, but he gave me a compliment. I told him either way, threats or compliments, he would be held accountable. He put his head down and went off to school concluding round #1.

Another factor critical to our success with these children is to work as a team and control all variables in the child's life — therefore producing a unified approach. In our program there is only changing buildings to go from the residence to the school; the approach and staff act in unison. We take time to work with caseworkers and family members so that the methods the child has used to irritate, control, and keep others distant, do not work on campus or with the family.

Treatment with these children not only must strip them of their remarkably intricate insulation and defenses, but also must provide a real and attractive alternative. How can getting close ever look attractive to a child with an attachment disorder? The answer is as simple as the first principle of negotiation — you get some of what you want only when you give something the other person wants. Despite attempting to look otherwise, these children have many material interests. They are generally extremely motivated by material belongings, although they believe that if you knew this, it would make them vulnerable, and thus they pretend to be apathetic to almost everything. When the child tells you with a calm tone, "Punish me, take away all my toys and ground me until I am 18, I don't care," don't believe it.

Children with attachment problems will take without giving, if you let them. You must teach them reciprocity and hold them accountable. There must be a constant pressure to connect. With normal children (has anyone seen one of these lately?) coercion is not a positive or useful approach. But with these children, they get dessert only after a polite request; they go to see the movie only after doing a chore for you; they play fifteen minutes of Play Station only after sharing two important events at school today. The approach is clear: You don't get something for nothing (except love and other basic needs).

The effectiveness of treating these children comes down to every interaction between all adults and the child. This means that every contact between a program staff member and the child is a very small part of the puzzle; but each interaction is critical to the overall picture. Manipulative children do not change if their tricks work on anyone. If the therapist and parents work together, but the school is out of the loop, the child will never change. When the child's manipulations work, the principle of intermittent variable reinforcement is involved, the same principle that brings confident gamblers to Las Vegas to lose their money time after time. Just like the hopeful gambler, the child tells himself that he will prevail in the end.

As stated before, these children are usually quite smart, and when they understand that they must work to get what they want, here is their sequence: they start by not doing it, to see if you get flustered; then they do it halfway and grudgingly (punishing you); then, if they must do it right, they will do it, but with a bad attitude; and eventually they just do it. These progressive steps occur only when they must do their part to get what they want. When this pattern is repeated over and over for years, the psychological principle of cognitive dissonance steps in, which says that if your behavior changes, eventually your attitude must change, and if your attitude changes, then your behavior must eventually change as well.

You must demand that children with attachment disorders do just what you want of them (which are progressive steps toward relationships). They need not do it with an open heart or with honesty, they just need to do it. What you begin to systematically show them is that they will not be abused when they are vulnerable, and that the world where you get what you want by being close to others is far superior to using others and being emotionally and personally alone in the world.

The last factor that makes a difference is a four-letter word: *time.* Time is a four-letter word in our culture because we don't want to take the time to do most anything right. We are irritated by the traffic light that delays us two minutes; we want the flu medicine that gives us fast, fast relief; and incredibly we are impatient when we need to wait two and a half seconds to store our documents on our older model computer. Is it any wonder that we flinch at the prospect of taking years to treat an attachment disorder? This may have something to do with the do-it-quick "holding" therapies that promise some bonding after an intensive weekend, or at least after the twelve-week special. Some may believe that the patterns of withdrawal and distance in a true attachment disorder can be extinguished relatively quickly, and a new pattern of interdependency and vulnerability learned soon after, but I do not believe there is any shortcut to the years of concentrated effort described above. For the *Star Trek* generation, where any galactic problem is solved within the hour, years of effort are inconceivable, but they are truly necessary to make progress with attachment disorders.

To be fair to all us parents who have a child with an attachment disorder in our home (we had one by adoption), we would have a better chance at putting in years of effort if only we saw some progress, even tiny successes, or at least the reassurance that we were heading in a direction other than futility and exasperation. This is precisely what our program tries to give parents — a road map. We all know that human beings take at least twelve years to raise before the onset of their teen years. Our current thinking is that the relearning process may take five to seven years. I believe parents can find the strength to persist if they are shown a way that works, as long as they don't get a false message that there is a quick fix.

The Jasper Mountain method works — whether it is the place, the people, approach, the time invested, or all of the above simultaneously. The important thing is that the program wears the child's defense down before the child wears the staff down. We do not describe the children as "cured" when they leave Jasper Mountain. Attaching is not only an instinct, it is also a skill. We should not leave children in a rather scary and indifferent world without their defenses, unless they are given new tools to succeed in the game of life. It takes a very long time to learn how to bond even after the children decide they want to. This is usually a process of unlearning and then relearning. It is important that we not lead these children down this long road to healing if we are not prepared to go the distance. In residential care this means that you never completely close a case. Our program's graduates keep in touch, come by, borrow money, and bring by their fiancés to meet the family. We have invited our children into our extended family, and nearly all accept.

In adoptions we must understand that there may be no other chance for these children. Due to the time it takes to free a child for adoption, to place the child in the right home, and to invest the five to seven years with him or her, there may not be time for a "Plan B" to start the process over with another family. This may sound like a great deal of responsibility for the adoptive family, but if real bonding doesn't happen in the first adoptive family, it may never happen.

Perhaps the ultimate betrayal is to take a child who is dependent on others for her very life, thwart her survival instinct by not placing her where she can form an attachment, fail to help her connect with others during her early years, and expect her to live the rest of her life emotionally and spiritually alone and separated from friends, a spouse, her own children, and even God. It comes very close to a definition of hell, doesn't it? I hope you agree with all of us at Jasper Mountain that years of hard work are not too high a price to pay to save the quality of life for a child with an attachment disorder.

Since the above was written over ten years ago, nearly all of what was said then is still true about our program today. We are now larger, we have a more critical role in our state's mental health system, and we have better defined what it is that works about our treatment of these children. We also have a decade worth of treatment outcomes to show that our efforts produce positive results in nearly all the children. Even some of the most serious children not only are forming significant relationships in their lives, but they even contact us with the unthinkable — a thank you for "not giving up on me and helping me learn how to be happy and successful." What has not changed over the last ten years is our belief that consistency over a long and difficult journey is the only road to success.

Assessing Attachment Problems and the Attachment Disorder Assessment Scale — Revised

A perplexing issue for therapists and parents is how to know if your child has an attachment disorder. Taking the child for a psychological or mental health evaluation does not always provide answers. At times the diagnosis Reactive Attachment Disorder is given to children when there is some other problem that better explains the child's behavior. Other times the diagnosis is not given when it should have been due to a lack of understanding of this issue. Most professionals agree that the starting place to determine the level of the attachment problems of the child is a comprehensive evaluation with close attention to the experience of the primary care provider as well as attention to the quality of the interaction between the family members and the child.

A recent review of the psychology literature came up with over 5,000 psychological instruments to help identify various problems of every sort imaginable. Of these measures, there are a small group of instruments designed to assess attachment issues in children. Attachment measures can be categorized into several types: laboratory observations, naturalistic observations, clinical interviews, narrative picture assessment, play therapy, and caregiver self-reports. In a review of the attachment literature, 37 instruments were found that are designed to assess the attachment problems in children (Fairchild-Kienlen, 2001). Each of the different categories of assessments have strengths and also weaknesses. However, for validity and practicality in assessment attachment, it is difficult to match self-report measures provided by care providers. Of the ten existing self-report measures concerning attachment issues in children, there is little research available that is independent, normed on a multi-ethnic and broad geographical population of children with and without attachment problems. One exception is the Attachment Disorder Assessment Scale — Revised or ADAS-R.

Originally developed 15 years ago, the ADAS was designed to be a quick and easy screening of the issues most likely to identify the level of attachment concerns presented by a child. This instrument does not require specialized training and is completed by a primary care provider of the child in less than 15 minutes. The scale is based on constructs of attachment found both in attachment theory and in diagnostic identification. The population upon which the author based the scale was severely disturbed children with and without serious attachment problems, as well as children with no mental health treatment history. The instrument has 40 questions in three areas of interest: developmental history, quality of relationships, and personality traits. The author found that all three areas were necessary for the accurate assessment of the level of attachment issues with a child. The ADAS was developed incrementally over a number of years and has been used as an assessment and outcome measure in the author's treatment program since 1989. After development, the instrument was subsequently modified in 1999 after 10 years of use.

The ADAS was the subject of a major independent research study in 2001 (Fairchild-Kienlen, 2001). The principal researcher used a sample of over 500 children ages 3-13 from five states (Texas, Georgia, Ohio, New Mexico and Virginia). This sample was large enough to provide statistical power as well as include an ethnic sample approximately similar to the U.S. population (68% Caucasian, 17% African American/Bi-racial, 10% Latino and 5% Asian). The sample was approximately equal as to gender, and the children lived in six types of family placements (biological 39%, foster 35%, adoptive 16%, grandparents 4%, kinship care 1% and step parents 1%). Thirteen descriptive characteristics were obtained including: medical condition, mental health treatment history, school history, age, parent status, and family income.

The results of the psychometric analysis indicated significant strengths of the ADAS. Reliability was evidenced by a excellent Chronbach Alpha internal consistency of .9372. The study found evidence of construct validity including reliance on construct and theory in development of the measure. It provides a continuum of attachment, which is superior to discrete categorization of attachment concerns. The instrument demonstrated an ability to allow for differences in the way various cultures and males and females express attachment (no significant differences in scores was found other than when ADHD is present).

Descriptive validity is reported based on four strengths of the instrument:

I.   A high ADAS score correlated with previous mental health diagnosis (significant at the .0001 level).

II. A high ADAS score correlated with severe disorders and with a previous diagnosis of Reactive Attachment Disorder (.0001 level).

III. The instrument was able to discriminate between children with a diagnosis of Attention Deficit Hyperactive Disorder and Reactive Attachment Disorder (significant at the .0001 level).

IV. The instrument also discriminated males and females with ADHD due to higher average scores of males with ADHD.

When the instrument was developed, it was intentionally not directly linked to the clinical criteria of the diagnosis of Reactive Attachment Disorder because of the author's belief that this criteria would change over time, which has occurred. The instrument was primarily designed to identify the continuum of attachment issues and not just the presence of a diagnosable disorder. However, the instrument was able to show with statistical significance a direct correlation with a diagnosis of Reactive Attachment Disorder (.0001 level).

Additionally, the ADAS was able to distinguish between children with attachment problems and no attachment problems. It also reflected higher scores among children in foster care versus other family settings, where it is known that children have higher incidents of attachment problems (.001 level).

Essentially this large multi-state research study indicated that the Attachment Disorder Assessment Scale does exactly what it purports to do, and does so with reliability and validity. As with all studies, there were limitations to this study of self-reported data. The study recommended several improvements to the instrument based on psychometric properties and factor analysis. The research supported the goals of the ADAS:

I.   It is quick, easy, and inexpensive to administer and requires no technical skills or training.

II. It identifies the child on a continuum of attachment from minimal attachment issues to a serious attachment disorder.

III. It discriminates attachment problems from other diagnoses that have similar behavior manifestations such as ADHD.

IV. It is sensitive to cultural and gender differences in the way attachment is manifested.

V. It provides recommendations based upon the level of attachment problems identified.

The Attachment Disorder Assessment Scale, based on the author's use over fourteen years and with the above study, is currently the most psychometrically validated instrument available of its type. The current version of the instrument, the ADAS-Revised is in the final process of development and will soon be available for use by contacting the author.

INTERVENTIONS FOR
ATTACHMENT PROBLEMS

✓ First understand the biological, neurological and trauma components of attachment problems.

✓ Attachment disorders are rare but most children in substitute care need some help for attachment problems.

✓ Interventions that promote attachment: ensure safety, do not withhold basic needs, continually issue invitations to connection, and demand reciprocity in all areas of the child's life.

✓ Repetition is neurologically critical, have the child "fake it until he or she makes it."

✓ Avoid: retraumatizing the child, quick and easy fixes, physically intrusive "holding therapies," and any approach that defies common sense.

✓ It takes a village to raise difficult children, a big village. Have all the adults in the child's life work together as a team.

✓ For children with very serious behaviors, residential treatment may need to be an initial step to address problems families cannot manage. When picking a residential program, choose wisely.

A seven-year-old who was hoping for something for school lunch other than the sandwich before him told a staff member, "If I eat bologna the unsleeping part of my brain wakes up. So if I were to eat this sandwich, I may never sleep again!" [A risk we'll just have to take.]

Chapter

12

School Success For The Difficult Child

No discussion of challenging children would be complete without taking a look at how to integrate school into the treatment plan for the child. After the family, the school is the second social system nearly all children encounter. School is both how we keep children active and is essentially their profession until we deem the individual ready to contribute in some way to the world of work. It can be said that the first career children have is as a student. Success or failure in school can set a tone that can have long-term ramifications that are either positive or negative.

There are some inherent problems integrating difficult children into the public or private school setting if we are hoping for a successful experience for the child and the school. By definition the majority of difficult children present conflicts and roadblocks to having the academic experience run smoothly when compared to their more normal peers. Fortunately, we have societal values represented in our laws that all children are to be afforded a free and appropriate education (although currently we are trying to determine if the "No child left behind" legislation should be renamed "No unfunded federal mandates left behind"). We are also fortunate in this country to have committed teachers and

285

administrators who take their jobs very seriously with every child in their schools. But unfortunately many schools and school staff have a collective pragmatic view of education, in which you provide the most you can to as many children as you can. To these schools, the individual needs of children are just too daunting a chore to be able to address, particularly those of troubled and behaviorally demanding children. As a parent, it takes about five minutes at the first school meeting of the year to find out whether your child's school is interested in meeting your child's needs, or if you and your child are expected to meet the needs of the school. The education process is not a one-way street, and there must be cooperation between parents and school personnel, but we cannot expect troubled children to easily fit into a large, complex social environment — with continual pressures and expectations that can be overwhelming to the child with special needs.

Although it has been going on for decades, over the last twenty years there has been a growing demand from our society to improve the quality of our educational system. This movement to take a hard look at the way we set up our schools and measure the outcomes, is an essential subject for troubled children. Early in the industrial revolution we changed many aspects of our society to adjust to "modern" times. We began to require schooling, which brought many more children to schools, some not wanting to be there. America had a massive exodus from the rural communities of the country to metropolitan urban communities during the first and second World Wars. A new way to provide schooling other than the one-room rural schoolhouse had to be developed. One model that caught, on particular in urban areas, was the "Henry Ford Model," where children were like a car frame that rolled down the assembly line from 1st to 8th grade while new components were added along the way. It is interesting that many of our schools began to look like assembly line plants as well as function like them. The principle problem with this model is that children are not like steel frames that are each indistinguishable and act exactly alike when provided their new components.

Our school system in this country has often taken the brunt of societal changes and dissatisfactions with the status quo. Although polls show that a quality education is perennially a high priority with the voting public, it is also true that the voting booth is a place that voters repeatedly decline to pay the costs of the education they want for at least their own children. In the 1970s whole communities were started particularly in the sun belt where children were not allowed, so that schools and school costs could be avoided. Schools have been given an ever-expanding role in our culture, and not always with forethought and agreement from all sides. Schools have always had the role to educate, but they have also either been forced into or have voluntarily taken on many roles that families used to fulfill. Schools supervise children not only during the day, but to and from school, and before and after school with extracurricular activities. Schools perform a health function, they provide basic needs and social service functions. In many communities schools, like churches, form the basic building block of the community, where neighbors interact around the schooling of their children. Schools are microcosms of our society. As such, schools deal with many competing needs and have the constant responsibility of successfully impacting many lives. I make these general comments in an attempt to say that I understand the challenges of schools to help and satisfy everyone. It is a daunting task that I do not envy. Now that I have said this, I can say that, particularly in our public school system, all our children do not succeed in their first career as a student. Difficult children make up a considerable percentage of the children who start out their social lives by failing in a school environment.

We can no longer be satisfied that 80% of our children succeed in our educational system, although failure and dropout rates appear to be considerably more than 20%. There is a direct relationship between the children who fail academically and socially in school, and adults who fail in our society. Some children tend to learn even with mediocre or poor teachers, but some children tend to fail even with the best of instruction. I believe there are some fundamental changes that are needed in our public educational system, but in this chapter I want to talk about the issues that come up when trying to educate and work with children who have a history of not wanting to, or not being able to cooperate and do their part in school.

Particularly in the school setting, troubled children at times do not present as behavioral problems, and these children can be even more worrisome. Of the two types of troubled children, the aggressive externalizers or the passive internalizers, the acting out children with behavior problems come to the attention of educators long before the other group. However, it has been my experience that acting-out children are often more successfully helped than children who internalize their problems. These two behavioral patterns require different strategies to address the needs of the child.

Before I go further, I want to make a disclaimer on my knowledge and experience related to academic instruction of children. As a psychologist and someone who works directly with children every day, I am not and do pretend to be a school teacher. However, my observations come from having an advanced degree in education, teaching courses in high school and college, and being the administrator of a elementary school for emotionally disturbed children for the last fifteen years. Despite this experience, I know much less about teaching reading, for example, than I do most other areas of working with difficult children.

Success in School Is Critical

The early predictors of future success in life are generally focused on the first two years and the attachment and inner working models the child develops during this time. The profound early impact of social learning is weighted as it should be because our views of ourselves and of the world are significantly established in the family. However, success in life also has a great deal to do with success in the second social institution that children encounter — school. Even if we have a very supportive parent or parents, the child may think, "Of course mom thinks I'm smart and capable, she's my mother, she's supposed to think that."

What most children want to find out is does anyone else beside their mother like them, their ideas, their art work, their skills, and their potential to be someone special in life. The place most of us find positive or negative answers to these questions is in school.

The American culture is steeped in competition. Competition is the basis of our capitalist economy. It is often more important that your product is #1, than if it is the best product available. We compete in sports, in politics, in business, in recreation, and even some churches say with pride that they have the largest membership in town. We teach children early to be competitive. We have sports programs for children, talent contests, art and poster competitions, beauty contests, science contests, spelling bees and geography contests, and the one common element in all our competitions is that one person or team wins and all the others lose. The competitive way of thinking is so ingrained in our culture that it is almost un-American to question why we have our children competing with each other — rather than learning more about cooperation and less about competition.

As children mature in school, the amount of competition they face grows. Some is sanctioned such as a student's academic rank in class, national honor society, or other groups that honor the cream of the crop. But children incorporate competition in other aspects of their world, and develop social ranking systems based on the ability of the young person to compete successfully with peers in whatever the groups value (from how many goals you can score for the team, to how much money you have to spend on the latest clothing fads). In many ways the social make-up of public schools prepares children for the rigors of what they will face when competing for a slot in graduate school, or competing with a dozen other applicants for a desired job.

A major disadvantage to our competitive system is that in every contest more children come up losers than winners. In a foot race, regardless if all eight children try their best, and perhaps run faster than ever before, the results are one winner and seven losers. In a culture that makes heroes out of sports figures, professional football coach Vince Lombardi's quote is often repeated, "Winning isn't everything, it is the only thing." Our children quickly internalize the value our culture places on winning and winners. Most of us are able to handle competition in our lives, even if some of us would prefer the world to be a bit less competitive. We adjust our perceptions and goals based upon the probable outcome of competing with others. For example, most adults do not join a weekend 10K road race with the hope of winning. We learn to compete with ourselves for a better time or a longer distance. When Time magazine annually chooses "The Person Of The Year" (it used to be the man of the year), most of us are not depressed that we did not get considered. But not everyone can handle our competitive world, in fact nearly 33% of our adult population does not meet our society's standards for a successful functioning member of our culture. America may have the highest percentage of failures of any culture in the world, this group is populated by people who are: incarcerated, homeless, addicted, on welfare, in and out of mental institutions, unable to sustain an intimate relationship, or a long list of criteria for people who are just not making it. I wonder how many languages have a term for this as we do — being a "loser," and if the term is mentioned as often as it is in our culture?

I felt like I needed to make the comments about competition to point out that competition is one of the obstacles to success for troubled children. To the degree that the educational environment is competitive, most troubled children will fail. It makes little difference that we are preparing these children to get accustomed to competition in their future, and to take their place in our competitive world. The problem is that these children often do just that, they take the place of the person who is picked last for the team, and who finishes last in most everything but getting attention. Not only troubled children, but most people tend to avoid the parts of their lives where they consistently fail.

Troubled children usually finish out of the running not because they don't have abilities; sometimes they have remarkable abilities. They lose the race before it has begun because they do not see themselves as a winner. They have never won, they have never been told they will win, and the few times they did their very best, the result was embarrassment and disappointment, and they decided not to feel that again. These children handle competition by avoiding it, they will act out so they will not be chosen for the team rather than be chosen last. They will make the class project a joke rather than be a part of it, and they will tear up their homework rather than get more criticism in red ink. If we want troubled children to experience academic and social success in school, we must eliminate the element of competition and give the child a taste of success and how success is linked to effort.

Positive Competition Is Possible

Our program has Olympic competition for the children every summer. We want the children to learn that competition can be fun as well as teach other lessons such as: trying hard, doing your best, and being a good sport. We ensure that all children are on an equal footing for each event. Accommodations are made for age and physical ability level so that with effort each child could win any event. We also have team events. In the end, we give Olympic medals for events. But more importantly, we give a trophy for children who participated with genuine effort. We also give the highest award for the child who demonstrated the best spirit of sportsmanship. Most of the children have never won medals and trophies before. They are always proud, and they looked forward each year to these Olympic games.

Failure in school usually takes the form of academic failure and/or serious behavior problems. We have special education categories for these two major forms of special needs. A child does not usually get placed in the difficult category only due to learning problems. I don't know of any teacher who would begrudge spending extra time with a child with a learning problem — if the child was asking for and appreciating the help. A difficult child is almost always the child who refuses help (acting out externalizing child) or avoids help (the internalizing child), and adults learn that any extra time will probably be wasted on these children, and there are so many other children to help who will accept what is offered.

Our schools have a strange tolerance for avoidant children, who sit in the back of the room and get by on little effort and poor performance, but who don't disrupt the class. We also have a strange intolerance for the acting out child who manipulates us into suspending or expelling them, and thus prevent them from going to school which they didn't want to do in the first place. A number of years ago, I had a challenging child in our program attending the local public school. He got up one morning and said, "That's it, no more school, I'm not going." I told him in the future he could make that choice for himself, but for now he needed to be in school. He replied, "Then I will get myself thrown out of school today!" I called the principal of the school and relayed the conversation, and I asked to be called if he was a problem and I would come to school, but it was important the child not get his way through negative behavior. I got a call 90 minutes later from the principal to come pick up the child, he was suspended from school for three days for "cussing out" the teacher in class. I went to the school and asked the principal why he didn't call me as agreed to work out a plan so the child didn't get his wish? With the child sitting in his office the principal said, "This child acts like a crazy person, and we are not prepared to deal with crazy children." I wish I were making this up, but as I drove the child home hearing, "I told you so," I promised myself that I would develop a school designed for these children when I had the opportunity. It took another three years, but we finally put together our own school.

One of my points with this true story mentioned in the past paragraph is that difficult children are smart enough to know how to use the rules to their advantage. Schools are even more hypersensitive now than they were five years ago to any sign of violence, such as a child saying, "I'll kill you," on the bus fooling around with peers, or "I'll get back at you for that," both statements that resulted in one of our children suspended from local schools. We neither want to ignore the signs of serious concern for safety in our schools, nor do we want to hand difficult children the power to get their way through negative behavior.

"Why Are You Making Jeff Worse?"

There are many reasons why our program had to develop its own school, but George and his brother Jeff were reason enough. The two siblings, who were one year apart, had a mother with paranoid schizophrenia. The impact of the resulting abuse and neglect was very different on the brothers. George was a serious behavior problem, but Jeff internalized his issues and was sullen and isolated. In the public school, George was well-known to the staff, particularly to the principal. In treatment we worked to have George learn self-regulation, and we helped Jeff to externalize his feelings of sadness and anger. As the two boys improved in their own ways, the school staff appreciated our work with George, but they demanded to know, "Why are you making Jeff worse?" The teacher told me Jeff was a "model student." When I asked about this I was told, "He is not learning as I would like, but he never talks out in class, is not a problem at recess and he sits quietly, he's every teacher's dream." Apparently sitting in the back row of class depressed, isolated and not learning was acceptable as long as he did so quietly. In our treatment program both made progress, George learned better control and Jeff learned to express his pain and anger, and became a challenge in school.

The challenge I see with educating difficult children is to find ways to manage their behavior, work with their attitude issues, and at the same time help them learn the skills and basics that they will need in life. Doesn't sound any harder than climbing Mt. Everest in sandals does it? Well, maybe a little harder.

True Individualized Education, the Only Way to Go

In most every classroom, teachers try to present the subject material to the 25 to 35 children in the class in a way that each child will grasp the concepts. In some way, all education must be individualized. Troubled children need us to go much further in the direction of individualized instruction. Essentially all of the troubled children I work with have been tested and qualify for special education, and have an individual education plan or IEP. Many of the children are bright with above-average intelligence. A major reason the majority of these children have trouble learning is the direct result of the neurological effects of trauma caused by early abuse and neglect. Previous traumatic experiences cause two academic problems found in most difficult children: 1. Behavior problems that prevent the child from fitting into the school environment successfully and 2. Deficiencies in academic skills that were caused by the child being focused on survival and missing early opportunities to learn.

As with psychological treatment, we cannot assume that we know what is going on inside the child without taking the time to find out for sure. We also cannot assume that we know what will take care of the child's problems in school without doing a full assessment of a broad range of academic skills. In other words we must truly individualize the learning plan for the child based upon a careful and complete educational assessment. Although this is exactly what is required by federal law for every child who qualifies for special education services, some of the shortcuts that schools circumvent with more normal children will not work with difficult children.

How Abused Children Succeed in School, What We Have Found over Time

Few services have been as carefully examined and tested as academic instruction for children. We know a great deal about how children learn to read, to understand math, and to spell words such as Albacurkey, or is it Albuquerque? What we know less about is what hampers learning with seriously troubled children, and how we can help these children succeed academically. To assist in addressing learning problems, special education has been the subject of years of research. What we know little about is what to do for the learner who has multiple impediments to learning that may include learning disabilities, behavior and attitude problems, traumatic histories, and the lack of personal resilience to overcome the difficulties in life, which everyone has their share of.

Resiliency has itself been the subject of scrutiny by educators. In the book *Resiliency in Schools*, Henderson and Milstein point out that resiliency promotes success in school and in life through a number of traits that include: social competence, using life skills such as problem solving, critical thinking, initiative, having special interests, being goal-directed, and motivated to achieve their potential (Henderson & Milstein, 2003). These authors borrow from the research on chemical dependency (Hawkins, Catalano & Miller, 1992) as well as learning (Benard, 1993) to develop an educational "Resiliency Wheel" of six factors: 1. Promote increased bonding, 2. Set clear and consistent boundaries, 3. Teach life skills, 4. Provide caring and support, 5. Set and communicate high expectations, and 6. Provide opportunities for meaningful participation (Henderson & Milstein, 2003).

In our fifteen years of experience providing a school for the most challenging children we have learned a great deal. Much of what we have learned fits well with the above thoughts on resiliency. Perhaps what we have learned most about is what does not work. It seems sometimes we must try a dozen approaches before we find something that will work. But we have found some themes that seem to work more often than they don't with troubled children. David Letterman likes to have his top ten, and here is my Dave's Top Ten ways to teach troubled children.

1. The school environment must be experienced by the child as safe and predictable as well as the other components of the Building Blocks (see Appendix, page 343). By now I have mentioned these two essential elements so many times that I do not have to say much more. Safety is both a matter of internal and external safety of the school facility (Walker, Irvin & Sprague, 1997), and safety is also a matter of the child's perception and internal experience. Without these first steps as a foundation, no healthy structure can be built whether for physical health,

emotional health, learning or any other developing area of the child.

2. The process of learning must allow active involvement. Forget about the child sitting quietly at a desk doing seat work, unless you want trouble. Instead have the child experience the learning. If the subject is trees, go for a hike and look at trees, if you are teaching math, have the child hand one child four poker chips and another child two poker chips and ask how many poker chips were handed out. All children, but particularly troubled children, learn best by doing (so do adults, by the way). If you want high interest, find a way to have active involvement.

I Was Traumatized by Spanish, or Was it the Spanish Teacher?

Trauma in the classroom for me was advanced Spanish. Half of the class spoke Spanish as their primary language. The class was required for me and I was not proficient in languages other than English. The professor spoke only Spanish in the class and did not go easy on anyone, particularly me. I still have nightmares where I am sitting at a desk and someone begins to speak Spanish and I hear, "Senior Ziegler, Como se dice..." And I wake up with a pounding heart. I could learn Spanish in Mexico (say during a leisurely cruise), but put me in a Spanish class and I would freeze up again. We need to break the negative mold that most difficult children associate with school, much like my reluctance to ever set foot in a Spanish class again.

---

3. We find that the "Unschool" works best. You are probably not starting from scratch and providing the child's first school experience. Most difficult children have been in schools, and they were not fun places. We have found that if we have an environment that looks, feels, smells and acts very differently than other schools, the "unschool," the children are more open to the process. In general, the more the setting is unlike school the better. Don't worry just yet about teaching the child to sit quietly to fit

into public schools; that can be tackled after he has been taught to love learning at school.

4. Learning must promote high interest and get a "buy-in" from the child. For some reason people think adults don't need to motivate children in school — that is the child's job. Perhaps, but not with difficult children. Toy makers, manufacturers of cereal, and producers of child TV shows know that they must start by gaining the child's interest, and if they don't do this quickly, they have lost the child. Products that target children go for high interest, flash, color and a variety of ways to gain "buy-in" by the child. We must do the same in school if we don't want to immediately lose the interest and investment of the troubled child.

5. Give the child some meaningful choices. This is one way to be an unschool; let the child make choices during the term and during the day concerning what they want to study, and what he wants to do to learn about a particular subject. There are many ways to offer meaningful choices, but the goal is for the child to make choices because he will show more interest if he decides rather than if you decide. You can guide the choices, but make them real and not, "Do you want to do the green math sheet or the blue math sheet?" Such a choice is often met with the difficult child indicating what you can do with both math sheets!

6. Only the correct kind of competition is allowed. We discussed competition earlier. Competition is a way of life in America. It is not competition that is the problem, it is the type of competition we have, particularly in school. The right kind of competition for troubled children is easy, it boils down to this — with every competition the child has an equal chance of winning as the other children. Before you allow any competition for running, spelling, math or handwriting, make sure that the troubled child has a good chance of winning every race. Chances are that if they feel they are not likely to win, they won't try. Would you?

7. Serve up extra praise, and hold the criticism. We have talked about stacking the deck in the positive direction. Essentially all of the elements we have talked about with difficult children in other settings can also be said for school, including five positives for

every criticism. That ratio doesn't sound like any school I ever attended.

8. Rather than holding them back, give the child room for expression. We have come to associate school with a place to sit down, be quiet and listen. Each of these tend to be challenges for difficult children. I am not saying that they don't need a chance to work on these necessary abilities, just don't require this to begin with. School for challenging children should be a place of action, of discovery and a place of expression: singing, dancing, talking, laughing, and even crying and yelling at times. If we communicate to the child that an emotional outburst from her will stop everyone in their tracks and all eyes will immediately come her way, watch out — you have just shown her how to be powerful. In our school, we allow children to get angry, yell, sing or speak their mind, but they need to leave the classroom and not come back in until they have concluded their diatribe and they are ready to join the group.

9. Give the child a chance to teach others. The best way for anyone to learn something is to review it, and then teach it to someone else. Learning through teaching also applies to problem children. They usually experience that no one is interested in what they have to say, and to be able to be the teacher is magical. Most any child can teach a younger child something of value, you just need to find what she has to offer.

10. Make sure there is room for mistakes. With the exception of the way Enron was managed, there are positives in every mistake. We learn from mistakes. We can't try something new without doing it wrong in the beginning. Unless we want the child to be fearful of trying, the school environment must be a place where mistakes are made and accepted. The adults must shape the learning and the behavior by pointing out the progress of the positive aspect of every mistake. Too often we give the child the message that a mistake is bad, and soon the child not only thinks she only makes mistakes but she IS one big mistake. Make sure you model mistakes, and tell the class when you make them.

To skillfully put together the above elements in a school creates an environment where learning is much more fun than not learning. There are many ways to do this, and many educational philosophies can be built into the above components of a successful classroom for difficult children. If this list looks interesting but impossible, I assure you it is not. All these elements exist in our school to some degree. I will now share the vision of our school, but I want to make it clear that this is only one model that works very well with extremely challenging children. Our approach works not only for our intensive psychiatric residential population but these children are integrated with day treatment students coming from many of the area's school districts. Day treatment children have a history of failure despite the best efforts of the district. So imagine a school that is made up of some of the most damaged children combined with the most difficult children from a dozen school districts. Doesn't that sound like fun? Actually it is quite fun for the children and the staff (usually).

I am not the only one to develop a list of how difficult children best learn. Ron Federici has identified twenty-five accommodations for children with attention and processing disorders. These include such ideas as: ensure you first get the child's undivided attention before providing instruction, sitting the child next to a child who has good learning skills, using gestures, emphasize key words, give one task at a time, have the child set goals, encourage personal organizational skills, and many more (Federici, 2003). It is clear that whatever list you consult, the process of learning for a difficult child will not be education as usual, and the adults will have to invest considerable time on the front end, with an individualized time consuming plan, or invest considerable time on the back end, with discipline problems and struggling with poor outcomes.

One Model — SCAR/Jasper Mountain School Vision

Jasper Mountain opened its doors in 1982, twenty-two years ago. It was not until 1989 that it began its academic program following years of conflict with the local public school district. The conflict involved the problem behavior of the children and the general inability of the public schools to meet the demanding needs of very difficult children. The beginning of our school was both a negotiated settlement with the local district and a desire to design a program for learning that would be tailor-made for abused children. From day one the program had a vision to maximize the learning possibilities for a very unique population — abused children who had little or no previous success in school.

Over the last thirteen years, the personnel and the facilities have changed a number of times, but not the intent to provide a special opportunity for abused children to find academic success. During this 20th year celebration for our agency and on the verge of moving into our newly constructed Jasper school facility, a team of agency board, staff and stakeholders reviewed the school's vision, and the goals and strategies needed to achieve the vision.

It was through the experience, suggestions, shared values, and participation of our staff, management, Board of Directors and community participants that the following vision emerged.

School Vision Statement

Our school exists to provide the best learning experience possible to the abused children we serve.

Program Goals

There are many reasons why seriously abused children generally do poorly in school regardless of their intellectual ability. SCAR/Jasper Mountain School must address these reasons. Developing an environment of academic success with our target population is a complex proposition that must be built on solid theory and practice. Three primary goals lead to the desired learning environment:

1. Educating abused children in the academic skills they will need to achieve personal goals and success in learning.

It is essential to provide children with the building blocks of academic success. These include not only reading, writing and math, but also listening, cooperating, accepting direction, and a host of social skills in and out of the classroom. Without the basic tools, gained through specific instruction, the children will not have the needed foundation.

2. Integration of the educational program with mental health treatment in order to turn personal growth into academic success.

Trauma and child abuse produce a multitude of challenges for young children. Nowhere is this more apparent than in a classroom. Treatment and academic instruction must be seamlessly integrated to maximize both. The primary reason to have an on-site school in a psychiatric treatment program is to provide such a seamless integration. Issues such as behavior management, medication management, and establishing a safe and predictable setting for all children, must all be effectively achieved.

3. Instill an attitude of enjoyment in lifelong learning.

Learning can and should be challenging, stimulating and fun. In the long run, it is less important that the child learn the multiplication tables than he or she learn to enjoy working with numbers. The ability to read is important, the love of reading will make a huge difference in academic success over time.

Learning Strategies to Achieve the Goals

Goal #1 Teaching Educational Skills

- Enhancing reading and comprehension skills

- Learning how to write and then deciding what to write

- Having fun with numbers

- True individualized education

- Teaching internal self-discipline

- Practicing concentration and focus

- Developing and meeting individual educational goals

- Teaching problem solving skills

- Assessing the child's style of learning

- Enhancing social skills

- Understanding learning styles of children and making adjustments accordingly

Goal #2 Integrating Treatment
- Improving self-confidence through achievement

- Treatment goals come into the classroom

- Consistency in treatment and academic rules and expectations

- Establishing behavioral limitations while providing conceptual freedom

- Enhancing expression of all types

- Taking small incremental steps and build on successes

- Providing learning at the child's pace

- Reducing anxiety and performance pressure

Goal #3 Developing an Attitude of Lifelong Learning
- Fostering self-directed learning

- Learning is active and enjoyable

- Children have choices in learning areas and help develop their personal educational plans

- Encouraging children to develop ownership of the content and process of their schooling

- Building in success: failure is not fun for anyone

- Experiential hands-on learning approaches

- Creative and innovative projects

- Adults are involved and excited

- Multiple learning methods are used

- Positive reinforcement/positive incentives

- Valuing mistakes as opportunities to learn

The following are components of a successful learning environment designed for abused children.

- Schooling should be year-round

- Building interest in learning through thematic units

- Involving children in teaching others to learn more themselves

- Making full use of the physical facilities to support educational outcomes

- Educating outside the box, developing learning zones, including outdoor education

- Providing opportunities to express creativity through exhibits of art, plays and performances, and music recitals

- Teaching children to set personal learning goals

- Focusing less on seat work and more on self-directed work

- Student-led learning

- Teachers adjusting their role from instructors to facilitators

- Teamwork in the classroom

- Teachers and aids all remaining actively involved

- Team teaching

- Children team teach with peers and adults

- Cooperative learning

- Methods of evaluating the child's and the program's strengths and weaknesses

- Age of children does not determine their status or placement

- Develop incentives for staff creativity

A Final Comment about School Success

Much like the treatment process of traumatized children, there are many approaches that can be used to educate troubled children. I have included some of the strategies that we are using in our school. Some we do better than others, and just as in our treatment center, we are always working to improve our school. Although there are some additional challenges in school, the guidelines are very similar to what needs to happen in families and in the community. It is important to remember that if a child does not find success in school, the result is not only the loss of academic skills, but a much deeper loss of personal worth and the belief that success is unattainable in life. This is one major reason why adults who failed in school often struggle throughout life. Early experiences set the stage for what comes later in life. However, regardless of the failure of the child in past school experiences, if he or she can succeed in your school, this plots a positive course for success in other areas of life.

How Traumatized Children Best Learn

✓ The classroom must be experienced as safe and predictable.

✓ Enhance active involvement in learning.

✓ Create the "Unschool."

✓ Create high interest and obtain a buy-in from the child.

✓ Give the child meaningful choices in what he learns.

✓ Allow only the right kind of competition.

✓ Serve up extra praise and hold the criticism.

✓ Make opportunities for expression.

✓ Give the child a chance to teach others.

✓ Make sure there is room to make mistakes.

Part IV

The Secrets of Success

Perhaps exposed to hip-hop music, the five-year-old girl told the staff member, "I am going on a visit today so I have to look bootiful!" [As in full of booty?]

Chapter

13

The Difference Between Failure and Success with Difficult Children

In this chapter I want to spell out in plain language what produces success in working with troubled children, and conversely, what too often results in frustration and failure. I will break this discussion into two parts. The first is to discuss internal qualities of people who succeed at this most demanding endeavor. The second part is to talk about strategies, or what approaches tend to produce better results with challenging children. Please don't read into this chapter or anywhere in this book that there is a surefire formula, or only one way to achieve success. We must be artists at work with the canvas of our relationships with the child. The style, the color and the textures are left to the artist, and each of us will create a one-of-a-kind work. However, this does not mean that anything goes, because how we approach our art will say a lot about the final product. I will conclude with a few comments on a concept that may interest you — no-lose parenting. Is it possible to work with a difficult child and not fail? I will offer my answer to this question.

Working with difficult children requires so much from us that it demands the focus of our mind, body and spirit. For this reason, in Chapter 12 of *Raising Children Who Refuse To Be Raised*, I called working with difficult children an excellent path to spiritual growth. Working with difficult children is also one of the best methods I have found for learning more about myself. This is particularly true in areas within myself that I was not aware of, and when they came to my attention, I was not particularly proud of, either. The directness of difficult children comes from the fact that they seldom like themselves, and they generally let you know in a multitude of ways that they don't like you either. They may follow the golden rule and treat you as they want to be treated, but this doesn't help much because they don't treat themselves very respectfully, nor do they often care how others treat them. You are likely to hear criticism of your appearance, your intelligence, and your personality more harshly from these children than from anyone in your life (unless you played basketball for Bobby Knight or went through Marine boot camp several times). As the saying goes, "listen to your friends, but pay closer attention to what your enemies tell you, you will often learn more." A challenging child will often be able to size you up quickly, and then begin the process of tearing you down. With an attitude adjustment (involving no alcohol), you will be able to view the child's criticism of you as a way for you to learn more about yourself.

Characteristics of Adults Who Are Successful

The following list of qualities is not unique to those working with difficult children. It could be a list describing adults who are successful in running a business, or adults who meet personal goals in life. But the items on this list are the qualities that will help us do a better job in relating to one or more difficult children in our lives.

- Personal stability — a difficult child does not want to be the only vulnerable person in the room, so he will attempt to level the playing field by pointing out the parent's obvious shortcomings. This is one reason why being a parent is a great way to undergo personal psychotherapy. Within days or perhaps minutes, a challenging child will provide you with a list of what you need to work on as a person. Only stable people need apply for the job. It takes personal strength to look at personal weakness. If you feel a little shaky, parenting a difficult child will make it worse. If your marriage is a little rocky, don't take on a difficult child to strengthen the marriage by having a mutual project; such a move may end the marriage.

- Taking care of yourself — if you don't, make sure your well does not run dry, who will? There is nothing in the job description of a difficult child that says he is to take care of you. It is either time out or it is burn out; you decide.

- Giving without needing to receive — only a saint can practice unconditional love all the time, but one characteristic of an effective parent is to understand that parenting is about putting the focus on giving, not receiving.

- Learning from every situation — no experience with a difficult child, regardless of how unpleasant, is a failure unless we have not learned from it. We must always be the student in life, or we miss the lessons that are all around us.

- Seeing below the surface — I have compared difficult children to icebergs. If you only consider what you can see on the surface, you may go down with the ship after colliding with what was below the surface. Much of what I have to say in this book is about seeing and feeling more than is immediately apparent, or what little the child wants you to see.

- Knowing when to ask for help — if you are the type who does not ask for help from others, don't even try parenting a difficult child. I ask for help from others all the time and I am considered by some an expert at this. The problem is that each new child has not read my books to know that resistance is futile, so there are no shortcuts, and help from others is essential. Learn when to ask for help (constantly), so that you don't find yourself so far behind that you can't catch up.

- Knowing what you need and accepting it when it is offered — it may be better to give than receive, but some of us need some practice in receiving. Freely offer your help to others and freely accept the help offered to you. Wise people know what they don't know, and they also know who might have the answer they lack.

- Ability to be tough in a loving way — who says that nurturing is always loving, and confrontation is always harsh and unloving? Not so. Love is honest, and it also has the best interests of the beloved as the motivation. With that said, we must learn to be tough with those we love as well as tender, and learn to be tough in a way the person feels loved and not rejected.

- Ability to be vulnerable in a personal way — not many of us enjoy being vulnerable to others, particularly to people who are not our best friends. If we struggle with this, how hard must it be for a child to be vulnerable to adults she is not sure have her best interests at heart? The best way to teach is to be a model, which we can do by being personally vulnerable so the child watches and learns from us.

- Meeting the child more than half way — we are the big people and the child is the little person (not always calculated by physical size). We must go to the child, we must take the first step, second step and third step, and we must be ready to take more steps toward the child than the child takes toward us.

- Never stop working on ourselves — I don't know if you are finished working on yourself, but my wife continues to find areas that I can improve upon. At the point that you think you have learned enough about yourself and have progressed as far as you need to, you are likely to not learn from your next encounter with a difficult child. At that point, it will simply be an unpleasant experience with no redeeming value. That doesn't sound like any fun. If you change your receptivity, what you can learn from the child is cheap therapy.

- Enthusiasm for the journey — so who says that hard work needs to be unpleasant? Bring energy to your parenting, your teaching or your therapy with challenging children — even after you get battered a little by the cold wind coming from the child. If you can't think of any reason to maintain your enthusiasm, you can stay positive because it will confuse the child trying to send you to the assisted care center early.

Strategies for Success

Now that we know the personal qualities that help us succeed, we can turn our attention to approaches I have found that have the best chance to produce positive results.

- **Take the time to understand this child and the roots of the child's problems.** Difficult children are like snowflakes; they can be cold, they make you slip and fall, and they are often flakes. Well, perhaps there is some truth to these statements, but my point is that difficult children are all one of a kind, just like snowflakes. That I know of, no flakologist has divided snowflakes into four types or seven categories. It just doesn't make sense, because there are literally trillions of deviations. The same is true for troubled children. One thing we know about human nature, we like to categorize things because it somehow makes us feel if we can first understand it, then we can control it. I think it is important to resist the temptation to say that Tiffany is a type 17 or Juan is a category 31. I understand the temptation to do this. After so many years and so many children, I look into young eyes and see the faces of other child I have worked with. But they are not the same. There is no reliable category 31 or type 17, there is this Tiffany and there is this Juan, and it is our job to understand the child not the classification or categorization. Individual differences is one reason why I suggest to parents to beware of therapists who specialize in a certain type of childhood problem. Too often these professionals put on their green-tinted glasses and each child they examine looks a little green to them.

Although it is usually helpful for foster and adoptive parents to have experience as a parent before bringing home Dennis Rodman Jr., there are times when previous parenting experience gets in the way. When I sit down to coach two parents who have done a great job with their own children, or have done well with their own adoptive child, I always suggest that they start their parent training all over again and start fresh. However, I know that few can leave past experience behind. Once we are successful at any enterprise, we can't help but trust that if we do it the same way it is just bound to work again. Past success is not necessarily predictive of future success when it comes to challenging children. You may have seen many snowflakes in your years as dog musher in the Yukon, but you haven't seen this particular snowflake, ever. If you have a plan in your head, get it out of your head now. If you are pretty sure how this is all going to come down with this child, think again. Parents or therapists who have an image of the way things should go, are often the first to throw up their hands the ninety-ninth time it does not go the way they thought it would or should.

No children sit in a high chair with their pureed lima beans and decide to drive adults crazy the rest of their lives. Children don't decide to be troubled or to have lives that are painful. Children are doing the best that they can. They are repeating patterns that they internally believe have actually helped them to survive and get through some very rough waters in their past. We must learn as much as we can about this child and what makes sense and does not make sense to him and to her. It takes time to know a child. As a psychologist, I am often baffled by the importance people give to a psychological evaluation. I write them, but if you really want to know this young man, it takes more than spending 3 or 4 hours with the child, you must live with him. Live with a child first, and only after you have looked at the world from the vantage point of the child can you begin to understand first the problem, and second the solution to the problem.

- **Translate the meaning of the child's behavior and develop a plan that best meets this individual child's needs and issues.**

The most critical element of understanding a difficult child is to translate the meaning of the child's behavior. With very few exceptions, behavior has meaning. It is not always clear to someone else what the meaning of your behavior is. How many times are you asked, "Why did you do that?" This question is asked even more often of difficult children. The meaning behind the actions requires some detective work. The first clue to the meaning of the child's behavior is that words are seldom helpful in finding the mystery motivation. Words are used by these children primarily as decoys to throw you off track. We must become very good at translating the meaning of what troubled children say and what they do.

Translating the Behavior

To address particularly unpleasant behavior, first understand its meaning to the child. For example, the child urinates in his clothes during the day. After going through the process in the previous paragraph, I give the child a chance to make decisions from several choices of what clothes to wear. Additionally, I take the child to buy some new clothes and the child is given some choice in what we get. The urinating goes away, why? I correctly translated that the child felt he had no control over anything in his life except when and where to pee. When he felt some control, he felt differently particularly in the clothing he picked out. Of course, you will not always be right the first or second time that you attempt to translate the behavior.

There is a procedure that I find useful to help me translate the meaning of behavior. First I identify what particular action I am trying to understand. Next I consider at least five possible reasons the child may have done this. If the child has made a statement about the action, I first consider the opposite of what the child has said. When considering the possibilities, I always add two additional motivations: 1. To get attention and 2. To control the environment. It is often helpful to come up with at least one long shot possibility, which helps you to think more like the child than like an adult. Then go through the list of possibilities and list those that are more likely and those that are less likely. Then I take the list of more likely, combine them and proceed on the basis that this is my best guess. I will then be looking to see if my best guess rings true with further contact with the child. This method of translating a child's message through his or her actions is not foolproof, but when used often, the parent will begin to get closer to the thinking of the child because the process helps the adult do just that.

We cannot come up with a solution until we correctly understand the problem. In the past some families have believed that I had some special intuitive powers since I was able to provide an intervention that had nothing to do with the problem, and it worked. Now I have outlined how I do that. When we come up with our best theory of the meaning of the behavior to the child, we need to address not necessarily the behavior but the motivation or problem behind the child's actions or words. When you are off, go through the process again and test your theory. Over time you learn to be very skilled at translating the behavior of your youngster.

- **Ensure the child feels supported by you and other adults.** I know that all the adults in a child's life at school, at home and in the community want the best for the child, but does the child feel this? Does the child belong in the classroom at school, and is this clear to the child? Is there anything about the church the family goes to that says welcome to the child, and we are glad you are here? Particularly for foster and adoptive children, are there signs around the house that show the child that she belongs here? For example, most families have group pictures sitting around. When a new foster or adoptive child comes into a home, I believe it is a good idea to take some group pictures, enlarge them, put them in a nice frame and sit them around the house. Does your refrigerator have something on it directly related to the child, such as a drawing? Troubled children are not fed by the words of adults, but by signs in the environment. These children have felt the sting of an abusive adult saying they wish the child had never been born, or possibly even worse. They have learned not to listen because they expect to be hurt by the words of adults. The child needs signs and symbols that say he is supported by the people in this class, in this youth group at church, on this team, and in this family.

Make sure you take the other adults in the child's life aside and fill them in on the challenge in front of them. Most adults I have worked with step up to a challenge and work very hard when they are approached personally at the beginning of the process. The child's teacher is a good example. Don't wait for the first suspension from school to sit down with the teacher and principal and outline the challenge for the school term. If there is even one adult the child experiences as potentially abusive, either with actions or words, you will have little success in inviting the child into a more supportive world than she has experienced in the past.

- **Give the child more positive statements of effort and improvement than negative corrections (five positive for every one negative).** If I were to pick the most difficult strategy in this list it would be this one. There are multiple reasons why giving a difficult child positive statements is like staying dry in Oregon in the winter. The first problem is that these children don't help you much. They just don't do a lot that you want to celebrate. The proportion of positive to negative is also a real problem. To give the child five positives to every one negative must mean that you have to continually lie about the positive behaviors that are nonexistent, and then you have to overlook most of the problem behaviors. Come on, admit it, you were thinking these things, weren't you? I will not soft-pedal this strategy — it is very hard to do. There is an important factor that must also be acknowledged — as hard as it is, it is also essential for success.

If the difficult child had a dollar for every time an adult expressed disapproval for behavior, ideas, requested needs and wants, and even disapproval for the fact that the child walks on the planet, the child could take these dollar bills and become the principal stock holder in a Fortune 500 company. When we are subjected to criticism that is never ending, and some of which we cannot do anything about, we pretend to tune it out. The soul and the inner spirit of the child cannot fully tune out everyone's criticism, but she will attempt to act like nothing phases her. I discussed in *Traumatic Experience and the Brain* that negative experiences produce neuro-pathways in the brain, through which other related events are processed. In other words, when we give a traumatized child criticism, the child's brain thinks, "Here they all go again, when will it end?" But it isn't "they," it is you, and you should not be viewed in the same category as the child's abusers. Unfortunately, logic will not save the day; the child's brain will lump your comments with the most unfair and degrading put-downs from the past.

What troubled children are not very familiar with are honest, positive comments from adults. Yes, I said honest. I am not a believer in vacuous praise to raise the self-esteem of everyone on the planet. I do believe in letting people know what they do that is good, as well as pointing out ways less than ideal performance could be improved. This formula helps with running my business (with one hundred employees), and it helps with difficult children. False praise for these children is often easier to think up, but neither you nor the child will believe it. If you must speak honestly, then the question is "are you willing to take the time to find what the child does well, or what the child tries to do that could be improved?" If not, I am sorry but I think you will not succeed with any child with whom you cannot do this. If you can't find the positive, you will be placed and eventually enshrined in the hall of critical adults within the child's brain. I know the hall of shame is not the desired destination of any of us, but we can easily find ourselves there if we respond as most people would respond to a difficult child.

I often suggest that we all get a coach to help us. It is not always that we don't know what to do, we just need someone to consult with at times when the going gets rough. Being continually positive with an exceptionally negative child is rough going indeed. I do not have an easy trick to accomplish this strategy. Like most other things about raising a difficult child, it is much easier to say what needs to be done than to do it. I will just say that, as you work on this, please know that I and thousands of other adults are working on it as well with the mouseketeers we have in our world.

I think we need to be honest with ourselves. We must admit it when we are sick of being positive and we just want to scream or break something expensive. Get this feeling out of your system, then go eat a large piece of chocolate and try to be a little sweeter on the outside. As I said, I don't have any easy ways to do this, but who said it would be easy to be successful with a difficult child?

- **Develop a team of people to work on the same goals with the child; team interventions have the best outcomes.** If you always wanted to be the Lone Ranger, then don't try to help a troubled child. I am not saying that you can't try to go it alone to help one of these children, but I am saying that you will probably fail miserably. As the saying goes, "It takes a village to raise a child," and that is a normal child. So it must take an industrialized nation to raise a troubled child or at least a major metropolitan area. Most parents are not as aware, as the parents of troubled children, how many adults the child comes into contact with. Now the parents of troubled children are more aware of this because we hear from each of the adults who encounter our little Ahab Junior. All the adults in the child's life want you to make sure they have no more problems with your child. When I get these calls, I quickly change the subject and say, "Now that I have you on the line, when can we meet so I can get your help with this child?" They may turn you down the first time, but soon they will see that either they become a part of the solution, or they pay a bigger price in frustration. Some of these adults will think, "this child may make me miserable, but if I am part of the team, at least I will not be the only one who is miserable." However, as soon as all the adults working together begin to see some signs of hope, there is no better feeling, and everyone on the team is hooked.

I suggest that adults in the child's life meet as a team several times initially, and then stay in contact with phone calls or group e-mails. On the team, I like to see the parents, teachers, therapist, coach, caseworker, attorney, CASA (Court Appointed Special Advocate), youth group leader, big sister, grandparents, and a high-ranking official in your state's national guard (in case the need arises). It is the job of the team to talk about where the child is and where the child needs to go, and to commit to working together to get there. If there are any negative adults in the group, ask them what the other option is to working positively as a team. The child is going to end up getting everyone's attention — do you want it to be a positive or negative experience for yourself and the child?

- **Come across to the child as confident in the role you play as parent, therapist, teacher, grandparent or coach.** It is not just the child who has to "fake it until you make it." It is essential that the child does not see fear in our eyes. Like the wild beasts that they are, fear promotes the attack response, which also happens to be a deep instinctual drive of students toward substitute teachers. This can be ugly, so it is important that you keep your knees from shaking, and you act like a presidential candidate in a debate — wing it and hope no one notices. I am not saying that you should not be emotional at times in trying to parent or work with a difficult child, I am saying not to be emotional within a mile of the child. These children have sensors that detect pain and frustration. Their mental computer puts a benchmark on this experience as a favorite location and they return often. It is neither essential nor possible to always be confident or sure of what you are doing, but put on your game face and make it seem to the child like you have been a winner in this contest all your life.

When I talk about confidence, I am not suggesting that you be rigid or unresponsive to needed adjustments in working with the child. However, whatever you do, I suggest you communicate to the child that you are the parent and you know what you are doing. OK, sometimes you have to stretch the reality a little. Your confidence is important because most of the adults these children have run across have not known what to do or when to do it. When the adult in the situation is confused or powerless, the child's internal alarm goes off, and he acts out to see if the situation is within anyone's control. It is amazing how much of the acting out done by difficult children disappears when the environment signals with confidence that whatever comes up will be managed. The child will need to test this a few times, but if you pass the test, he will turn his attention to some other poor adult to see if he can facilitate early onset dementia.

- **Don't just focus on behaviors, intervene with the whole child: feelings, thoughts, attitudes, beliefs, moral development, and goals.** There may be a strong urge to look mainly at the behaviors of the child; avoid such an urge. Behaviors are what they call you about from school. Behaviors are what we are looking at when the child is having another one of those days. You can even find some experts who talk mainly, or even exclusively, about behaviors. Don't do it! Behaviors are important but they are not the sum total of what we need to understand, work with, and attempt to change. Instead we need to understand, work with and attempt to change the child as a whole person.

Behaviors are seductive in the same way a child's words entice us to overemphasize. We have already covered the limited value of the content meaning of a troubled child's words. Why would his or her behaviors be any more reliable or valid? When the child acts good, does that mean the child is sincere? When a child acts bad, does that mean the child is insincere? I hope you answered no to both questions.

If behaviors are not always good indications of what is going on inside the child, then what is? The times when behaviors are the best indicators of what is going on inside the child is when the child is not aware you are closely observing. When she knows you are watching, she will likely be as phony as a Nigerian e-mail offer to make you a rich person. Behaviors can tell us about the thoughts, feelings and motivations of the child, but we must add more depth to our information. We must include feelings, but only honest emotions. We can find out about the child's thoughts from things she writes or what he shows in his art.

Behaviors are the end result of thoughts impacted by the child's experiential history, flavored by motivations, and filtered through feelings. If we only try to change the behavior, it is like trying to melt the part of the iceberg that protrudes from the frigid water; the more it melts the more that comes from below to take its place. Always ask yourself what the child's motivation is for doing things. Ask what the child is feeling and thinking. These questions will help explain what is behind the behavior and help you plan a course of action to change the conditions that produced the problem behaviors.

Difficult children are complicated. In a way this is good, because when they are young, very few of them understand themselves. This gives us the chance to have the upper hand when we understand the child's thoughts, feelings and behaviors better than the child does. If we can do this, we may be able to provide to the child what he really wants and needs before he figures out how to sabotage getting something worthwhile and truly valuable.

- **Provide an alternative to the problem behaviors that works for the child.** There are very few children who have no goals in life. Troubled children have goals, they are just not the goals we would like them to have, such as controlling everyone and getting everything they can through any means possible. These and other such goals are instilled in the minds and hearts of children who do not wait to be invited to the birthday party, they come early and try to steal the cake. Most difficult children have many goals in life and constantly ask the question, "What can I get out of this?" Don't be fooled by the children who pretend not to want anything in life. Most of the time they are trying to deceive you into believing they want nothing from you, and therefore you can't affect their lives.

> ### Todd's Goal Was to be Noticed
>
> This morning I was working with one of the most difficult children currently in my program. I decided to do one of my frequent experiments. Todd is a child who has a vast repertoire of reprehensible behaviors and attitudes. He is so extreme that he gives himself away. No one would struggle as much as Todd unless there was something to be gained for the effort. I translated the message from Todd that he wanted me to notice him, and he was willing to do most anything to get my notice. Some of his past methods have been urinating on the floor, responding to "good morning" with "Go fuck yourself," and similar pleasantries.
>
> This morning I decided to test my theory of him wanting to be noticed. He tried several of his exaggerated attempts to get attention, each of which I ignored. However, I made sure that every few minutes I checked in on him making his bed and picking up his room before school and let him know I noticed him. He tried to be as negative as possible, among other things he made himself vomit today, which I promptly ignored. What happened in the process of him trying to get noticed with negative behavior and my noticing him behind all the drama was that for the first time in a month, Todd made his bed, picked up his room, dressed himself in school clothes (it took three outfits to get it right), brushed his teeth and was off to school on time. It would have looked ghastly to an outsider — he cried, cursed, rolled on the ground, yelled at others, vomited and after each attempt he looked around to see if I or anyone was noticing. What I did notice was him, not what he was doing.

Once we translate the behavior and the motivations of these children, we have an opportunity to come up with other possible ways the child can get some of what he wants. If it is attention, positive can be more fun the negative, but only if the child learns that positive attention is obtainable. Control over the world may not be possible, but how about control over some aspects of the child's world? The substitution of positive methods over negative methods, to obtain the desired result, is only possible if we determine the desired goal.

I work from the principle that you can't take something away unless you put something in its place. If you don't like what the child is doing, what could meet the need of the child that you could live with? It takes some creativity on your part, but if you try to eliminate a negative trait in the child, unless you fill the space with something else, a more negative trait will often show up to take its place.

- **Separate the child from the behavior and use other aspects of positive discipline in Chapter 3.** It seems simple enough, but just try it for the whole day. Let's see, there is the dear child and there is the odious behavior, don't confuse the two. I think I understand — that is, until the day starts rolling, and I get slapped in the face with the totally ridiculous actions from the child, that I don't deserve. When this happens I must go back and repeat: there is the child and there is the behavior, don't confuse them.

One month after the experience with Todd described above, he is completing the work I expect of him each morning. His tantrums have reduced by 90%, and now we just need to work on the rest of his day. Early on I don't think Todd even realized that he did everything I wanted from him. If he did he probably would have made sure he didn't. From Todd I have received more evidence that what Todd wants out of life is to be noticed, one way or the other. I would prefer the other!

- **Don't lock the child into old behaviors; make sure you are ready for the child to make changes when the child gets to this place.** Human beings are creatures of habit. We develop routines and we settle into established patterns in our daily lives. This is often a good thing and helps us to better manage our lives. There are also times that our habits and patterns lock us into unhelpful behaviors and old attitudes. This pattern can sometimes get in the way when working with a troubled child.

It may very well be that the last 50 times the child was very unpleasant to deal with. However, on the 51st time, if the child was even a little better, would you see the subtle change, or would you stay in the pattern of seeing the child as perpetually unpleasant? If we cannot see improvement or changes made by the child, then we inadvertently lock the child into old behaviors. This is a trap for the child and for the adult as well.

If the child who you have struggled with for years, were to wake up one morning and do a better job, would you notice? We all want to say yes, but would we really be ready for the child to try on some new and more positive behaviors? Many of us would be tempted to say to ourselves or to the child, "So today you want to be the good boy, well I remember what you did last weekend and I'm not buying it." There are many derivations to this message. Some parents would like to take privileges away from the child for the rest of the school year, if not for life. We can become suspicious of any improvement and communicate directly or indirectly to the child, "So what are you up to now?" I am not saying to get fooled by the child's manipulative behavior; but I am saying that if the child begins to see that maybe some positive attention may be a nice change, wouldn't you be interested in the child finding out that positive attention can be considerably better than negative attention? To find this out, you will need to do your part to provide the positive attention; otherwise the child changes and you don't, and the child walks away with the terrible conclusion that it doesn't make any difference, so why even try?

- **Have very clear and firm expectations of the child regardless of how many times the child has not met your expectations.** If I were writing this chapter to help troubled children be more difficult to adults, I would include a section on training adults to lower their expectations. The best way to do this is to never give adults what they ask for, and make sure you turn the situation into a battle so they have to put in much more effort than the result is worth to them. Now that we know these children think in this way (take my word for it), we know what to do and what not to do as adults.

325

What we need to do with difficult children is to be very clear what our expectations are. Be specific and include the goal, the methods, the time frame and the standards you will use to measure the outcome. For example, if the child is to make his bed in the morning, the goal is to have the bed neat, the method is to have both sheets spread out on the bed with the four corners on the four corners of the bed. The blankets neatly cover the sheets and the pillow has a pillow case over the pillow and placed at the head of the bed. The expected time frame is to complete the job in 10 minutes or less, and the final result is an orderly bed that looks good all day and one the child will want to climb into at the end of the day. Now you may be thinking that I am crazy to use this as an example, but stick with me a minute.

For the first three years of our program with difficult children, we were satisfied that the child got up on a school day, managed to eat something without throwing it, and if a toothbrush passed over a few teeth, the child had appropriate clothes and he was off to school before midmorning, we felt we had done what we could. Despite our efforts, we tried and were never successful at getting the children to make their beds and clean their room before they took on the day. We had repeated discussions about the mess in the rooms, unmade beds, and the stuffed animals, clothes and toys scattered all over. The children would return from school and wade through the mess, change out of school clothes, throw them on the floor and the pattern continued. I look back at this period of time as an excellent example of the children training us to believe that they were not capable of meeting our expectations.

To change this pattern we first had to be very clear what our expectations were. The expectations need to be set just a bit higher than you are prepared to accept, because the children will need to give you at least a little less than you want each time (a bit like setting the price for a used car higher to allow for some negotiation room). We finally came to the position that we could not expect the children to behave well in a chaotic environment (their rooms). We established high expectations, we had incentives for completion, and we had disincentives for not meeting the expectations. It took a few weeks but from that point through the last 18 years, every child in our program starts his or her day meeting our expectations on making his or her bed and having a neat room before they proceed with the day. Having an organized space and starting the day following orderly instructions symbolizes the job of the child for the rest of the day. Now I can't imagine it being any other way, but I do remember when it wasn't that way, and it was primarily an adjustment the adults had to make, and the children quickly caught on once we got our act together.

There are many similar examples like the one I used of making a bed. The task is not difficult even for the four-year-olds we have had in our program. The challenge is to communicate the expectation, follow through and not allow the child to lower your expectations by consistently not giving you what you want. Most every difficult child will try this strategy, but you need to spot this immediately. Now every new child coming into our program gets up the first day and says some form of the following, "I don't know how to make a bed," or "I don't make my bed in the morning, adults do that for me." To which I reply, "Does this look like a Holiday Inn?" When new children start with the excuses, nearly every time one of the other children in the program will reply, "Dave will not buy that line, don't even waste your energy."

Consider your expectations of your child; are they fair, are they possible, and are they helpful to the child in the long run? If yes to each, then consider which expectations are not being met, and ask yourself if the child has trained you to either give up on this issue, or has trained you into lowering your expectations. My formula is that if you set the goal (on a standard of a 10 being perfect) at 7 you will get a 5.5 from the child, but if you set the goal lower at 5.5 you only get a 4. My suggestion is that you hold your high expectations to the child with a clear message that you know the child can do it, and then be internally prepared to live with a little less than 100%. As time goes by, raise the bar gradually and you will be surprised how much improvement you will notice.

- **Get the consultation and help you need.** Working with difficult children is a team sport, it is not for loners or adults who think they can do it all. You can't do it all. Learn to ask for help because you will need it nearly every day. I have been working with dozens of difficult children nearly every day of the last 21 years, and I do not get through the day without asking someone for information or ideas about a plan for a child. Some of my newer staff look at me with surprise at this and say, "Wait a minute, aren't you the expert on these children, why are you asking for my ideas?" They soon learn that we all need other eyes, ears and ideas to do the best job we can do.

Finding the Consultation You Need

Nearly each day I hear from people around the country with the question, "Can you refer me to someone in my town who can help coach me with my troubled child?" Whether they live in Fresno, Fargo or Ft. Lauderdale, my answer is the same. It may take a little time, but it will be worth it in the end to follow this approach. Make three calls: to a counselor in the yellow pages, a large local non-profit that works with children, and the local county or state mental health organization. Ask each for a list of three local therapists with experience with very difficult children. Compare the lists and see who is mentioned more than once. Call the person and ask if they understand the concept of helping you with your child by being a coach for you and your family. If there is only silence on the other end of the phone, thank the person and return to your list and try again. Once you find someone to coach you with your child, you must be clear what type of help you are asking for (and it is probably not to resolve your issues with your own mother). The clearer you are about what you want, the better your chance of getting it.

For too long we have had a belief in our culture that parenting should come naturally to people; and therefore it is a sign of ignorance to ask for help. The only sign of ignorance I can imagine is to believe you know all you need to know, and you don't need ideas from others. Fortunately, difficult children teach us in a big hurry that we do not have all the answers, and our desperation will ask for the help if our wisdom does not. The critical point is to ask for the type of consultation that you need, and do so when you need it, which is long before you have reached your breaking point.

- **Ensure adequate supervision of the child.** There is no substitute for adult supervision. In our program we have violent children and we have children who sexually act out and attempt to victimize others. We also have boys and girls together. At first glance this sounds like a formula for disaster. The first question I am asked about the program is, "How do you manage all this?" The two word answer is proper supervision. How do parents make sure their child is not sexually acting out with the neighbor children? Adequate supervision. How do you know if the child bathes, eats, plays, dresses, brushes, studies, works and plays appropriately? Adequate supervision. Some parents respond, "Sure, I can keep the child on the straight and narrow if I follow him around all day long, but that is impossible." If it is impossible, then you will not have the child on the straight and narrow.

I repeat — there is no substitute for good supervision. The unsupervised times that normal children are given cannot be afforded to difficult children. It may be impossible for you to follow the child around all day, but other adults must play this role when you are not there. Without the level of supervision needed, you will be meeting with the principal or the policeman about the result of the unsupervised time for your little Hell's Angel in training. In addition to common sense, all the professional research points out that parental supervision of children is a necessary factor in long-term behavioral improvement of difficult children regardless of the problem.

- **Make sure you get some time away from the child; if your batteries are low, you are both in trouble.** "OK, if I have to supervise the child 24 hours a day, how do I keep from losing my ever-loving mind?" Obviously you can't personally supervise the child 24 hours a day. This is where the village comes in, and why parenting is a team sport. If you tried to play volleyball by yourself, you have no one to pass the ball to and no one to rely on. Some parents even make life more challenging by home schooling their budding Einstein. Although I don't recommend this with a troubled child because of the complexity of meeting the child's academic needs, the parents who do this need to ensure more than other parents that they have some time away from the child.

What kind of parents make plans to get away from their child? My answer is a good parent. No one is served well when a parent and a troubled child are figuratively handcuffed to each other all day, every day. If you have not found a need for other help with your child, then this will give you instant reason to pass the torch to other adults while you go off and tango, golf, participate in civil war reenactments, or join the tag team needle point league. You will need to decide how to best recharge your batteries, and do it in a hurry. I am not talking about having a week off from your child every few weeks, I am talking about a few hours every day and perhaps a day every few weeks. If you are not sure you need the time away from the child, after checking your vital signs, take the time anyway for the child's benefit. She needs a break from you as much as you need a break from her.

- **View every situation as an opportunity to learn.** As a student yourself you are expected to make some mistakes along the way. I have saved the most important success strategies for last. The first is change your thinking from, "How do I get through the day?" to "How can I learn the most today?" Your child will be teaching you constantly what works and doesn't work, and the question is: are you constantly learning? There is a minor shift in thinking but a major change in results, from targeting the goal to having as little conflict as possible in a day, to using every daily opportunity to learn to be a better parent.

If I was to pick one factor that was present in all the parents and staff I have known that I would consider successful with difficult children, it would be that these successful adults viewed every challenge, not as a disruption in their day, but as an opportunity to get better at understanding and being successful with the child. If this is an adjustment you do not believe you can ever make, then I do not hold out much hope that you will in the long run be what the child needs, and be able to personally grow and find satisfaction for yourself. But don't be too hasty in saying this change in thinking, or any other adjustment described in this book, is not something you can do. Others before you have made the adjustment and with effort, support, consultation and sometimes prayer, you can probably make the adjustment as well.

- **Do your best and don't take the outcome personally.** The final strategy is a mind set to first, do your best and second, not to be emotionally attached to the outcome. Don't make the mistake of thinking that your best is some form of perfection. By definition your best, on this day and in this situation, is the very best you can do today and with the situation as it is. Fritz Perls, a psychoanalyst once said that when you look closely at behavior, everyone is doing the best they can at any particular time. What we all need is the confidence, the support, and a plan to do even better. From this framework we should all accept that we are doing our best, which is not to say that we can't improve in the future.

Parenting, coaching and teaching are tasks that are not unilateral — they require an interactional relationship. We cannot look at only one side of the interaction. The world's best teacher could work with a child who does not learn from the interaction. It is possible that a mediocre teacher could have a student who learns a great deal. There are many potential factors here, but there is no formula that guarantees a certain outcome. Although we all want the children we work with to succeed in life (otherwise you wouldn't be reading this book, you would be reading Stephen King because you would be short on nightmares), the only thing we can control is our part of the interaction.

There is another needed adjustment in thinking here. The best measure of success for an intervention is how well we did our part, and not what the child did with the opportunity. If we measured our ability and success as a parent the way parents with normal children do (how the child turns out), we are asking for trouble. The only way to hang-in-there day after day and year after year, is to keep doing your part and improving what you have control over — you. My experience is that this and other adjustments in thinking will positively affect the child, but there are no guarantees. When all is said and done, you must accept that your best is good enough, or in the future there is a padded room waiting for you with your name on it.

Not All Traumatized Children Are Still Young

We must recognize an unmistakable fact: traumatized children grow up and become adults. Because trauma can affect the individual throughout his or her life, the effects of trauma will often continue to be a factor throughout adulthood. Many of the individuals who are working with difficult children were traumatized themselves during childhood. This would include parents, teachers and therapists. Due to the prevalence of trauma, the odds are good that approximately 50% or more of the people doing their best to help traumatized children have their own history of trauma. This situation can present complicated dynamics, and requires attention by both the individual with the traumatic background and others who try to be of support to the person.

Trauma memories are recorded in the limbic area of the brain, and new events that remind the individual of their past, bring up old feelings and struggles from the past. It is highly likely that working with someone else who has been abused or otherwise traumatized will remind the brain of the past. This can put the individual at a disadvantage in trying to meet the needs of a child, while struggling with very similar personal needs at the same time.

How the adult's past trauma affects the present depends in part on the role the adult is called upon to play. Most often this role is being a parent — biological, foster or adopted. However, a portion of professionals, (therapists, teachers and caseworkers) also have a history of trauma. It is important for traumatized parents to have an understanding of how the past is playing a part in the present. It is even more important for professionals, who have the responsibility to help the child and the parents, to have the self-awareness of internal responses to situations involving abuse.

Parents can make mistakes on both ends of a continuum. Parents may have a tendency to be empathetic and focus on supporting the child by going easy on expectations and rules, which is not what the child needs. Or parents may go to the other extreme and replay some of the harsh or unresponsive adult energy they encountered as a child. A therapist may be unaware of picking sides, or of becoming the child's protector and advocate and viewing the parents and the system as the problem. As soon as this happens, the therapist's influence with the family is minimized. Caseworkers are often in the role of making decisions over the child's life. Caseworkers may project their own past when they decide to remove a child from an adequate home, or keep a child in an inadequate home based more on their own past than the present situation. What complicates this dynamic is that the adult often has no idea how much influence the past has on present thoughts, opinions and decisions.

It is incumbent upon all of us to consider how our own past plays a role in our present. If we have been through serious trauma in our lives, we will likely be affected when we encounter someone else who has also been abused. The key is self-awareness and obtaining outside consultation to help us see what we don't see within ourselves. Professionals are often called upon to help parents with their difficult child. Some of us also supervise therapists or caseworkers in the roles they play in the lives of children and families. How past trauma can impact our role in helping others can get very complex, but the principles we discussed in Section 2 of this book can help — not only in understanding and working with traumatized children, but also working with adults with a history of trauma.

The following is a list of the most frequent effects of trauma. If you have a trauma history, it is important that you ask yourself if you are aware of how these factors affect you. If you are in the role of helping an adult with a history of trauma assist a traumatized child, these are the issues that you must be aware of and prepared to address. Without our collective ability to stop the cycle of trauma, and the frequent subconscious impact on our lives and our impact on others, the negative cycle of reactivity based on trauma will continue with children, with parents and with professionals who are attempting to help.

Problem	Solution
Trauma produces a tendency to get stuck and organize our lives around negative experiences.	*Cognitive restructuring, which means to use our reasoning abilities to self-reflect and work through or around the roadblocks we encounter due to the past.*
Affective blindness toward the needs of others due to unmet needs within the self.	*Model the acceptance of feelings and the experiences of the other person to help them get beyond their own restricted emotional development.*
Feelings of powerlessness produce an exaggerated need to control others and the environment.	*Help the individual experience control in appropriate areas.*
The loss of self-regulation resulting in behavior, feelings and words that damage others.	*Help the person experience internal controls.*

Problem	Solution
The inability to use personal feelings as a guide to make wise decisions.	*Understand and learn to work with depression, guilt and fear in the person you are working with. Help the person reflect on the role feelings can play in making good decisions.*
Primary focus on what is wrong and the negative.	*Provide an external reality check that includes the positive as well as the negative.*
Loss of the ability to play and have fun.	*Help the person learn to enjoy activities, people and life in general.*
Lack of personal confidence.	*Help the individual experience small successes through skill building and external feedback.*
Lack of trust in others.	*Develop a supportive relationship with the individual that eliminates threat.*
Personal isolation.	*Develop environmental supports for the individual.*

You will see that the above list can be used for helping a traumatized child, or an adult with a history of abuse, or supervising a professional who is charged with intervening in a trauma case. How you accomplish the above solutions is up to you, your creativity and your style. However, if many of the above problems are not addressed, the outcomes may not be positive. Each of the above problems are often present in some form, but the way the dynamics play out often depends on the particulars of the situation. What is true for children is also true for adults, the effects of trauma do not tend to improve without some form of outside intervention. Encourage the adult you are working with to get the type of help that aids moving beyond the traumatic past.

Which Children Are Reachable and Which Are Not?

The quick answer to which children can be helped and which cannot is that it is not always possible for us to know. Because we cannot always be sure at the time, every child must be approached with the belief that the child is reachable. It can be difficult to know when a child has improved. In our treatment program, we have had children deteriorate and have the public school call us and say how much better the child is in class. When an angry child with behavior problems becomes depressed and gives up fighting, this can look like progress, but the child is going in the wrong direction. Other children who internalize their problems often have to act out as a part of their growth and healing, and this positive step can look like the child has deteriorated. Working with difficult children is not rocket science — it is much more complex and difficult. For this reason the parent of a difficult child never graduates from parenting school.

We must use our intuition to understand what is going on inside of the child, information the child often does not know. As we progress in our ability to work with difficult children, we learn to use and trust our intuition. There are times when problems are at their worst, but we may sense there is a breakthrough on the horizon. At other times, everything around the child seems calm, but you have a feeling that either something doesn't seem right, or this calm is not going to last. All we can do is our best, and it is a full-time job to try to figure out what to do next.

The parent of a difficult child can put too much energy into wondering how this child may turn out. Investing energy in short-term goals can be more important than long range goals. The real work is right now, not two years or five years from now when the child goes into junior high school, or may be infected by the drug, sex and rock and roll virus. Either as a parent, therapist or teacher, you have plenty on your plate to get through today helping the child become more successful, while ensuring that you don't take up bungee jumping without the bungee.

The voice of experience reminds me that I don't often know the impact that I have on the children I work with. This voice is helped by the hundreds of times the children tell me about this impact, but do so 5, 10 or even 15 years later. It is very similar to when teenagers leave the family home for college or other independent pursuits, and only after they have been gone awhile can some of them tell you thanks for giving them the structure that taught them how to succeed. Some of the children who are the most angry with me at the time are the ones who later tell me they hated me when I held them accountable, but they learned what accountability was. I find it interesting that I have many more children who get back to me years later and thank me for being very firm with them, than say thanks for being kind and patient with them. But I know that, without the child's inner sense that I am kind and supportive of them while being firm out of love, I would just be another demanding adult who wants something from the child but gives little in return.

I consider myself a good psychologist and an excellent judge of character. Despite this, I do not always judge correctly children with whom I have worked. Most of the children that I believe I have reached turn out to show that I was correct. However, I am happy to say there are some children that I am sure I did not reach, only to hear from the child later and find out that my determination was wrong and I had an impact. My point here is that we do not always know how much of an influence we have had on difficult children. Sometimes we are so involved, and rightfully so, with the work at hand that we are not the best at recognizing subtle improvements; much less at foretelling the future. We can never underestimate the impact on the child of even one adult who wants nothing of the child other than the child's success in life. I have learned to say that I don't have a sense that I reached a particular child, but I cannot be sure. Whether I made a difference or not on the child, the process of helping and loving with or without being loved in return has made a difference within me. At the end of the day, I can only be held accountable for my part. Doing my part, to the best of my ability, needs to be enough to qualify for personal success.

No-Lose Parenting

With the odds of success seemingly against our efforts to parent, to coach, and to teach difficult children, how is it possible to consider this task a no lose proposition? Our ultimate success in life is not a matter of external acts and grand accomplishments. Nearly every religion in the world stresses internal, not external, progress. Major factors in external accomplishments are timing and luck, and not always hard work and great ideas, although these certainly help. In contrast, internal success involves essentially no luck and requires the right kind of hard work throughout the journey; and as the Nike advertisements tell us, there is no finish line.

The best measure of our progress as a parent is not to look to our accomplishments, but to look inward at who we have become. It is possible to work for years only to have a child who still tells you that she hates you, and she can't wait to get out on her own to be able to make poor decisions. The teacher cannot control the internalization of the learner. The best of coaches cannot get out on the field and make the plays for the athlete. Despite the pervasive values of our culture, winning is not the best measure of a good coach. There is only one coach who wins the Superbowl or World Series; but there are many good coaches, some on teams with losing records, and others who are fired at the end of the season.

As a child matures, it is your responsibility to provide opportunities for him or her to make better decisions. This is true even with difficult children, although we need to take many factors into consideration. Unless you want to stretch your parenting job into a 30- or 40-year endeavor, at some point you will need to stand back and see what the child does with all the help and learning you have provided. When it is the troubled child's turn to make the decisions, the results are not always pretty. So if the young man loses his driver's license due to traffic tickets, or shoplifts and spends a couple nights in jail, have you failed as a parent? The only meaningful answer to that question is your own answer. However, my answer is that if you have done your best to teach the child that there are consequences for our actions, and being responsible is a necessary personal quality, then what the child decides to do is his report card, not yours.

So much of parenting is about our thinking. Many of the factors that will affect whether you fail or succeed at working with difficult children will depend on your thinking; as I said, this is not rocket science, this is much more difficult.

Yes, I believe we can take on the hardest challenge in parenting or working with a difficult child, and we can proceed with the confidence that we can learn, we can influence, and we can succeed. As I am sure you do as well, I prefer to succeed along with the child, but this doesn't happen every time. Whether you succeed along with the child has a lot to do with your own outlook and disposition in working with the child. Please understand that I am not letting anyone off the hook for doing a mediocre job of parenting. Just like in teaching, there are some children who grow and develop in spite of the poor parenting they receive. There are other children who take what a parent offers and surprises everyone with the quality of their decisions. In both these cases, I give the major credit to the child. But if we do all we can, and the child throws our gifts in the trash bin, then I give the credit to the parent and not the blame.

So the way to work with a difficult child and have it a no-lose proposition is to: do your homework, never stop learning, use your mental skills, model being healthy, continue to reach out regardless of the response, take care of yourself, get the help you need, change most of your thinking about parenting, learn to enjoy the process, and don't give up! I didn't say it was easy, but I do believe it is possible.

Thank you for all you do for every child described in this book. Like you, these children are trying to navigate difficult waters, sometimes not very well. If we choose to help, then we are in this together with the child and the support system we develop. And if we remember it is not only about the child, and not only about the external results, we can find deeper meaning in our efforts. To all of you I wish you great challenge, much struggle, and above all continual success.

SUCCEEDING RATHER THAN FAILING REQUIRES

✓ Taking care of yourself.

✓ Learning from every situation.

✓ Seeing below the surface of behavior problems.

✓ Being firm and even tough in a loving way.

✓ Knowing when and from whom to ask for help.

✓ Never ceasing to work on yourself; it is great modeling.

✓ Having fun along the way.

✓ Taking the time it requires to understand the child.

✓ Always translating the meaning of the behavior.

✓ Making sure the child feels your support.

✓ Giving more praise than criticism.

✓ Showing confidence to the child.

✓ Developing a team of adults to work together.

✓ Separating the child from the child's behavior.

✓ Affecting the child's mind, body and spirit and not just behavior.

✓ Not locking the child into problem behaviors.

✓ Ensuring adequate supervision.

✓ Not letting the child lower your expectations.

✓ Doing your best and not taking the outcome personally.

Appendix: Building Blocks of Treating Emotional Disturbance

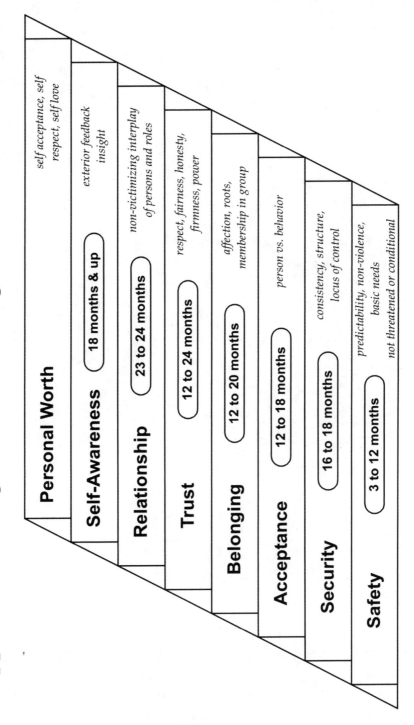

Personal Worth — 18 months & up — *self acceptance, self respect, self love*

Self-Awareness — 23 to 24 months — *exterior feedback insight*

Relationship — 12 to 24 months — *non-victimizing interplay of persons and roles*

Trust — 12 to 20 months — *respect, fairness, honesty, firmness, power*

Belonging — 12 to 18 months — *affection, roots, membership in group*

Acceptance — 16 to 18 months — *person vs. behavior*

Security — 3 to 12 months — *consistency, structure, locus of control*

Safety — *predictability, non-violence, basic needs not threatened or conditional*

References and Suggested Reading

Altimari, D., Weiss, E.M., Blint, D.F., Poitras, C. & Megan, K. (1998). *Deadly Restraint: Killed by a system intended for care. Hartford Courant*, Hartford, Connecticut (8/16/98).

American Academy of Pediatrics—Committee on Pediatric Emergency Medicine (1997). *Pediatric, 99* (3), 497-498.

American Psychiatric Association. (2000). *Diagnostic and Statistical Manual of Mental Disorders, Fourth Edition Text Revision.* Washington, DC: American Psychiatric Association.

Bath, H. (1994). The physical restraint of children: Is it therapeutic? *American Journal of Orthopsychiatry, 64* (11), 40-48.

Barkley, R.A. (1987). *Defiant Children: A Clinician's Manual For Parent Training.* New York: Guilford.

Barth, R.P. (2001). *Institutions vs. Foster Homes: the Empirical Base for the Second Century of Debate.* Chapel Hill, NC: UNC, School of Social Work, Jordan Institute for Families.

Baudewyns, P.A., Hyer, L., Woods, M.G., Harrison, W.R. & McCranie, E. (1990). PTSD among Vietnam veterans: An early look at treatment outcomes using direct therapeutic exposure. *Journal of Traumatic Stress, 3,* 359-368.

Belsky, J. & Nezworski, T. (1988). *Clinical Implications of Attachment.* Hillsdale, NJ: Lawrence Erlbaum Associates.

Benard, B. (1993). *Turning the corner from risk to resiliency.* San Francisco: WestEd Regional Educational Laboratory.

Berrick, J.D., Barth, R.P., Needell, B. & Jonson-Reid, M. (1997). Group Care and Young Children. *Social Service Review,* June.

Bickman, L. (1996). A Continuum Of Care, More Is Not Always Better. *American Psychologist, 51* (7), 689-701.

Blake, D.D. (1993). Treatment outcome research on posttraumatic stress disorder. *CP Clinician Newsletter, 3,* 14-17.

Bowlby, J. (1982). *Attachment.* New York: Basic Books Inc.

Brom, D., Kleber, R.J. & Defares, P.B. (1989). Brief psychotherapy for posttraumatic stress disorders. *Journal of Consulting and Clinical Psychology, 57* (5), 607-612.

Caspi, A., Elder, G.H. & Bem, D.J. (1987). Moving against the world: Life course patterns of explosive children. *Developmental Psychology, 23,* 308-313.

Chamberlain, P. & Reid, J.B. (1998). Comparison of two community alternative to incarceration for chronic juvenile offenders. *Journal of Consulting and Clinical Psychology, 66* (4), 624-633.

Cooper, N.A., & Clum, G.A. (1989). Imaginal flooding as a supplementary treatment for PTSD in combat veterans: A controlled study. *Behavior Therapy, 20* (3), 381-391.

Cotton, N. (1989). The developmental-clinical rationale for the use of seclusion in psychiatric treatment of children. *American Journal of Orthopsychiatry, 59,* 442-450.

Council on Accreditation for Children and Family Services (2002). *Accreditation Standards 7ᵗʰ Edition.* New York, NY.

Crespi, T.D. (1990). Restraint and Seclusion with Institutionalized Adolescents. *Adolescence, 25,* (100), 825-828.

Crisis Prevention Institute, Inc. (2001). *Nonviolent Crisis Intervention Training Manual.* Brookfield, WI.

Eisen, M., Donald, C.A., Ware, J.E., & Brook, R.H. (1980). *Conceptualization and measurement of health for children in the health insurance study.* The Rand Corporation: Santa Monica, CA. R-2313-HEW.

Elliott, D.S. Hamburg, B. & Williams, K. (Eds.) (1998). *Violence in American Schools.* New York: Cambridge.

Elliott, D.S. Huizinga, K, & Menard, S. (1989). *Multiple Problem Youth: Delinquency, Substance Use and Mental Health Problems.* New York: Springer-Verlag.

Erickson, M., Sroufe, A. & Egeland, B. (1985). The relationship between quality of attachment and behavior problems in preschool in a high-risk sample. *Monograph for the Society for Research in Child Development, 50,* 147-166.

Fahlberg, V.I. (1991) *A Child's Journey Through Placement*. Indianapolis: Perspective Press.

Fairchild-Kienlen, S. (2001). The Clinical Assessment Of Attachment Disorder In Children 3-13: An Evaluation Of the Attachment Disorder Assessment Scale. Doctoral Dissertation from The University of Texas at Arlington.

Federici, R.S. (2003). *Help for the Hopeless Child: A Guide for Families*. Alexandria, VA: Federici and Associates.

Felitti, V.J., Anda, R.F., Nordenberg, D., Williamson, D.F., Spitz, A.M., Edwards, V. & Koss, M.P. (1998). The relationship of adult health status to childhood abuse and household dysfunction. *American Journal of Preventive Medicine, 14*, 245-258. 1

Foa, E.B., Keane, T.M. & Friedman, M.J. (2000). *Effective Treatments for PTSD*. New York: Guilford Press.

Foa, E.B., Rothbaum, B.O., Riggs, D.S. & Murdock, G.B. (1991). Treatment of posttraumatic stress disorder in rape victims: Comparison between cognitive behavioral procedures and counseling. *Journal of Consulting and Clinical Psychology, 59*, 715-723.

Foa, E.B., Steketee, G. & Rothbaum, B.O. (1989). Behavioral/cognitive conceptualizations of post-traumatic stress disorder. *Behavior Therapy, 20*, 155-176.

Fulghum, R. (1990). *All I Really Need To Know I Learned In Kindergarten*. New York: Villard Books.

Hawkins, J.D. (Ed.) (1996). *Delinquency and Crime: Current Theories*. New York: Cambridge University Press.

Hawkins, J.D., Catalano, R.F. & Miller, J.Y. (1992). Risk and protective factors for alcohol and other drug problems. *Psychological Bulletin, 112* (1), 64-105.

Henderson N. & Milstein M.M. (2003). *Resiliency in Schools, Making it happen for students and educators*. Thousand Oaks, CA: Corwin Press, Inc.

Hyde, P.S., Falls, K., Morris, J.A. & Schoenwald, S.K. (2003). *Turning Knowledge Into Practice*. Boston: The Technical Assistance Collaborative.

Hoagwood, K. (2003). The Evidence For And Against Evidence Based Practices. Keynote address to the National Symposium on Evidence Based Practices, Portland, OR.

Hollander, E. & Stein, D.J. (Eds.) (1995). *Impulsivity and Aggression*. Toronto: Wiley.

Hughes, J. & Hasbrouck, J. (1996). Television violence: Implications for violence prevention. *School Psychology Review, 25* (2), 134-151.

James, B. (1994). *Handbook for Treatment of Attachment-Trauma Problems in Children*. New York: Lexington Books, Macmillan Inc.

Joint Commission On Accreditation of Health Care Organizations (1996). *Accreditation Manual for Hospitals: Volume 1 – Standards*. Oakbrook Terrace, Il.

Keane, T.M., Fairbank, J.A., Caddell, J.M. & Zimering, R.T. (1989). Implosive (flooding) therapy reduces symptoms of PTSD in Vietnam combat veterans. *Behavior Therapy, 20* (2), 245-260.

Kirkwood, S. (2003). Practicing Restraint. *Children's Voice, 12* (5), pp. 14-19.

LaGreca, A.M., Vemberg, E.M., Silverman, W.K. & Prinstein, M.J. (1996). Symptoms of posttraumatic stress in children after Hurricane Andrew: A prospective study. *Journal of Consulting and clinical Psychology, 64,* 712-723.

Lambert M.J. & Bergin, A.E. (1994). The effectiveness of psychotherapy. In A.E. Bergin and S.L. Garfield (eds.), *Handbook of Psychotherapy and Behavior Change*. New York: John Wiley & Sons.

Lamberti, J.S. & Cummings, S. (1992). Hands-on restraint in the treatment of multiple personality disorder. *Hospital and Community Psychiatry, 43* (3), 283-284.

Larson, J. (1994). Violence prevention in the schools: A review of selected programs and procedures. *School Psychology Review, 23*(2), 151-164.

LeDoux, J.E. (2002). *Synaptic Self: How Our Brains Become Who We Are*. New York: Viking.

Lewis, M., Feiring, C., McGuggog, C. & Jaskir, J. (1984). Predicting psychopathology in six-year-olds from early social relations. *Child Development, 55,* 1123-1136.

Lieberman, C. (1994). *Television and Violence.* Westlake Village, CA: Council of State Governments Conference on School Violence.

Loeber, R., Farrington, D.P. & Washchbusch, D.A. (1998). *Serious and violent juvenile offenders: risk factors and successful interventions.* Thousand Oaks, CA: Sage Publications.

Masters, K.J. & Bellonci, C. (2002). Practice Parameters for the Prevention and Management of Aggressive Behavior in Child and Adolescent Psychiatric Institutions, With Special Reference to Seclusion and Restraint. *Journal of American Academy of Child and Adolescent Psychiatry, 41*(2), 4-25.

Matos, L., Arend, R.A. & Sroufe, L.A. (1978). Continuity of adaptation in the second year: The relationship between quality of attachment and later competence. *Society for Research in Child Development, 49,* 547-556.

Maylath, N.S. (1990). Development of the Children's Health Ratings Scale. *Health Education Quarterly, 17*(1), 89-97.

VanAntwerp, C. A. (1995). The Lifestyle Questionnaire for School-aged Children: A tool for primary care. *Journal of Pediatric Health Care, 9,* 251-255.

Measham, T.J. (1995). The acute management of aggressive behaviors in hospitalized children and adolescents. *Canadian Journal of Psychiatry, 40* (6), 330-336.

Miller D., Walker, M.C. & Friedman D. (1989). Use of a holding technique to control the violent behavior of seriously disturbed adolescents. *Hospital and Community Psychiatry, 40* (5), 520-524.

Monahan, J. & Steadman, H. (1994). *Violence and Mental Disorder.* Chicago: University of Chicago Press.

Mordock, J.B. (2002). A model of milieu treatment: its implementation and factors contributing to "Drift" from the model over a 30-year period. *Residential Treatment for Children & Youth, 20*(1), 29-51.

National Association of Psychiatric Health Systems, Washington, D.C.

National Technical Assistance Center for State Mental Health Planning (2002). *Networks*, Alexandria, VA.

Patterson, G.R., Reid, J.B. & Dishion, T.J. (1992). *Antisocial boys (Vol. 4): A social interactional approach.* Eugene, OR: Castalia.

Pepler, D. & Rubin, K. (Eds.) (1991). *The Development and Treatment of Childhood Aggression.* Hillsdale, NJ: Lawrence Erlbaum.

Perry, B.D. (1997). Incubated in Terror: Neurodevelopmental Factors in the 'Cycle of Violence.' In *Children, Youth and Violence: The Search for solutions.* J. Osofsky, (Ed.) New York: Guilford Press.

Perry, B.D., Pollard, R.A., Blakely, T.L., Baker, W.L. & Vigilante, D. (1995). Childhood trauma, the neurobiology of adaptation, and "use-dependent" development of the brain: How "states" become "traits." *Infant Mental Health Journal, 16,* 271-291.

Peniston, E.G. (1986). EMG biofeedback-assisted desensitization treatment for Vietnam combat veterans with post-traumatic stress disorder. *Clinical Biofeedback and Health, 9*(1), 35-41.

Resick, P.A. & Schnicke, M.K. (1992). Cognitive processing therapy for sexual assault victims. *Journal of Consulting and Clinical Psychology,* 60(5), 748-756.

Rich, C. (1997). The use of physical restraint in residential treatment: an ego psychology perspective in residential treatment for children and youth. *Residential Treatment for Children and Youth, 14,* 1-12.

Rolider, A., Williams, L., Cummings, A. & Van Houten, R. (1991). The use of a brief movement restriction procedure to eliminate severe inappropriate behavior. *Journal of Behavioral Therapy and Experimental Psychiatry, 22* (1), 23-30.

Rubin, K.H. & Lollis, S.P. (1988). Origins and consequences of social withdrawal. In J. Belsky & T. Nezworski (Eds.), *Clinical Implications of Attachment.* Hillsdale, NJ: Lawrence Erlbaum Asociates.

Rutter, M., Giller, H. & Hagell, A. (1998). *Antisocial Behavior By Young People.* New York: Cambridge.

Satcher, D. (2001). Youth Violence: A Report of the Surgeon General. United States Department of Health and Human Services.

Schore, A.N. (1994). *Affect Regulation and the Origin of the Self: the Neurobiology of Emotional Development*. Hillsdale, N.J.: Erlbaum.

Sgroi, S.M. (1989). *Handbook of Clinical Intervention In Child Sexual Abuse*. Toronto: Lexington Books.

Seigel, D.J. (1999). *The Developing Mind: Toward a neurobiology of Interpersonal Experience*. New York: Guilford Press.

Smith, P.A. (1993). *Training Manual for Professional Assault Response Training Revised*.

Snyder, H.N. & Sickmund, M. (1999). *Juvenile offenders and victims: 1999 National Report*. Washington, DC: United States Department of Justice.

Sourander, A., Aurela, A. & Piha, J. (1996) Therapeutic holding in child and adolescent psychiatric inpatient treatment. *Nordic Journal of Psychiatry*, 50 (5), 375-380.

Sprague, J. (2003) *Improving School Climate, Safety and Student Health*. Eugene, OR: Institute on Violence and Aggressive Behavior.

Stephens, R.D. (1995). *Safe Schools: A Handbook for Violence Prevention*. Bloomington, IN: National Educational Service.

Stirling, C. & McHugh, A. (1998). Developing a non-aversive intervention strategy in the management of aggression and violence for people with learning disabilities using natural therapeutic holding. *Journal of Advanced Nursing, 27* (3), 503-509.

Sugar, M. (1994). Wrist-holding for the out of control child. *Child Psychiatry and Human Development, 24* (3), 145-155.

Teather, E.C. (2001). A Peek into the Trrenches: Changes and Challenges in Residential Care. *Residential Treatment for Children & Youth, 19* (1), 1-20.

Terr, L.C. (1993). *Unchained Memories*. New York: Basic Books.

Troutman, B., Myers, K., Borchardt, C., Kowalski, R. & Burbrick, J. (1998). Case study: When restraints are the least restrictive alternative for managing aggression. *Journal of the American Academy of Child and Adolescent Psychiatry, 37* (5), 554-555.

Van der Kolk, B.A. (1996). The complexity of adaptation to trauma: Self-regulation, stimulus discrimination, and characterological development. In van der Kolk, M.A., McFarlane, A.C., & Weisaeth, L. (Eds.), *Traumatic Stress: The Effects of Overwhelming Experience on Mind, Body and Society,* pp. 182-213. New York: Guilford Press.

Verhaagen, D. (2003). Assessing and managing violence risk in juveniles. Presentation at Medford, OR.

Walker, H. M., Colvin, G. & Ramsey, E. (1995). *Antisocial Behavior in School: Strategies and Best Practices.* Pacific Grove, CA: Brooks/Cole.

Walker, H.M., Irvin, L.K. & Sprague, J.R. (1997). *Violence Prevention and School Safety: Issues, Problems, Approaches, and Recommended Solutions.* University of Oregon Institute on Violence and Destructive Behavior.

Webster, C. & Jackson, M. (Eds.) (1997). *Impulsivity: Theory, Assessment, & Treatment.* New York: Guilford Press.

Whittaker, J.K. (2000). The Future of Residential Group Care. *Child Welfare 79* (1), 59-77.

Whittaker, J.K. (2000) Reinventing Residential Child Care: An Agenda for Research & Preactice. *Residential Treatment for Children and Youth, 17* (3), 13-30.

Whittaker, J.K. & Maluccio, A.N. (2002). Rethinking "Child Placement": A Reflective Essay. *Social Service Review, 76* (1), 108-134.

Wong, S.E. (1990). How therapeutic is therapeutic holding? *Journal of Psychiatric Nursing & Mental Health, 28* (11), 24-28.

Ziegler, D.L. & Littlebury, J.A. (1994). *Mission Impossible, or Is It?* Jasper, OR: SCAR/Jasper Mountain.

Ziegler, D.L. (2001). To Hold, or Not to Hold...Is That the Right Question? *Residential Treatment for Children & Youth, 18* (4), 33-45.

Ziegler, D.L. (2000). *Raising Children Who Refuse To Be Raised.* Phoenix: Acacia Publishing.

Ziegler, D.L. (2002). *Traumatic Experience and the Brain, A handbook for understanding and treating those traumatized as children.* Phoenix: Acacia Publishing.

Ziegler, D.L. (2004). Attachment Disorder Assessment Scale — Revised. Jasper, OR: SCAR/Jasper Mountain.

Achieving Success with Impossible Children

How to Win the Battle of Wills

Dave Ziegler, Ph.D.
Executive Director,
SCAR/Jasper Mountain,
Jasper, Oregon

SCAR/Jasper Mountain
37875 Jasper Lowell Rd.
Jasper, OR 97438-9704
E-Mail: Davez@scar-jaspermtn.org

ISBN: 0966657292

LCCN: 2004112674

Cover design by The Cricket Contrast
Published by Acacia Publishing, Inc.
Phoenix, Arizona
www.acaciapublishing.com
Printed and bound in the United States of America

This volume is dedicated to Judy Littlebury.
In our many years of working together, she has challenged me,
taught me, and supported me. Many of the ideas presented here
either came from her or have been influenced by her.
My life has been enriched
by our partnership.

Also from the author of

Achieving Success with Difficult Children...

Raising difficult children can be a daunting task, but Dr. Dave Ziegler can help. *Raising Children who Refuse to Be Raised* (2000) deals with problems ranging from ADHD to attachment issues, from manipulation to deeply antisocial behavior.

"If you are a parent or therapist of a child who lies, steals, is hyperactive, traumatized, distrustful, aggressive, belligerent, or explosive, you will find in this book the fundamentals of parenting such a child. Dr. Ziegler looks at traditional understandings of children with a critical fresh eye."
– Janine Gordon, M.D., Board Certified Child & Adolescent Psychiatrist

Traumatic
Experience
and the
Brain

A Handbook for Understanding
and Treating Those
Traumatized as Children

Dave Ziegler, Ph.D.

Some of us wish for our childhood to go on and on. Others, however, wish it would finally end. *Traumatic Experience and the Brain* (2002) describes how trauma experienced early in life physically affects the brain, actually rewiring one's perceptions of and reactions to self, others, and the world. The book vividly describes how, with love, therapy, and support, parents and therapists of these "broken" children can help them to overcome their past experiences and lead normal adult lives.

"Ziegler melds together years of clinical experience in treating severely traumatized children with an up-to-date understanding of how trauma affects the brain. This valuable book will help therapists and professionals recognize how the traumatized brain produces trauma symptoms and how best to intervene."
—David V. Baldwin, Ph.D., Author/Editor, Trauma Information Pages

ISBN 0-9671187-5-1; 172 pages; $19.95 + $2.50 shipping and handling
To order, call Acacia Publishing toll-free: 866-265-4553